Compendium of Antitrust Damages Actions

International Chamber of Commerce (ICC)

2nd edition

John W.H. Denton AO
François Brunet
Sarina Williams
Caroline Inthavisay

Compendium of Antitrust Damages Actions (2023)
International Chamber of Commerce (ICC)

This document, as well as any data and map included herein, are without prejudice to the status of or sovereignty over any territory, to the delimitation of international frontiers and boundaries and to the name of any territory, city or area.

Publisher: Concurrences
First Printing, December 2023
ISBN 978-1-954750-52-4 (Hardcover)
Library of Congress Control Number: 2023951514
Cover Design: Yves Buliard, www.yvesbuliard.fr
Book Design and Layout implementation: Nord Compo

Concurrences Books

Tributes

Eleanor M. Fox – Antitrust Ambassador to the World, *2021*

Herbert Hovenkamp – The Dean of American Antitrust Law, *2021*

Frédéric Jenny – Standing Up for Convergence and Relevance in Antitrust, (Vol. I & II), *2019 & 2021*

Albert Foer – A Consumer Voice in the Antitrust Arena, *2020*

Richard Whish – Taking Competition Law Outside the Box, *2020*

Douglas H. Ginsburg – An Antitrust Professor on the Bench (Vol. I & II), *2018 & 2020*

Wang Xiaoye – The Pioneer of Competition Law in China, *A. Emch, W. Ng (eds.), 2019*

Ian S. Forrester – A Scot without Borders (Vol. I & II), *A. Komninos (eds.), 2015*

William E. Kovacic – An Antitrust Tribute (Vol. I & II), *2013 & 2014*

Practical Books

Pharmaceutical Antitrust: An Analysis of US and EU Law, *M. Thill-Tayara, G. Gordon, 2023*

Innovation Paradox in Merger Control, *G. Gurkaynak, 2023*

State Aid & the Energy Transition, *D. Buschle, L. Hancher, M.-T. Richter-Kuhnert (eds.), 2023 (in collaboration with the Energy Community)*

State Aid & National Enforcement, *J. Derenne, D. Jouve, C. Lemaire, F. Martucci (eds.), 2023*

Antitrust and the Digital Economy, *Y. Katsoulacos (ed.), 2023 (in collaboration with CRESSE)*

Judicial Review of Competition Cases, *D. Ginsburg, T. Eicke (eds.), 2023*

Competition Law Treatment of Joint Ventures, *B. Bleicher, N. Campbell, A. Hamilton, N. Hukkinen, A. Khan, A. Mordaunt (eds.), 2022 (in collaboration with the IBA)*

Information Exchange & Related Risks, *Z. Marosi, M. Soares (eds.), 2022 (in collaboration with the IBA)*

Rulemaking Authority of the US Federal Trade Commission, *D. Crane (ed.), 2022*

The International Competition Network at Twenty, *D. Anderson & P. Lugard (eds.), 2022*

Competition Case Law Digest – 5th Edition, *F. Jenny, N. Charbit (eds.), 2022*

Competition Inspections in 21 Jurisdictions – A Practitioner's Guide, *N. Jalabert-Doury (ed.), 2022*

Perspectives on Antitrust Compliance, *A. Riley, A. Stephan, A. Tubbs (eds.), 2022 (in collaboration with the ICC)*

Turkish Competition Law, *G. Gürkaynak, 2021*

Competition Law – Climate Change & Environmental Sustainability, *S. Holmes, D. Middelschulte, M. Snoep (eds.), 2021*

Merger Control in Latin America – A Jurisdictional Guide, *P. Burnier da Silveira, P. Sittenfeld (eds.), 2020*

Competition Inspections under EU Law – A Practitioner's Guide, *N. Jalabert-Doury, 2020*

Gun Jumping in Merger Control – A Jurisdictional Guide, *C. Hatton, Y. Comtois, A. Hamilton (eds.), 2019 (in collaboration with the IBA)*

Choice – A New Standard for Competition Analysis? *P. Nihoul (ed.), 2016*

PhD Theses

Abuse of Platform Power, *F. Bostoen, 2023*

Reform of Chinese State-Owned Enterprises, *X. Bai, 2023*

Competition & Regulation in Network Industries – Essays in Industrial Organization, *J-M. Zogheib, 2021*

The Role of Media Pluralism in the Enforcement of EU Competition Law, *K. Bania, 2019*

Buyer Power, *I. Herrera Anchustegui, 2017*

General Interest

Global Dictionary of Competition Law, *D. Healey, W. Kovacic, P. Trevisan, R. Whish, 2024*

Great Antitrust Enforcers, *W. E. Kovacic, 2023*

Competition – How to Speak Like an Expert, *E. Combe , 2023*

Women and Antitrust – Voices from the Field (Vol I & II), *E. Kurgonaite & K. Nordlander, 2020*

Conference Proceedings

Antitrust in Emerging and Developing Countries – (Vol I & II), *E. Fox, H. First, 2015 & 2016*

Global Antitrust Law – Current Issues in Antitrust Law and Economics, *D. Ginsburg, J. Wright, (eds.) 2015*

Competition Law on the Global Stage – David Gerber's Global Competition Law in Perspective, *D. Gerber, 2014*

e-Book versions available for **Concurrences+** subscribers

About ICC

As the institutional representative of over 45 million businesses, reaching more than 170 countries, the International Chamber of Commerce (ICC) operates with a mission to make business work for everyone, every day, everywhere. We are the primary voice of the real economy in a range of intergovernmental organisations – from the World Trade Organisation to the UN climate process – championing the needs of local business in global decision making. The convening power of our global network enables us to set rules and standards that facilitate over USD 10 trillion dollars in trade each year – in addition to providing tailored products and digital services that directly address the real challenges faced by businesses operating internationally. We also provide the world's premier private global dispute resolution services, leveraging ICC's unique independence, integrity and expertise.

About the ICC Global Competition Commission

ICC's international antitrust agenda is spearheaded by its Global Competition Commission. With over 300 members from nearly 45 countries, the commission intends to remain the lead voice of business in global competition policy and to develop practical tools and guidance to help companies of all sizes in their daily activities. The ICC Global Competition Commission strives to enhance the harmonization and convergence among jurisdictions in key competition policy areas with the aim to minimize regulatory costs for international companies. It also works toward increasing the efficiency of antitrust enforcement at a global level both from a legal and economic perspective. The commission has been particularly active in areas such as merger control, sustainability and competition law, antitrust enforcement in the digital economy, antitrust compliance programmes and advocacy, antitrust damages actions, non-target RFIs, State aid and subsidies, and the new EU Horizontal Guidelines.

How to join the ICC

If you wish to participate in the work of the ICC Global Competition Commission, please contact caroline.inthavisay@iccwbo.org.

OVERVIEW

Biographies III

Foreword V

Acknowledgements VII

Introduction XI

Publisher's Note XIII

Glossary XV

Table of Cases XVII

Table of Contents XLVII

EUROPEAN UNION 1
François Brunet and Pierre Chellet

AUSTRIA 19
Andreas Traugott, Bernt Elsner, Lothar Hofmann, Florian Neumayr, Markus P. Fellner, Christoph Haid, Stefanie Stegbauer, Martin Eckel, David Konrath, Philipp Strasser, Guenter Bauer and Robert Wagner

BELGIUM 29
Gerrit Oosterhuis, Angela Ortega González and Vincent Mussche

BRAZIL 41
Joyce Honda, Thales de Melo e Lemos, José Gabriel Assis de Almeida and Mickael Viglino

CHILE 53
Benjamin Grebe and Andrea Von Chrismar

FRANCE 61
Sergio Sorinas and Marie Louvet

GERMANY 73
Christian Ritz and Carolin Marx

ITALY 87
Guido Carducci, Irene de Angelis, Jacques Moscianese, Pietro Merlino and Veronica Pinotti

KOREA 97
Cecil Saehoon Chung, Woo Yul Lee and Tae Yong Kim

MEXICO 105
Ivan Szymanski Curiel and Fernando Ruiz Alva

NETHERLANDS 111
Gerjanne te Winkel and Niels van Loon

POLAND 121
Marcin Trepka and Elżbieta Buczkowska

PORTUGAL 131
Eduardo Maia Cadete, Miguel Miranda, Miguel Gorjão-Henriques, Gonçalo Anastácio, Leyre Prieto, Nuno Cruz and Miguel Pena Machete

SPAIN 139
Juan Pablo Correa Delcasso, Laura Pérez, Rais Amils, Ana Parés, Belén Irissarry, Fernando Giménez-Alvear and Laura García-Valdecasas

SWEDEN 157
Claes Langenius and Sofia Falkner

TURKEY 165
Sahin Ardıyok

UKRAINE 177
Olexander Martinenko and Daryna Ushchapivska

UNITED KINGDOM 187
Andrew Bartlett and Penny Coombs

UNITED STATES OF AMERICA 201
Benjamin Holt

BIOGRAPHIES

John W.H. Denton AO is the Secretary General of the International Chamber of Commerce (ICC). He is a global business leader and international advisor on policy and a legal expert on international trade and investment. In 2022, John was appointed by the United Nations Secretary General to represent the global private sector on the newly formed Steering Committee of the UN Global Crisis Response Group on Food, Energy and Finance. This year, John was appointed by the WTO Director General to represent ICC at the WTO Business Advisory Board group. He also currently serves on the WHO Foundation Strategic Advisory Group and the Global Task Force on Refugee Labour Mobility. John is a Board member of the UN Global Compact and was appointed Chair of the UN Business and Human Security Initiative advisory board in February 2023. John is a founding member of the Business 20 (B20), Co-founder of the Australia–China CEO Roundtable and Patron of UNHCR in Australia. He serves on the Board of IFM Global Investors, a leading institutional investment manager, and is Chair of the Moeller Institute Advisory Board at the University of Cambridge. He additionally serves on the Boards of the UN Development Programme's Impact Investing Steering Group and UNICEF's global education initiative, GenU, and he is a member of the Advisory Board of the African Green Infrastructure Investment Bank (AfGIIB) and the G7 Working Group on Impact Investment. A former diplomat, John co-led the Australian Government's 2012 White Paper on "Australia in the Asian Century" and previously chaired the APEC Finance and Economics Working Group. Prior to joining ICC, he served for two decades as Partner and CEO of Corrs Chambers Westgarth, Australia's leading independent law firm. In 2015, John was appointed an Officer of the Order of Australia for his services to the business community, the arts and the rights of refugees, including as a founder of Human Rights Watch (Australia) and Teach for Australia.

François Brunet is a French Avocat, who has been actively practicing EU and French competition laws over more than three decades. Previously, he was Partner at Hogan Lovells (2017-2021) and at Cleary Gottlieb Steen & Hamilton (2000-2017). Mr. Brunet has represented clients in a significant number of cartel/monopolization investigations and M&A transactions in the television, car equipment, pharmaceuticals, cement, paper and sugar Industries. In June 2021, he was appointed Chair of the Global Competition Commission of the International Chamber of Commerce (ICC), which comprises more than 400 prominent antitrust practitioners operating in over 80 jurisdictions. Professor at the University Paris 5-René Descartes (2000-2009), he is also widely published on various aspects of EU and French competition laws. He has been distinguished as a leading competition/antitrust lawyer by Chambers Global, The World's Leading Lawyers and The International Who's Who of Business Lawyers.

Sarina Williams is a Partner in the Litigation team at Linklaters in London and Co-Head of Linklaters' global competition litigation practice. She has been involved in many of the market-leading UK competition damages cases before the English courts and the Competition Appeal Tribunal, including proceedings relating to interchange, FX, ATM transactions, power cables, diesel emissions and app stores. She is a member of the

UK Competition Appeal Tribunal User Group and is Chair of the ICC Global Competition Commission's Task Force for Antitrust Damages Actions.

Caroline Inthavisay is Global Policy Lead for Competition at the International Chamber of Commerce (ICC) Headquarters in Paris. She ensures the successful implementation of the strategic priorities of the ICC Global Competition Commission and oversees its work. In addition to managing international policy advocacy campaigns, she has contributed to the development of numerous practical tools for business in a variety of areas related to international trade and investments, notably Anti-Corruption & Corporate Responsibility and Transport & Logistics.

FOREWORD

Antitrust laws and antitrust enforcement are essential to deter and prosecute abusive pricing and other anti-competitive business conducts, which are detrimental to international trade and investment and can be harmful to innovation and consumer welfare.

Once limited to the United States for decades, the role of private competition law enforcement in ensuring fair and undistorted market conditions has been pushed to the fore after the full implementation of the European Union of Directive 2014/104. The European Directive removes practical obstacles to compensation for all victims of anti-competitive conduct and refines the interplay between private damages actions and public enforcement of the EU competition rules within the region. As a result, other countries beyond Europe have adjusted their private enforcement regimes either by establishing new rules or reinforcing existing ones, making the global business regulatory framework increasingly complex.

The consequences for businesses, regardless of their sizes and markets, are enormous. Companies involved in anti-competitive behaviours can face heavy fines and sometimes criminal sanctions from the public enforcement of competition law. But with the importance that private enforcement has gained over the last few years, they may find themselves at greater loss due to private legal actions filed against them by victims seeking compensation for damages.

It is in this particular context that the first edition of the *Compendium of Antitrust Damages Actions* (the "Compendium") was published by the International Chamber of Commerce (ICC) in 2021.

As the institutional private sector partner to businesses, governments, and international organisations, our intent back then – as it is now – was, first and foremost, to help business understand the heightened risks they face of being sued for damages while raising awareness on the trends that will inevitably influence the international antitrust regulatory environment for the long term.

Indeed, antitrust enforcement is not static. Enforcement agencies are rethinking the way the laws are applied because our economies are undergoing profound changes. And the interesting question remains: how will enforcers, practitioners, businesses, and economic actors as a whole, respond to the new challenges of our time, be they digital, environmental, or political in nature?

ICC is proud to partner with Concurrences to continue bringing clarity and guidance in an area of law that is in constant evolution. The Second Edition of the Compendium gathers the latest developments in antitrust litigation proceedings and new case law in a number of key jurisdictions. These decisions are also available in the Concurrences e-Competitions Bulletin.

The Compendium does not seek to provide a detailed analysis of private litigation practices in different countries. Instead, it aims to profile the legal regime related to antitrust damages actions in a variety of key jurisdictions by providing an overview of the key legal principles that are illustrated by a selection of leading cases across various economic sectors and industries.

With nearly 350 court cases, including salient facts and insights on important judgments, the Compendium is a unique tool for all economic actors – antirust experts and non-experts alike – and was designed to address the concerns of both multinational companies and SMEs that may be exposed to, or already involved in, antitrust litigation. It provides details on the method of calculating damages in numerous jurisdictions as well as the amount of damages awarded, to increase companies' understanding and awareness of the issue.

We hope that the Compendium of Antitrust Damages Actions will continue to serve as a key reference for antitrust practitioners and enforcers across the globe.

John W.H. Denton AO
ICC Secretary General

François Brunet
Chair, ICC Global Competition Commission

Caroline Inthavisay
ICC Global Policy Lead – Competition

ACKNOWLEDGEMENTS

This publication was made possible thanks to the invaluable contributions and commitment of the authors listed in this section. We are forever grateful to the members of the Editorial Committee whole roles have been essential to the release of the new edition.

The Editorial Committee includes:

- Sarina Williams, Partner, Linklaters, and Chair of the ICC Task Force on Antitrust Damages Actions
- Daniel Jowell KC, Barrister, Brick Court Chambers, and Vice-Chair of the ICC Task Force on Antitrust Damages Actions
- Joyce Honda, Partner, Cescon Barrieu Vice-Chair of the ICC Task Force on Antitrust Damages Actions, with the support of Thales de Melo e Lemos, Senior Associate, Cescon Barrieu
- Carolin Marx, Partner, Hogan Lovells International, and Vice-Chair of the ICC Task Force on Antitrust Damages Actions
- Caroline Inthavisay, ICC Global Policy Lead – Competition, with the support of Francesco Felici, ICC Global Policy

The authors are (in alphabetical order by last name):

- Rais Amils, Partner, Pérez-Llorca (Spain)
- Gonçalo Anastácio, Partner, SRS Advogados (Portugal)
- Sahin Ardıyok, Partner, Dentons (Turkey)
- José Gabriel Assis de Almeida, Partner, J.G. Assis de Almeida & Associados (Brazil)
- Guenter Bauer, Partner, Wolf Theiss Attorneys at Law (Austria)
- Andrew Bartlett, Partner, Osborne Clarke (United Kingdom)
- François Brunet, Avocat at the Paris Bar, Chair of the ICC Global Competition Commission (France, EU)
- Elżbieta Buczkowska, Counsel, Baker McKenzie Krzyżowski Wspólnicy sp.k. (Poland)
- Guido Carducci, Attorney-at-Law, Carducci Arbitration (Italy)
- Pierre Chellet, Associate, Hogan Lowells (France, EU)
- Cecil Saehoon Chung, Head of International Antitrust, Yulchon LLC (South Korea)
- Penny Coombs, Associate Director, Osborne Clarke LLP (United Kingdom)
- Juan Pablo Correa Delcasso, Partner, Laguard (Spain)
- Nuno Cruz, Partner, JP CRUZ (Portugal)
- Ivan Szymanski Curiel, Associate, Santamarina y Steta, S.C. (Mexico)
- Irene de Angelis, Head of Antitrust Affairs, Intesa Sanpaolo (Italy)
- Miguel Mota Delgado, Junior Lawyer, Morais Leitão Advogados (Portugal)
- Martin Eckel, Partner, Taylor Wessing e|n|w|c Natlacen Walderdorf Cancola Rechtsanwälte (Austria)

- Bernt Elsner, Partner, CMS Raich-Rohrwig Hainz Rechtsanwälte (Austria)
- Agathe Esch, Senior Associate, Herbert Smith Freehills Paris LLP (France)
- Sofia Falkner, Partner, Advokatfirman Hammarskiold & Co (Sweden)
- Markus P. Fellner, Partner, Saxinger, Chalupsky & Partner Rechtsanwälte (Austria)
- Laura García-Valdecasas, Lawyer, Clifford Chance (Spain)
- Fernando Giménez-Alvear, Counsel, Clifford Chance (Spain)
- Miguel Gorjão-Henriques, Partner, Sérvulo & Associados (Portugal)
- Benjamin Grebe, Partner, Prieto Abogados (Chile)
- Christoph Haid, Partner, Schönherr Rechtsanwälte (Austria)
- Lothar Hofmann, Lawyer, HLAW (Austria)
- Benjamin Holt, Partner, Hogan Lovells, (United States of America)
- Joyce Honda, Partner, Cescon Barrieu (Brazil)
- Belén Irissarry, Lawyer, Counsel, Clifford Chance (Spain)
- Tae Yong Kim, Counsel, Yulchon LLC (South Korea)
- David Konrath, Senior Associate, Taylor Wessing e|n|w|c Natlacen Walderdorf Cancola Rechtsanwälte (Austria)
- Claes Langenius, Partner, Advokatfirman Hammarskiold & Co (Sweden)
- Woo Yul Lee, Partner, Yulchon LLC (South Korea)
- Niels van Loon, Counsel, Jones Day (Netherlands)
- Marie Louvet, Of Counsel, Herbert Smith Freehills LLP (France)
- Eduardo Maia Cadete, Partner, Morais Leitão Advogados (Portugal)
- Gonçalo Machado Borges, Partner, Morais Leitão Advogados (Portugal)
- Efigénia Marabuto Tavares, Managing Associate, PRA | Raposo, Sá Miranda & Associados (Portugal)
- Carolin Marx, Partner, Hogan Lovells International LLP (Germany)
- Thales de Melo e Lemos, Senior Associate, Cescon Barrieu (Brazil)
- Pietro Merlino, Partner, Orrick, Herrington & Sutcliffe (Italy)
- Miguel Miranda, Partner, PRA | Raposo, Sá Miranda & Associados (Portugal)
- Jacques Moscianese, Head of Institutional Affairs, Intesa Sanpaolo (Italy)
- Vincent Mussche, Partner, Liedekerke (Belgium)
- Florian Neumayr, Partner, bpv Huegel Rechtsanwälte (Austria)
- Gerrit Oosterhuis, Partner, Houthoff (Belgium)
- Angela Ortega González, Professional Support Lawyer, Houthoff (Belgium)
- Jill Ottenberg, Knowledge Lawyer, Hogan Lovells (United States of America)
- Ana Parés, Lawyer, Pérez-Llorca (Spain)
- Miguel Pena Machete, Partner, Cuatrecasas (Spain)
- Laura Pérez, Lawyer, Laguard (Spain)
- Veronica Pinotti, Partner, White & Case (Italy)
- Leyre Prieto, Partner, Telles Advogados (Portugal)
- Christian Ritz, Partner, Hogan Lovells International LLP (Germany)
- Judith Solzbach, Senior Associate, Hogan Lovells International LLP (Germany)
- Sergio Sorinas, Partner, Herbert Smith Freehills LLP (France)

- Holden Steinhauer, Senior Associate, Hogan Lovells; (United States of America)
- Stefanie Stegbauer, Counsel, Schoenherr Rechtsanwälte (Austria)
- Philipp Strasser, Partner, VHM Legal (Austria)
- Andreas Traugott, Partner, Baker McKenzie (Austria)
- Marcin Trepka, Partner, Baker McKenzie Krzyżowski Wspólnicy sp.k.(Poland)
- Mickael Viglino, Partner, J.G. Assis de Almeida & Associados (Brazil)
- Andrea Von Chrismar, Counsel, Prieto Abogados (Chile)
- Robert Wagner, Counsel, Wolf Theiss Attorneys at Law (Austria)
- Hanna Weber, Senior Associate at Hogan Lovells International LLP (Germany)
- Gerjanne te Winkel, Partner, Jones Day (Netherlands)

INTRODUCTION

Over the last decade, there has been a significant evolution of the antitrust litigation landscape. We have moved from a world where antitrust law was principally a matter of public enforcement, essentially carried out by competition authorities (particularly outside North America), to a world where private enforcement abounds and legislatures look to implement regimes that facilitate mass claims. Not long ago, antitrust class actions were an almost uniquely North American phenomenon. Not anymore. As new "opt-out" class action regimes have evolved in the UK and Europe, we have seen a surge of third-party litigation funding, making feasible mass claims that would not have been cost-effective if brought on an individual basis.

While some claims continue to piggy-back on investigations by competition authorities, others – emboldened by new regimes and backed by funders – look to bring "stand-alone" cases (*i.e.* cases not reliant on an infringement decision) based on novel theories of harm which push the boundaries of what might traditionally have been thought of as competition law claims. Many of these claims seek eye-watering sums in damages, which would in many cases dwarf fines by antitrust regulators. Claimants are also increasingly emboldened to pursue class actions in multiple jurisdictions in parallel.

The significant increase in these types of claims has had a corresponding impact on leniency regimes, with businesses needing to take difficult decisions around their risk profile, usually across multiple jurisdictions (and therefore regimes). It has also had a significant commercial impact, with any consumer-facing business needing to be conscious of the possibility of antitrust damages claims at multiple levels of the supply chain.

Civil liability rules apply to private enforcement. Claimants have to provide evidence of a competition law infringement, the harm suffered from such an infringement, the amount of the damages and a causal link between the infringement and the damages. We have seen development of the procedural and evidential rules in many jurisdictions around the globe to facilitate access to justice, including in the European Union, the United Kingdom, Brazil, Chile, Mexico, South Korea and China.

The difficulty is that not all jurisdictions have adopted the same rules, and antitrust litigation has become extremely complex. Several issues provide a good illustration of these differences: for example, punitive or treble damages are not available in all jurisdictions; rules governing discovery vary from country to country; infringement decisions by competition authorities may or may not have binding effect depending on national law; and not all countries permit claims by indirect purchasers. The diversity of national procedures means that legal practitioners need to have an in-depth and "global" understanding of the different legal frameworks, before bringing or defending a case.

In addition to these procedural and substantive discrepancies, lawyers and companies may also need to take into account the diversity of jurisdictional rules from an international private law standpoint. Indeed, a single anti-competitive behaviour may involve companies from various countries and affect businesses and consumers in different places. As such, national rules on jurisdiction may limit or promote international claims for damages.

With this Compendium, we intend to contribute to a greater awareness by decision-makers of this new legal environment and the correlative higher risks. The Compendium reflects contributions from leading antitrust law specialists from a number of key jurisdictions around the world. It does not try to explore the complexity of each legal system but strives to capture a comprehensive picture of the matter, organised around nine topics, and completed in some jurisdictions by an additional section highlighting key issues.

In addition to the overview, the Compendium provides an unprecedented collection of decisions issued in a wide range of jurisdictions, which are also available in the Concurrences e-Competitions Bulletin. This database complements the overviews and will allow a better understanding of how the rules presented in the Compendium have been applied by the judiciary in each country. Each case summary provides users with a brief description of the facts of the case and outlines key rulings from the courts in respect of issues in the case. Rather than performing keyword searches through the common online databases in each jurisdiction, antitrust practitioners and enforcers will have all key decisions to hand. Courts will be able to see what courts in other jurisdictions have decided on a given issue, which may contribute to a greater consistency and, within the European Union, to enhance integration. This Compendium is also intended to support competition authorities by giving them a general view on the consequences of their decisions.

By providing decision-makers with a comparative overview of the issues most frequently arising in private antitrust litigation in key jurisdictions, we hope to help them navigate through a new, fast-changing legal environment.

Sarina Williams
Chair of the ICC Task Force on Antitrust Damages Actions

PUBLISHER'S NOTE

The 1st edition of the Compendium of Antitrust Damages Actions, developed by the Global Competition Commission of the International Chamber of Commerce (ICC)" in March 2021 in electronic format, had the aim to provide guidance on antitrust litigation practices in an array of key jurisdictions and to raise awareness on the trends that are evolving across borders.

Two years later, Concurrences is delighted to also have the opportunity to collaborate with the ICC at the occasion of the 2nd edition of the Compendium, and to publish, for the first time, this remarkable work in print and ebook formats.

This book aims to profile the legal regime related to antitrust damages actions in 19 jurisdictions by examining the key legal principles, structured in 9 topics as well as an additional section highlighting key issues in some jurisdictions. In addition, case summaries on nearly 350 judgments are being made available in the e-Competitions Bulletins, and are providing readers with not only crucial facts of the cases, but also further details on the method of calculating damages as well as the amount of damages awarded.

Whether you are an academic, private practitioner, economist, judge, business, competition enforcement agency, or policy maker, the Compendium offers a comprehensive and accessible resource that equips you with the knowledge and tools needed to navigate the evolving terrain of antitrust litigation practices.

Concurrences would like to express its sincere gratitude to the editors for their expertise as well as well as to the authors of the 19 jurisdictions for the quality of their analysis and to the ICC Global Competition Commission for its unique support.

Nicolas Charbit - Sébastien Gachot - Patricia Hagleitner

GLOSSARY

Appeal: a proceeding undertaken to have a decision reviewed by a higher authority whose jurisdiction may include (i) an entirely new assessment of the case, (ii) a limited review of manifest errors of law and facts, or (iii) a specific review limited to legal issues.

Article 101 TFEU: This provision prohibits as anti-competitive all agreements, decisions and practices between undertakings and concerted practices which may affect trade between EU member States, and which have as their object or effect the prevention, restriction or distortion of competition within the internal market.

Article 102 TFEU: This provision prohibits any abuse by one or more undertakings of a dominant position within the internal market or in a substantial part of it. Those behaviours are incompatible within the internal market in so far as it may affect trade between EU member states.

Award: a final judgment or decision, especially one by an arbitrator or by a jury assessing damages.

Burden of proof: The responsibility for a party during legal proceedings to prove the facts it asserts; the burden of proof may be shifted to the opposing party once the Standard of proof has been met.

Cartel: Any horizontal collusion between competitors whose purpose is to fix prices or quantities, allocate markets, while sharing sensitive commercial information.

Cease-and-desist order: a court's or agency's order prohibiting a person from continuing a particular course of conduct which is deemed harmful. In competition law proceedings, these orders also include a prohibition from adopting future conducts likely to have the same effects as the one which is prohibited.

Claimant: the party who brings a civil suit in a court of law.

Class action: a lawsuit where a person or a group seeks damages for a larger group of claimants. Class action proceedings typically include a preliminary stage to define the characteristics of the group, which needs to gather persons with identic cases and who have suffered a prejudice from the same tort.

Competition authority: Any public authority, whether independent of forming part of a government administration, whose role is to enforce rules which prohibit unilateral and coordinated behaviours that restrict competition.

Damages: money claimed by, or ordered to be paid to, a person as compensation for loss or injury.

Defendant: a person sued in a civil proceeding.

Discovery: Proceeding whereby a party has to disclose information and documents relating to the litigation upon the request of the opposing party. This procedure is usually implemented during the pre-trial phase of the lawsuit.

Directive 2014/104/EU: European Union Directive issued on 5 December 2014 on certain rules governing actions for damages under national law for infringements of the competition law provisions of the member states and the EU. The purpose of this text is to set forth common rules among EU member States in order to enhance private enforcement of Articles 101 and 102 TFEU and full compensation for victims of anti-competitive conducts. The text also provides for specific rules on the interplay between civil lawsuits and enforcement proceedings before competition authorities.

Follow-on: A competition law claim for damages where the alleged infringement has previously been found by a final decision of a competition authority.

Immunity: Total exemption of fine for a company that is the first to reveal the existence of a competition law infringement to a competition authority.

Infringer: Any company that has implemented unilateral or coordinated behaviours infringing competition law, where a competition authority has found such infringement in a decision.

Joint-and-several liability: liability that may be apportioned either among two or more parties or to only one or a few select members of a group of Infringers upon the decision of a competition authority or a civil court.

Leniency: A competition law procedure that rewards companies that adopt anti-competitive conducts with Immunity or reduction of fine, if they inform a competition authority of an infringement that it it did not previously have knowledge of.

Limitation period: a statutory period after which a lawsuit or prosecution cannot be brought in court.

Passing-on defense: a competition law defence that relies on the civil law principle of unjust enrichment. During civil proceedings, a defendant may argue that the plaintiff's claim for compensation should be totally or partially denied as it passed the alleged overcharge resulting from a competition law infringement on its own customers.

SME (Small- and Medium-sized Enterprise): categories of micro, small and medium enterprises defined based on their staff headcount, and either their turnover or balance sheet total.

Stand-alone action: A competition law claim for damages where the alleged infringement has not previously been found by a final decision of a competition authority.

Standard of proof: In any legal procedure, the level of evidence that is required to establish with certainty a fact or a liability.

Tort: A civil wrong, other than breach of contract, for which a remedy may be obtained, usually in the form of damages; a breach of duty that the law imposes on persons who stand in a particular relation to one another.

EUROPEAN UNION

François Brunet
Avocat, Paris Bar
Chair, ICC Global Competition Commission

Pierre Chellet
Associate, Hogan Lovells

For many decades, private enforcement of competition rules was not part of EU law DNA. The Treaty on the Functioning of the European Union ("TFEU") primarily entrusted the European Commission (the "Commission") with the duty to enforce competition law provisions.[1] As a result, the European system of enforcement has mostly relied on administrative proceedings before dedicated agencies (the Commission and national competition authorities ("NCA")). Victims of anti-competitive behaviours would therefore submit complaints to these authorities, expecting them to order appropriate remedies to bring the infringement to an end.

Depending upon the applicable national law, customers, competitors or suppliers could claim damages, ask for a cease-and-desist order, or interim measures. Article 101 (2) TFEU even provided that anti-competitive clauses and agreements should be ruled null and void. However, no unified procedural framework allowed claimants to rely on an effective enforcement of competition law in private litigation. They faced various obstacles from access to evidence to limitation periods. In particular, the relationship between the private claim and the administrative proceedings gave rise to several conflicts.

In particular, the Commission and NCAs were concerned that disclosure of their files could undermine the attractiveness of their respective leniency programmes.[2] Although leniency applications to the Commission dropped over the last ten years, it is worth noting a recent revival in the interest of companies towards leniency (i.e., the Commission received 6 applications in 2021 and 13 in 2022), which may be caused by stronger *ex officio* proceedings and increased dawn raids activity following the Covid-19 pandemic.[3]

In order to fill the gap and to overcome such hurdles, the EU adopted Directive 2014/104/EU[4] (hereinafter the "Damages Directive") that sets forth common rules among Member States in order to foster private enforcement.

1. Jurisdiction

Jurisdiction within the EU is governed by the Brussels I recast Regulation.[5] Although it does not specifically address competition law issues, it provides for a common European framework in order to assess jurisdiction in civil and commercial matters. Case law of the Court of Justice of the European Union (hereinafter the "Court of Justice") has enlightened its meaning in competition law related claims.

---

1 Article 105 TFEU.

2 Adeline Archimbaud, Les programmes de clémence européens et les actions privées de concurrence : Les liaisons dangereuses, September 2020, Concurrences N° 3-2020, Art. N° 95697, www.concurrences.com

3 Francesca McClimont, "'Very significant' increase in leniency filings amid cost of living crisis, DG Comp official says", Global Competition Review, 26th May 2023.

4 Directive 2014/104/EU of the European Parliament and of the Council of 26 November 2014 on certain rules governing actions for damages under national law for infringements of the competition law provisions of the Member States and of the European Union, OJ L 349, 5.12.2014, p. 1–19.

5 Regulation (EU) No 1215/2012 of the European Parliament and of the Council of 12 December 2012 on jurisdiction and the recognition and enforcement of judgments in civil and commercial matters OJ L 351, 20.12.2012, p. 1–32.

1.1 *Jurisdiction of the Member State where the defendant is domiciled*

As a principle, under Article 4 of the Brussels I recast Regulation, courts of the Member State where the defendant is domiciled, shall have jurisdiction to hear the case. In case of plurality of defendants, Article 8 (1) provides that the claim may be brought in the courts of the place where any of the defendant is domiciled (the "anchor defendant"), subject, in summary, to close connection between the claims. This is particularly relevant in cartel cases, where multiple companies colluded and may then be sued collectively. The Court of Justice has provided guidance for cases where the claimant reaches a settlement with the anchor defendant and withdraws his claim towards him. In such a case, the initially court seized with the case does not lose jurisdiction, except if it is demonstrated that the settlement was purposely delayed to bring the case before that specific court.[6]

1.2 *Alternative jurisdiction*

The Brussels I recast Regulation also provides for alternative *fora* of jurisdiction depending on specific circumstances:

- **When the claim relates to the operations of a branch, agency or other establishment**, the courts of the place where such branch, agency or other establishment is located may have jurisdiction.[7] In competition law related claims, it is necessary to demonstrate that the branch actually participated in some of the actions constituting the infringement.[8]
- **When the claim relates to a contract**, the courts of the place of performance of the obligation may have jurisdiction.[9]
- **The parties may agree to submit their case to the courts of a Member State, which shall have jurisdiction.**[10] This ground may be challenging in competition law claims. Indeed, it is not sure that the parties have been willing to include antitrust infringements in the scope of the clause. Drafting of these provisions is therefore essential. Although the Court of Justice has shown caution when they relate to cartel infringements,[11] it has been more open to these clauses in matters relating to abusive behaviours.[12]
- **When the claim relates to tortious liability**, the courts of the place where the harmful event occurred or may occur may have jurisdiction.[13] In practice, identification of this place may be difficult. In *CDC Hydrogen Peroxide*, the Court of Justice ruled that claimants may choose between:
  - **The place of the causal event leading to the damage**. In cartel cases, it is the place where the anti-competitive agreement was concluded.[14] In abuses

6 CJEU, Case C-352/13, Judgment of 21 May 2015, *Cartel Damage Claims (CDC) Hydrogen Peroxide SA*, ECLI:EU:C:2015:335.

7 Article 7 (5) of the Brussels I recast Regulation.

8 CJEU, Case C-27/17, Judgment of 5 July 2018, *AB "flyLAL-Lithuanian Airlines"*, ECLI:EU:C:2018:533.

9 Article 7 (1) of the Brussels I recast Regulation.

10 Article 25 of the Brussels I recast Regulation.

11 CJEU, Case C-352/13, Judgment of 21 May 2015, *Cartel Damage Claims (CDC) Hydrogen Peroxide SA*, ECLI:EU:C:2015:335.

12 CJEU, Case C-595/17, Judgment of 24 October 2018, *Apple Sales International*, ECLI:EU:C:2018:854.

13 Article 7 (2) of the Brussels I recast Regulation.

14 CJEU, Case C-352/13, Judgment of 21 May 2015, *Cartel Damage Claims (CDC) Hydrogen Peroxide SA*, ECLI:EU:C:2015:335.

of dominant position, such place is easily determined as the place where the abusive conduct was implemented.[15]

- **The place where the damage materializes for the victim.**[16] In *CDC Hydrogene Peroxide*, the Court of Justice ruled that such place could be the statutory seat of the victim. More recently, in *FlyLAL* it refined its assessment and ruled that such place could be the Member State where the affected market is located.[17]

Questions arose regarding indirect purchasers. It was unsure whether their damage could provide basis for jurisdiction. In *Tibor-Trans*, the Court of Justice ruled that indirect customers suffer from additional costs incurred because of artificially high prices. Such damage is direct and may be sufficient to provide jurisdiction.[18]

2. Relevant legislation and legal grounds

Litigants may rely on rules stemming from EU law and from national specific provisions.

In addition to this, EU directives do not, in principle, have a direct effect for individuals. It is the responsibility of the Member States to implement a directive in national law. Therefore, private litigants willing to bring a claim for a competition law infringement need to rely on national rules that implement the Damages Directive. The 28 Member States[19] had until 27 December 2016 to implement this text. Under the principle of conforming interpretation, the national court is required, after 27 December 2016, to interpret, wherever possible, its national law so as to render it compatible with the provisions of that Damages Directive, without however interpreting national law *contra legem*.[20]

The Damages Directive does not completely harmonize the legal framework for antitrust claims. It simply sets forth common basic principles to ensure that EU competition rules are enforced. The Court of Justice has long ruled that private enforcement of the TFEU provisions on competition is necessary to comply with the principles of equivalence and effectiveness of EU law.[21]

However, Member States retain procedural autonomy, subject to the principles of equivalence and effectiveness. Consequently, national law may differ on issues relating to civil procedure. It is for the parties to analyze relevant national legislation in order to find the appropriate legal grounds, which may relate to several issues including (i) emergency proceedings, (ii) interim measures, (iii) cease-and-desist orders, and (iv) collective redress mechanisms.

---

15 CJEU, Case C-27/17, Judgment of 5 July 2018, *AB "flyLAL-Lithuanian Airlines"*, ECLI:EU:C:2018:533.

16 CJEU, Case C-352/13, Judgment of 21 May 2015, *Cartel Damage Claims (CDC) Hydrogen Peroxide SA*, ECLI:EU:C:2015:335.

17 CJEU, Case C-27/17, Judgment of 5 July 2018, *AB "flyLAL-Lithuanian Airlines"*, ECLI:EU:C:2018:533.

18 CJEU, Case C-451/18, Judgment of 29 July 2019, *Tibor-Trans Fuvarozó és Kereskedelmi Kft*, ECLI:EU:C:2019:635.

19 The United-Kingdom was still a member of the European Union at the time of the transposition.

20 CJEU, Case C-267/20, judgment of 22 June 2022, *Volvo and DAF Trucks*, ECLI:EU:C:2022:494, para. 77.

21 CJEC, Case C-453/99, Judgment of 20 September 2001, *Courage and Crehan*, ECLI:EU:C:2001:465 and CJEC, Cases C-295/04 to C-298/04, Judgment of 13 July 2006, *Manfredi*, ECLI:EU:C:2006:461.

3. What types of anti-competitive conduct are damages actions available for?

The Damages Directive offers procedural tools in order to submit a claim relating to breaches of EU competition rules laid down in the TFEU.

First, it relates to breaches of Article 101 (1) TFEU, which prohibits anti-competitive agreements and concerted practices. Practitioners not familiar with the EU legal system shall pay attention to the fact that this provision covers both horizontal and vertical agreements. Several behaviours are generally prohibited under this article, including but not limited to:

- Price-fixing;
- Output limitation;
- Market sharing;
- Exchanges of information between competitors;
- Resale price maintenance;
- Prohibition of passive sales in a selective distribution system;
- Prohibition of online sales in a selective distribution system;

Second, the Damages Directive covers infringements of Article 102 TFEU, which prohibits unilateral behaviours that amount to an abuse of a dominant position. Enforcement of this provision is subject to the prior demonstration that the undertaking in question holds a dominant position. Such circumstances are met when a company holds a significant market power that allows it to act independently from competitors on the market. Dominant position is presumed when the company holds at least a 50% market share.[22] Behaviours which may be qualified as an abuse include *inter alia*:

- Refusal to supply;
- Discrimination;
- Excessive pricing;
- Predatory pricing;
- Tying and bundling;
- Self-preferencing;

The Damages Directive also addresses breaches of corresponding provisions of national law.

Finally, it is worth noting that the Damages Directive does not cover harm that may result from the breach of the EU Merger Control Regulation.[23] Likewise, the Damages Directive does not address failure to comply with State aid provisions of EU law.[24]

---

22 CJCE, Case C-62/86, Judgment 3 July 1991, *Akzo v Commission*, ECLI:EU:C:1991:286.

23 Council Regulation (EC) No 139/2004 of 20 January 2004 on the control of concentrations between undertakings, OJ L 24, 29.1.2004, p. 1–22.

24 Member States may incur liability for infringement of State aid rules under the *Francovitch* case law (CJEC, Case C-9/90, Judgment of 19 November 1991, *Francovich and Bonifaci v Italy*, ECLI:EU:C:1991:428).

4. What forms of relief may a private claimant seek?

EU law essentially ensures two kinds of relief for private claimants.

First, under Article 101 (2) TFEU, anti-competitive agreements shall be deemed null and void. Private parties may therefore directly or indirectly invoke that provision before national courts. The Court of Justice recently ruled that the Damages Directive does not cover claims for annulment as it is limited to damages claims. However, the overall principles of equivalence and effectiveness of Article 101 TFEU may provide ground for relief before national courts.[25]

Second, the Damages Directive provides for various procedural and substantive requirements in order to ensure full compensation of the victims of anti-competitive behaviours.

Yet, other forms of remedies may be available subject to national law.

5. Passing-on defence

EU law aims at ensuring full compensation for victims. However, it does not include overcompensation.[26] This means that punitive or treble damages are not available under the Damages Directive. Conversely, it means that national courts shall consider the fact that a victim of anti-competitive overcharge may have passed it on to its own customers. Compensation is limited to the actual loss (including any possible loss of profit).

The Damages Directive provides for a coherent procedural framework in order to assess passing-on, whether it is invoked as a defense (5.1) or as supporting a claim from indirect purchasers (5.2)

5.1 *Passing-on defense*

Article 13 of the Damages Directive provides that the defendant shall bear the burden to prove that the claimant passed on the overcharge to its own customers. However, the text of the Damages Directive remains silent as to the standard which needs to be met in order to satisfy the burden of proof.

Disclosure of evidence

The defendant may request the national court to order the claimant or any third party to disclose relevant information or document to support the passing-on defense.

Article 5 of the Damages Directive, which deals with disclosure of evidence to the claimant, requires a reasoned justification for disclosure to be ordered. Conversely, the Commission Guidelines on the assessment of passing-on[27] explain that the defendant

---

[25] CJEU, Case C-25/21, Judgment of 20 April 2023, *ZA e.a. v Repsol Comercial de Productos Petrolíferos SA*, ECLI:EU:C:2023:298, para. 58-59.

[26] Recital 13, Damages Directive.

[27] Communication from the Commission – Guidelines for national courts on how to estimate the share of overcharge which was passed on to the indirect purchaser, C/2019/4899, OJ C 267, 9.8.2019, p. 4–43.

requesting disclosure under Article 13 shall make a "*plausible assertion that the overcharge harm has been passed on by the direct purchaser onto the indirect purchaser*".[28] While assessing this assertion, national courts shall pay attention to the facts which are already reasonably available to the defendant.

Assessment of economic evidence

The Commission Guidelines present relevant quantitative and qualitative evidence that shall be taken into account.

The Commission insists on the fact that econometric analysis is the most accurate way to demonstrate the price effect of passing-on. The Guidelines present various regression methods in order to perform this assessment: (i) comparison between prices across time referred to as "before-during-after approach",[29] (ii) comparison with another geographic market or with a closely related product market referred to as "cross-sectional approach",[30] (iii) comparison across time and across markets referred to as "difference-in-differences approach".[31]

Nevertheless, a fully-fledged econometric study may not always appear to be proportionate in view of the amount of damages claimed. In such cases, the Commission recommends using alternative methods. In particular, it suggests to analyse how previous changes in a company's costs have affected its prices before or after the infringement ("the passing-on rate approach").[32] An economic expert may as well perform a simulation of the effect of the overcharge on the claimant's profit during the infringement ("the simulation approach").[33]

Price effects of the anti-competitive conduct may not be sufficient to assess passing-on. Therefore, the Commission recommends using comparison methods[34] as well as elasticity analysis[35] to consider volume effects.

In any case, the Commission made clear that all cases do not require complex economic assessments. In light of the principle of proportionality, national courts may validly rely on qualitative evidence (internal documents, information relating to the firms or industry at stake) in order to make their assessment of passing-on.[36]

5.2 *Claims from indirect customers*

Article 14 of the Damages Directive provides that claimants shall prove the existence and the quantification of passing-on when their claim arises from their status of indirect customer of the infringing parties.

---

28 Ibid. para. 41.
29 Ibid. para. 91-92.
30 Ibid. para. 93-94.
31 Ibid. para. 95-99.
32 Ibid. para. 120-127.
33 Ibid. para. 132-133.
34 Ibid. para. 139-141.
35 Ibid. para. 146.
36 Ibid. para. 155-156.

The standard of proof is presumed to be met when:

- the defendant has committed an infringement of competition law;
- the infringement of competition law has resulted in an overcharge for the direct purchaser of the defendant; and
- the indirect purchaser has purchased the goods or services that were the object of the infringement of competition law or has purchased goods or services derived from or containing them.

However, the presumption may be reversed if the defendant proves that the overcharge was not, or was not entirely, passed on to the indirect purchaser.

In any case, when several claims arise at different levels of the value chain, national courts shall be cautious to equally avoid overcompensation and undercompensation. Therefore, they should take into account other claims related to the same infringement, previous judgments relating to a given infringement, as well as relevant available information.[37]

6. Pre-trial discovery and disclosure, treatment of confidential information

The main achievement of the Damages Directive is to create a common framework for disclosure of evidence in competition law damages claims. In that respect, the Damages Directive distinguishes main principles (6.1) from specific rules that apply to evidence included in the file of a competition authority (6.2)

6.1 *Main principles that apply to disclosure of evidence*

The Damages Directive sets a standard for a request for disclosure to be granted. The requesting party shall present "*a reasoned justification containing reasonably available facts and evidence sufficient to support the plausibility of its claim for damages*".[38] A defendant may be required to produce new documents, by compiling or classifying information, knowledge or data in its possession.[39]

While dealing with requests for disclosure, national courts shall apply the principle of proportionality. In particular, they need to take into account (i) available facts and evidence, (ii) the scope and cost of disclosure, and (iii) the confidential nature of information.

The Commission has also adopted a Communication on the protection of confidential information to provide assistance to national courts.[40] The Commission recommends national courts to order disclosure of a non-confidential version of the requested documents. Other methods may include the use of confidentiality rings, or the appointment of experts. During the course of proceedings, national courts may organize *in camera*

---

37 Article 15 of the Damages Directive.

38 Article 5 (1) of the Damages Directive.

39 CJEU, judgment: 10 November 2022, Case C-163/21, *PACCAR e.a.*, ECLI:EU:C:2022:863.

40 Communication from the Commission Communication on the protection of confidential information by national courts in proceedings for the private enforcement of EU competition law 2020/C 242/01, C/2020/4829, OJ C 242, 22.7.2020, p. 1–17.

hearings and ensure publication of a non-confidential version of their judgments. They may also subsequently limit access to court records.

Finally, the Damages Directive clearly states that these rules may not undermine legal professional privilege.

As Member States remain free to adopt wider rules relating to disclosure of evidence, chapters of the Compendium relating to national legal frameworks may provide additional relevant information for practitioners.

6.2 *Specific rules to disclose evidence included in the file of a competition authority*

The Damages Directive creates an *ad hoc* disclosure regime for evidence included in the file of a competition authority. The purpose of this regime is to ensure consistency between the leniency and settlement programs of competition authorities and the right to full compensation for victims of anti-competitive behaviours.

When dealing with such requests, national courts shall take into account (i) the degree of detail of the request, (ii) the purpose of the request, in particular if it relates to a claim for damages, and (iii) the need to protect effective public enforcement of competition law.

Evidence included in the file of a competition authority enjoy various levels of protection pursuant to Articles 6 and 7 of the Damages Directive:

- **Absolute protection** is granted to leniency statements and settlements submissions. Those documents can never be disclosed in the context of private enforcement and should be regarded as inadmissible by national courts.
- **Temporary protection** is granted to (i) information that was prepared for the administrative proceedings of a competition authority, (ii) information that the competition authority has drawn up and circulated to the parties during the administrative proceedings, and (iii) settlement submissions that have been withdrawn. Those documents cannot be disclosed and must be regarded as inadmissible in private litigation until the administrative proceedings of the competition authority have been closed. In that respect, the Court of Justice clarified that the decision of an NCA to suspend proceedings to let the Commission investigate does not equate to a closing of proceedings.
- **Limited protection** is granted to all other information in the file of the competition authority. National courts shall simply ensure that no other party or third party is reasonably able to provide that evidence.

In order to accurately assess the nature of documents in view of the above mentioned three categories, national courts are encouraged to order defendants to disclose those pieces of evidence to the court only under sequestration mechanisms (i.e., and not to other parties to the proceedings). The national court may then review the documents in question and decide whether or not they warrant absolute or temporary protection.[41]

[41] CJEU, Case C-57/21, Judgment of 12 January 2023, *RegioJet v České dráhy*, ECLI:EU:C:2023:6, para. 115 et seq.

Prior to the entry into force of the Damages Directive, the Court of Justice had tried to strike a balance between the right to full compensation and the attractiveness of leniency and settlement programs. It provided some elements of guidance to national courts in order to assess requests for disclosure. In particular, the Court of Justice ruled that "*it is necessary to ensure that the applicable national rules are not less favourable than those governing similar domestic claims and that they do not operate in such a way as to make it practically impossible or excessively difficult to obtain such compensation* (...) *and to weigh the respective interests in favour of disclosure of the information and in favour of the protection of that information provided voluntarily by the applicant for leniency*".[42]

The Court of Justice had even rejected the national law provisions which prevented any access to leniency submissions and did not leave any possibility for national courts to weigh up the interests involved. The Court of Justice required that "*refusal* [to disclose leniency documents] *to be based on overriding reasons relating to the protection of the interest relied on and applicable to each document to which access is refused*".[43]

The relation between these cases and the Damages Directive remains to be tested. In particular, claimants could try to rely on those judgments in order to trump the absolute protection granted to leniency submissions under the Damages Directive.[44]

7. Limitation periods

The limitation periods to lodge a claim is at least five years within the EU.

This period starts to run when (i) the competition law infringement has ceased and, (ii) the claimant knows of:

- the behaviour and the fact that it constitutes an infringement of competition law;
- the fact that the infringement of competition law caused harm to it; and
- the identity of the infringer.

Finally, limitation period is subject to suspension or interruption when the Commission or an NCA investigates the infringement that supports the claim. The suspension ends at the earliest one year after the infringement decision has become final or after the proceedings are otherwise terminated.

The Court of Justice has recently recalled the importance for Member States to draft their limitation periods paying due regard to the principle of effectiveness of EU law. In *Cogeco*, although the Damages Directive was not applicable, the Court of Justice ruled that short limitation periods could not start running when the victim was not aware of the identity of the infringer. It also required limitation periods to be suspended or interrupted from the moment the NCA starts investigating the infringement and until a final decision is issued.[45]

---

42 CJEU, Case C-360/09, Judgment of 14 June 2011, *Pfleiderer AG*, ECLI:EU:C:2011:389, para. 30.

43 CJEU, Case C-536/11, Judgment of 6 June 2013, *Donau Chemie AG*, ECLI:EU:C:2013:366, para. 47.

44 Luis Ortiz Blanco, *EU Competition Procedure*, 3rd edition, Oxford University Press, Oxford, 2013, para. 6.49.

45 CJEU, Case C-637/17, Judgment of 28 March 2019, *Cogeco Communications Inc.*, ECLI:EU:C:2019:263. See also CJEU, Case C-267/20, judgment of 22 June 2022, *Volvo and DAF Trucks*, ECLI:EU:C:2022:494.

8. Appeal

The Damages Directive does not address the issue of appeal of the final judgment, which is left to national civil procedure law. Likewise, the Damages Directive does not affect the possibility to appeal disclosure orders under national law.[46]

9. Class actions and collective representation

The Damages Directive has not created a common collective redress mechanism. The "Collective action" Directive adopted in November 2020 does not cover competition law claims.[47] However, the Commission has issued a recommendation in 2013 on collective redress mechanisms which covers competition related matters.[48] This text is nevertheless not binding on Member States.

In any case, several collective mechanisms already exist under EU law. In particular, victims may assign their claim to a special purpose vehicle, which gathers various claims in order to seek compensation. Although the validity of this operation is subject to national law, Article 2 (4) of the Damages Directive acknowledges that an action for damages may be brought by a person "*that succeeded in the right of the alleged injured party, including the person that acquired the claim*". In that respect, the Court of Justice ruled that claim assignments shall not have any consequence regarding the jurisdiction of the national court.[49]

Finally, the lack of class action mechanism at the EU level for private litigation does not preclude Member States from adopting specific national procedures. In that respect, chapters of the Compendium covering national law may be helpful for companies and their counsels.

10. Key issues

10.1 *Probative value of the Commission and NCA decisions*

EU law equally allows claimants to bring follow-on and stand-alone actions.

Although stand-alone claims do not call for many comments, follow-on actions require an assessment of the administrative proceedings. The probative value of the final decision depends on the authority which made it:

- Final decisions of the Commission finding an infringement are binding on national courts;[50]

---

46 Recital no. 19 of the Damages Directive.

47 Directive (EU) 2020/1828 of the European Parliament and of the Council of 25 November 2020 on representative actions for the protection of the collective interests of consumers and repealing Directive 009/22/EC.

48 Commission recommendation of 11 June 2013 on common principles for injunctive and compensatory collective redress mechanisms in the Member States concerning violations of rights granted under Union Law.

49 CJEU, Case C-352/13, Judgment of 21 May 2015, *Cartel Damage Claims (CDC) Hydrogen Peroxide SA*, ECLI:EU:C:2015:335.

50 Article 16 (1), Council Regulation (EC) No 1/2003 of 16 December 2002 on the implementation of the rules on competition laid down in Articles 81 and 82 of the Treaty, OJ L 001, 04.01.2003, p. 1 – 25.

- Final decisions of a Member State's NCA (or review courts) finding an infringement are binding on national courts of this Member State;[51]
- Final decisions of another Member State's NCA (or review courts) finding an infringement must be regarded as *prima facie* evidence of this infringement.[52]

A debate arose regarding the probative value of commitment decisions of competition authorities. These decisions express concerns of the Commission or the NCAs regarding legality of some behaviours. However, they do not reach a final conclusion on a possible breach of Article 101 or 102 TFEU. Instead, they simply make commitments submitted by companies binding. These commitments are deemed sufficient to address the initial concerns of the competition authority. In that respect, the Court of Justice ruled in *Gasorba* that commitment decisions could be used in private proceedings before national courts as *prima facie* evidence of an infringement.[53]

Furthermore, the scope of the Damages Directive is limited to claims for compensation, which means that its provisions relating to the probative value of Commission and NCAs decisions do not cover claims for annulment of an anticompetitive agreement. In *Repsol*, the Court of Justice recently ruled that national courts should nevertheless consider that such decisions are *prima facie* evidence of an infringement provided that (i) the contract which is subject to the annulment claim corresponds to the nature and the material, personal, temporal and territorial scope of the infringement found in the decision; and (ii) the defendant does not bring any proof of the contrary.[54] The Court of Justice further indicated that even in the event the contract at stake does not completely fall in the scope of the decision finding an infringement, "*the findings in such a decision are not necessarily irrelevant, but constitute an indication of the existence of the facts to which those findings relate*".[55]

10.2 *Private enforcement and the corporate veil*

EU competition law is addressed to undertakings, which is an autonomous concept of EU law that goes beyond legal personality. As such, an undertaking is any entity engaged in an economic activity, regardless of its legal status. For the purpose of imputability of competition law infringements, a parent company is liable for the infringements of its subsidiary when it exercises decisive influence on the behaviour of the latter, such influence being presumed when the parent company owns 100% of the capital of the subsidiary.[56]

Private enforcement represents a challenge in that respect.

First, restructuring of business structures is likely to question the possibility to claim damages. Indeed, the legal entity which was found to have breached competition law may

---

51 Article 9 (1) of the Damages Directive.

52 Article 9 (2) of the Damages Directive.

53 CJEU, Case C-547/16, Judgment of 23 November 2017, *Gasorba SL*, ECLI:EU:C:2017:891.

54 CJEU, Case C-25/21, Judgment of 20 April 2023, *ZA e.a. v Repsol Comercial de Productos Petrolíferos SA*, ECLI:EU:C:2023:298, para. 62.

55 Ibid. para. 64.

56 CJUE, Case C-516/15 P, Judgment of 27 April 2017, *Akzo Nobel v Commission*, ECLI:EU:C:2017:314.

no longer exist when claimants bring their actions for damages. In such a case, the Court of Justice indicated that civil liability would lie in the companies which (i) acquired and dissolved the infringing legal entity and (ii) pursued its commercial activities.[57]

Second, a subsidiary, which was not the addressee of the Commission or NCA decision, may be held liable for an infringement of its parent company depending on (i) the formal links between the subsidiary and its parent company (i.e., a unitary organisation of personal, tangible and intangible elements, which pursues a specific economic aim on a long-term basis); and (ii) the concrete links between the economic activity of the subsidiary and the infringement (i.e., which exists where the anticompetitive agreement made by the parent company relates to the products sold by the subsidiary).[58]

10.3 *Civil liability among cartel members*

As a matter of principle, the Damages Directive considers all companies that have taken part in a given infringement shall be held jointly and severally liable for the harm caused.[59]

However, the EU legal framework provides for two exceptions.

First, small and medium-sized enterprises ("SMEs") may not be subject to joint and several liability. SMEs are defined as undertakings which employ less than 250 persons and which have an annual turnover below EUR 50 million, and/or an annual balance sheet total below EUR 43 million.[60] In the context of damages claims, an SME is liable only to its own direct and indirect purchasers when:

- Its market share in the relevant market during the infringement period was below 5%;
- Enforcement of joint and several liability towards it would (i) irretrievably jeopardize its economic viability and (ii) cause its assets to lose all their value;
- Its role in the infringement did not involve coercion nor ring-leading;
- It was not previously found to have breached competition law;[61]

Second, the Damages Directive has adapted the regime of liability to take into account the attractiveness of leniency mechanisms. A company which has been granted total immunity from fines during the administrative procedure enjoys some level of protection during subsequent private litigation.

- It is jointly and severally liable only to its direct and indirect purchasers and providers. However, it can also be liable towards any other injured party when the latter cannot obtain full compensation for its damages from the other infringers.[62]
- Contribution of such company in its relations to other infringers is limited to the harm it caused to its own direct or indirect purchasers or providers.[63]

---

57 CJEU, Case C-724/17, Judgment of 14 March 2019, *Skanska Industrial Solutions Oy*, ECLI:EU:C:2019:204.

58 CJEU, Case C-882/19, Judgment of 6 October 2021, *Sumal*, ECLI:EU:C:2021:800.

59 Article 11 (1) of the Damages Directive.

60 Article 2 (1) of the Annex to the Commission Recommendation of 6 May 2003 concerning the definition of micro, small and medium-sized enterprises, C(2003) 1422, OJ L 124, 20.5.2003, p. 36–41.

61 Article 11 (2) (3) of the Damages Directive.

62 Article 11 (4) of the Damages Directive.

63 Article 11 (5) of the Damages Directive.

- When the claim is brought by a party which was not a customer or provider of the infringers, contribution of the immunity recipient in its relations to other infringers shall be limited to its relative responsibility for the harm.[64] This rule is, for example, relevant for claims that are based on umbrella effect.

10.4 *Who can be a claimant?*

The Court of Justice has been very open to damages claims, as it regards them as a relevant instrument to ensure the effective enforcement of Articles 101 and 102 TFEU. Hence, it has ruled that any person harmed shall have the right to be compensated.[65]

The Court of Justice has therefore refused to limit availability of damages claims to the sole direct and indirect customers. In *Kone*, it acknowledged the umbrella effect, which is the damage suffered as a result of the general price increase on the relevant affected market, even when the claimant was a customer of a company that did not take part in the cartel.[66]

More recently, the Court of Justice went further and considered that damages claims are not limited to suppliers and customers of the market affected by the cartel. The Court of Justice held that "*any loss which has a causal connection with an infringement of Article 101 TFEU must be capable of giving rise to compensation*".[67] The case related to a public body which granted subsidies to buyers of the affected market.

10.5 *Entry into force of the Damages Directive*

The issue of entry into force of the Damages Directive remains heavily debated. Article 22 creates two frameworks depending on the nature of the provision at stake, whether it is substantive or procedural.

Substantive provisions may not apply retroactively, which means that it may not affect situations that already arose on the date on which the Damages Directive was implemented into national law.

However, procedural provisions may apply to all actions for damages brought after 26 December 2014. The Court of Justice acknowledged that "*Member States enjoyed a measure of discretion in deciding, when transposing that directive, whether the national rules intended to transpose the directive's procedural provisions would apply to actions for damages brought after 26 December 2014 but before the date of transposition of that directive or, at the latest, before the expiry of the period prescribed for its transposition.*"[68] A case-by-case analysis is therefore necessary in each Member State. Other chapters of the Compendium dedicated to national law of EU Member States may be helpful in that respect.

---

64 Article 11 (6) of the Damages Directive.

65 CJEC, Case C-453/99, Judgment of 20 September 2001, *Courage and Crehan*, ECLI:EU:C:2001:465.

66 CJEU, Case C-557/12, Judgment of 5 June 2014, *Kone AG*, ECLI:EU:C:2014:1317.

67 CJEU, Case C-435/18, Judgment of 12 December 2019, *Otis GmbH*, ECLI:EU:C:2019:1069, para. 30.

68 CJEU, Case C-637/17, Judgment of 28 March 2019, *Cogeco Communications Inc.*, ECLI:EU:C:2019:263, para. 28.

Although this distinction may seem theoretically appealing, it may be difficult to implement in practice. Knowing whether a provision of the Damages Directive is of substantive of procedural nature is a complex exercise. The Court of Justice has held that the determination of whether a provision of the Directive is substantive or procedural is a matter of EU law in relation to which Member States have no margin of discretion[69]

Methodology for the selection of cases

The Court of Justice does not directly hear cases of private enforcement. It has developed its case law in that area through preliminary rulings under Article 267 TFEU. This mechanism allows national courts from all EU Member States to request the Court of Justice's interpretation of EU law. Consequently, the Court of Justice does not directly rule on the cases but rather provides guidance on specific issues.

Cases presented hereinafter may refer to national proceedings developed in other chapters of this Compendium. However, it makes sense to gather them under the European Union chapter as they are binding on all national courts of the EU. They represent the law that can be directly invoked at national level.

---

[69] CJEU, Case C-267/20, judgment of 22 June 2022, *Volvo and DAF Trucks*, ECLI:EU:C:2022:494 paras.39-41. Cf Philipp Kirst, The Temporal Scope of the Damages Directive: A Comparative Analysis of the Applicability of the New Rules on Competition Infringements in Europe (21 October 2019). European Competition Journal (2019, Forthcoming), Available at SSRN: https://ssrn.com/abstract=3478604.

List of Cases

All the case comments mentioned are available in the Concurrences e-Competitions Bulletin

Court of Justice of the European Union

20/04/2023, CJEU, Case C-25/21, *Repsol Comercial de Productos Petrolíferos*, ECLI:EU:C:2023:298, e-Competitions Bulletin, Art. N° 116294
www.concurrences.com/112694
François Brunet, Pierre Chellet

16/02/2023, CJEU, Case C-312/21, *Tráficos Manuel Ferrer*, ECLI:EU:C:2023:99, e-Competitions Bulletin, Art. N° 116292
www.concurrences.com/116292
François Brunet, Pierre Chellet

12/01/23, CJEU, Case C-57/21, *RegioJet*, ECLI:EU:C:2023:6, e-Competitions Bulletin, Art. N° 116290
www.concurrences.com/112690
François Brunet, Pierre Chellet

22/06/2022, CJEU, Case C-267/20, *Volvo and DAF Trucks*, ECLI:EU:C:2022:494, e-Competitions Bulletin, Art. N° 116288
www.concurrences.com/112688
François Brunet, Pierre Chellet

06/11/2021, CJEU, Case C-882/19, *Sumal*, ECLI:EU:C:2021:800, e-Competitions Bulletin, Art. N° 116193
www.concurrences.com/116193
François Brunet, Pierre Chellet

12/12/2019, CJEU, Case C-435/18, *Otis GmbH*, ECLI:EU:C:2019:1069, e-Competitions Bulletin, Art. N° 111913
www.concurrences.com/111913
François Brunet, Pierre Chellet

29/07/2019, CJEU, Case C-451/18, *Tibor-Trans Fuvarozó és Kereskedelmi Kft*, ECLI:EU:C:2019:635, e-Competitions Bulletin, Art. N° 111878
www.concurrences.com/111878
François Brunet, Pierre Chellet

28/03/2019, CJEU, Case C-637/17, *Cogeco Communications Inc.*, ECLI:EU:C:2019:263, e-Competitions Bulletin, Art. N° 111882
www.concurrences.com/111882
François Brunet, Pierre Chellet

14/03/2019, CJEU, Case C-724/17, *Skanska Industrial Solutions Oy*, ECLI:EU:C:2019:204, e-Competitions Bulletin, Art. N° 111884
www.concurrences.com/111884
François Brunet, Pierre Chellet

24/11/2018, CJEU, Case C-595/17, *Apple Sales International*, ECLI:EU:C:2018:854, e-Competitions Bulletin, Art. N° 111876
www.concurrences.com/111876
François Brunet, Pierre Chellet

05/07/2018, CJEU, Case C-27/17, AB "flyLAL-Lithuanian Airlines", ECLI:EU:C:2018:533, e-Competitions Bulletin, Art. N° 111877
www.concurrences.com/111877
François Brunet, Pierre Chellet

23/11/2017, CJEU, Case C-547/16*, Gasorba SL*, ECLI:EU:C:2017:891, e-Competitions Bulletin, Art. N° 111883
www.concurrences.com/111883
François Brunet, Pierre Chellet

21/05/2015, CJEU, Case C-352/13, *Cartel Damage Claims (CDC) Hydrogen Peroxide SA*, ECLI:EU:C:2015:335, e-Competitions Bulletin, Art. N° 111875
www.concurrences.com/111875
François Brunet, Pierre Chellet

05/06/2014, CJEU, Case C-557/12, *Kone AG*, ECLI:EU:C:2014:1317, e-Competitions Bulletin, Art. N° 111912
www.concurrences.com/111912
François Brunet, Pierre Chellet

27/02/2014, CJEU, Case C-365/012 P, *EnBW Energie Baden-Württemberg AG*, ECLI:EU:C:2014:112, e-Competitions Bulletin, Art. N° 111874
www.concurrences.com/111874
François Brunet, Pierre Chellet

06/06/2013, CJEU, Case C-536/11, *Donau Chemie AG,* ECLI:EU:C:2013:366, e-Competitions Bulletin, Art. N° 111873
www.concurrences.com/111873
François Brunet, Pierre Chellet

14/06/2011, CJEU, Case C-360/09, *Pfleiderer AG*, ECLI:EU:C:2011:389, e-Competitions Bulletin, Art. N° 111872
www.concurrences.com/111872
François Brunet, Pierre Chellet

Court of Justice of the European Communities

20/09/2001, CJEC, Case C-453/99, *Courage and Crehan*, ECLI:EU:C:2001:465, e-Competitions Bulletin, Art. N° 111879
www.concurrences.com/111879
François Brunet, Pierre Chellet

13/07/2006, CJEC, Cases C-295/04 to C-298/04, *Manfredi*, ECLI:EU:C:2006:461, e-Competitions Bulletin, Art. N° 111880
www.concurrences.com/111880
François Brunet, Pierre Chellet

AUSTRIA

Andreas Traugott
Partner, Baker McKenzie

Bernt Elsner
Partner, CMS Raich-Rohrwig Hainz Rechtsanwälte

Lothar Hofmann
Lawyer, HLAW

Florian Neumayr
Partner, bpv Huegel Rechtsanwälte

Markus P. Fellner
Partner, Saxinger, Chalupsky & Partner Rechtsanwälte

Christoph Haid
Partner, Schönherr Rechtsanwälte

Stefanie Stegbauer
Counsel, Schoenherr Rechtsanwälte

Martin Eckel
Partner, Taylor Wessing e|n|w|c Natlacen Walderdorf Cancola Rechtsanwälte

David Konrath
Senior Associate, Taylor Wessing e|n|w|c Natlacen Walderdorf Cancola Rechtsanwälte

Philipp Strasser
Partner, VHM Legal

Guenter Bauer
Partner, Wolf Theiss Attorneys at Law

Robert Wagner
Counsel, Wolf Theiss Attorneys at Law

Private antitrust litigation has a long tradition in Austria, specifically since 1993 when individual *locus standi* before the Cartel Court was introduced. It is not limited to damages claims. The recent implementation of the EU Directive 2014/104/EU on Antitrust Damages Actions (the "Directive") into national law will further facilitate private antitrust damages litigation in Austria.

1. Jurisdiction

Private antitrust damages actions can be brought before Austrian civil courts on the basis of Section 37c (1) of the Austrian Cartel Act ("KartG"), the general tort law provisions of the Austrian Civil Code ("ABGB") and of the Unfair Competition Act ("UWG").

In addition, certain private claims, in particular (i) applications for a declaratory decision that an undertaking has infringed EU or Austrian competition law, and (ii) applications for cease-and-desist orders regarding an infringement of EU or Austrian competition law, may be brought before the Cartel Court by all undertakings that have a legal or economic interest in the decision. However, the Cartel Court does not have jurisdiction to award damages.

2. Relevant legislation and legal grounds

Sections 37a to 37m KartG implement the Directive into national law. Pursuant to Section 37c (1) KartG, any entity that culpably – *i.e.,* intentionally or negligently – infringes Articles 101 or 102 TFEU or their Austrian equivalents (Sections 1 and 5 KartG) or equivalent provisions of the national law of a Member State of the European Union or of a Contracting State to the Agreement on the European Economic Area, is obliged to provide compensation for the harm caused by the infringement.

An action for damages resulting from a competition law infringement can also be based on the general tort law provisions of the ABGB. The Austrian Supreme Court confirmed that such an action may be based on Section 1311 ABGB, according to which anyone who intentionally or negligently infringes an act of law that aims to protect somebody or something from harm shall be liable to provide compensation for the harm arising out of this behaviour (Case 4 Ob 46/12m). The Supreme Court found that the prohibitions of restrictive agreements and abuse of dominance under EU and Austrian law qualify as such protective rules within the meaning of Section 1311 ABGB.

In addition, a private antitrust cause of action may also arise on the basis of Section 1 UWG in conjunction with articles 101 or 102 TFEU or their Austrian equivalents (Sections 1 and 5 KartG). According to Section 1 UWG and established case law, a breach of the law which is capable of conferring on the infringer an advantage over its law-abiding competitors constitutes an infringement of Section 1 UWG unless the breach can be justified by a reasonable interpretation of the law. Under the rules of the UWG, claimants may bring actions for injunctions and actions for damages and may have the decision published.

Finally, private antitrust litigation in a broader sense may also arise where one party to an agreement argues that the agreement or part of it is null and void because it infringes competition law.

Ratione temporis application of the Austrian rules implementing the Directive

The provisions of Austrian law which implement the substantive provisions of the Directive apply to the compensation of damages which occurred after 26 December 2016. Some of the rules provided for in the Directive were however already part of Austrian law prior to the implementation of the Directive (e.g. the binding effect of decisions of the competition authority or joint and several liability of joint infringers).

As regards the new rules on limitation periods, which implement the corresponding provisions of the Directive, a specific transitional provision provides that the new rules on limitation apply to claims for antitrust damages which had not yet become time-barred under the old rules on limitation on 26 December 2016 (unless the old rules on limitation are more favourable to the claimant than the new rules).

The provisions of Austrian law which implement the procedural provisions of the Directive, in particular the rules on disclosure of evidence, apply in proceedings on actions for antitrust damages which were initiated after 26 December 2016.

3. What types of anti-competitive conduct are damages actions available for?

In accordance with Section 37a (1) KartG, damages actions are available for infringements of competition law as defined in Section 37b (1) KartG.

These include violations of the prohibition of restrictive agreements (Article 101 TFEU), the prohibition of abuse of a dominant market position (Article 102 TFEU), as well as their Austrian equivalents in Sections 1 and 5 KartG respectively and the prohibition of retaliatory measures (Section 6 KartG). Violations of provisions of the national law of a Member State of the European Union or of a Contracting State to the Agreement on the European Economic Area, which are pursuing the same objectives as Articles 101 and 102 TFEU, are covered as well.

4. What forms of relief may a private claimant seek?

The primary objective of damages actions is compensation for harm caused by an infringement of competition law.

The undertaking that culpably commits a breach of competition law may be required to pay compensation for any harm caused thereby. Section 37c KartG contains the rebuttable presumption that a (horizontal) cartel between competitors causes harm. This standardised reversal of the burden of proof makes it easier for the injured party to assert its claims. As a result, the claimant does not have to demonstrate that it has suffered harm in the first place; it however still has to prove the quantum of harm.

Private claimants can request that the damage caused by an infringement of competition law is compensated; this damage includes positive damage, loss of profits as well as interest (Section 37d (1) KartG). The KartG does not contain rules on the calculation of damages. A civil court deciding on an antitrust damages claim can ask the Cartel Court, the Federal Cartel Attorney and the Federal Competition Authority for assistance in determining the amount of damages.

If several undertakings have infringed competition law through joint behaviour (e.g., in the case of a cartel), they are jointly and severally liable for the resulting damage (see Section 37e KartG). It is not required that they have a joint intention to cause damage.

Special provisions apply to "crown witnesses" (leniency applicants granted immunity from fines) and SMEs in Section 37e KartG. A "crown witness" is only liable to its direct and indirect purchasers and suppliers unless the other injured parties cannot obtain full compensation from the other undertakings involved in the same infringement of competition law. An SME is not liable to its direct and indirect purchasers and suppliers if either (i) its market share in the relevant market was below 5% at any time during the infringement of competition law, (ii) its unlimited liability would irretrievably jeopardise its economic viability and cause its assets to lose all their value, (iii) it has not been the leader of the infringement of competition law and has not coerced other undertakings to participate therein, and (iv) it has not previously been found to have infringed competition law.

5. Passing-on defence

Section 37f KartG provides that the defendant in an action for antitrust damages can invoke as a defence against a claim for damages the fact that the claimant passed on the whole or parts of the overcharge resulting from the infringement of competition law. The burden of proving that the overcharge was passed on is on the defendant. Even if the defendant can show that the overcharge was passed on, the claimant may still claim compensation for loss of profits due to the passing-on of the overcharge (e.g., if the claimant's sales to its customers were reduced as a result of the passing-on of the overcharge).

In the case of an action for antitrust damages brought by an indirect purchaser, the law provides for a presumption of passing-on of the overcharge to that indirect purchaser if it has been established that (i) the defendant has committed an infringement of competition law resulting in a price increase for the direct purchaser of the defendant and (ii) the indirect purchaser has purchased the goods and services that were the object of this infringement of competition law. The infringer (defendant) can rebut this presumption by way of *prima facie* evidence.

To prevent overcompensation, the defendant in proceedings involving passing-on can summon the respective third party (e.g. the direct or indirect purchaser) to join the proceedings. In such case, the findings concerning passing-on will be legally binding for the third party irrespective of whether it joins the proceedings (Section 37f (4) KartG).

6. Pre-trial discovery and disclosure, treatment of confidential information

Effective rules on the disclosure of evidence in antitrust damages proceedings were only introduced into Austrian law with the provisions implementing the Directive in 2017: Section 37j (2) KartG provides that a party may submit a reasoned request for disclosure of evidence to the court together with, or after having lodged, an action for damages. Apart from requesting disclosure of certain pieces of evidence, a request for disclosure may also cover categories of evidence. The evidence and the categories of evidence need to be defined by the party requesting disclosure as precisely and as narrowly as possible, taking into account the facts and information reasonably available to it.

The court may then order the disclosure of evidence by third parties or the opponent party. The court has to limit a disclosure order to take account of the principle of proportionality, considering the legitimate interests of all parties concerned. An interest to avoid actions for damages caused by an infringement of antitrust law is not relevant for this assessment. The disclosure may also comprise evidence containing confidential information. The confidentiality of the information has to be taken into account by the court when assessing the proportionality of a disclosure request. If necessary, specific measures to protect confidentiality of such information have to be mandated (e.g., excluding the public from the proceedings).

Moreover, the party being ordered to disclose evidence may request that certain pieces of evidence are only disclosed to the court by invoking a legal obligation of secrecy (e.g., legal professional privilege) or any other right to refuse to give evidence (Section 157 (1) no. 2-5 Austrian Criminal Procedure Act).

Documents which are part of files of competition authorities may also be disclosed upon application. However, certain documents can only be disclosed once the competition authority has completed its proceedings (Section 37k (3) KartG). Leniency statements and settlement submissions are not subject to disclosure (Section 37k (4) KartG).

So far, there is only limited guidance by the courts, as to how the new rules on disclosure of evidence shall be applied.

Apart from these new rules on disclosure of evidence after proceedings in antitrust damages claims have been filed, general Austrian civil procedural law does not allow for (pre-trial) discovery as found in Anglo-American legal systems. Rather, each party has to substantiate the facts favourable to its legal position by putting forward evidence, including private expert opinions. The court can, and in most cases will, also appoint an expert to produce a report on questions which require specific economic knowledge (e.g., on the quantification of harm).

7. Limitation periods

The limitation period in Austria is five years, starting from the date on which the injured party becomes aware, or can reasonably be expected to know (i) the identity of the infringer, (ii) the damage it suffered and (iii) the behaviour concerned as well as the fact that it constitutes an infringement of competition law (Section 37h KartG).

In any case, the claim for compensation becomes time barred ten years after the date of the occurrence of the damage.

However, the limitation periods referred to above shall not begin to run before the infringement of competition law has ceased.

Also, the limitation periods are suspended for the duration of proceedings before the European Commission or any national competition authority in the EU related to an infringement of competition law. The suspension ends one year after the closure of the competition authority's investigation or the final decision of the respective competition authority. On-going settlement negotiations also suspend the limitation period.

8. Appeal

District courts are the courts of first instance for cases with a maximum amount in dispute of EUR 15,000. Regional courts have jurisdiction for first instance rulings on all legal matters not assigned to district courts. The respective regional courts as court of second instance decide appeals against decisions of the district courts.

Appeal decisions may be challenged before the Austrian Supreme Court if the case at hand involves a significant legal issue. "Significance" refers to one of the following scenarios:

- the respective decision deviates from earlier Supreme Court case law;
- the legal question at hand is novel; or
- there are diverging decisions from the Supreme Court regarding the matter under consideration.

Also, usually an appeal to the Supreme Court requires that the dispute value in the respective case exceeds EUR 30,000, or the dispute value exceeds EUR 5,000 and the first appellate court grants a right to an appeal (e.g., if the appellate court agrees that the question at hand is significant, as per the above).

9. Class actions and collective representation

Austrian law does not provide for collective actions or class actions in the strict sense of the term. The Austrian Code of Civil Procedure provides for the possibility for proceedings to be joined if (i) these proceedings have been brought individually by several claimants, (ii) against the same defendant, (iii) are pending before the same court and (iv) the joinder of proceedings is likely to lead to an acceleration of the proceedings or a reduction of procedural costs (joinder of proceedings under section 187 of the ZPO).

Due to the absence of a genuine collective action, or class action in the strict sense, the Austrian legal practice has developed a mechanism that has been (unofficially) labelled as 'class action Austrian style'. In these cases, the injured parties (mostly consumers) assign their claims to a legal entity that is willing to act as a claimant, typically a trade or consumer association or a special purpose vehicle in the form of a limited liability company or an association (*Verein*), which then brings an ordinary (two party) lawsuit over the assigned claims (theoretically also a natural person could act as the claimant to which the claims of the other potential claimants are assigned). The monetary benefits are redistributed among the class. The Austrian Supreme Court confirmed the legal admissibility of these lawsuits under the condition that all claims are essentially based on the same grounds (see for example OGH, 27 February 2013, Case 6 Ob 224/12b, where the Supreme Court also confirmed the legality of third-party funding of such Austrian-style class actions).

10. Key issues

The focus of the Austrian Supreme Court's case law in the area of antitrust damages so far was on the issues of jurisdiction, limitation, the requirements of a sufficiently substantiated claim, burden of proof, passing-on and the standing of indirect purchasers (decisions of lower courts in civil matters are usually not publicly available). As regards limitation, the Supreme Court took a very claimant-friendly position already before the implementation of the Directive.

The Austrian Supreme Court also dealt with the question of umbrella pricing effects and asked for a preliminary ruling of the CJEU on this point which has become relevant for antitrust damage claims across the European Union (CJEU, Case C-557/12, *Kone et al.*).

There is yet no case law of the Supreme Court on the new rules on disclosure of evidence which implement the Directive. As disclosure of evidence is a novelty to the Austrian system of civil procedure, guidance by the Supreme Court and appellate courts will be needed in order to establish a uniform practice in the application of these rules by the courts of first instance. However, the Austrian Supreme Court has made a number of important clarifications in a decision on 12 May 2022 on the relationship between the new disclosure rules and the right of third parties to request access to the files of the competition authorities (Supreme Court 22 May 2022, 16 Ok 1/22s). In addition, the Appeal Court of Vienna has requested the European Court of Justice to clarify the scope of protection of leniency statements and settlement submissions in criminal proceedings (CJEU, C-2/23) in light of the provisions of the Directives 2014/104/EU and (EU) 2019/1. Although this case relates to a criminal proceeding, the outcome will have a great impact on antitrust damage actions as well as the application of the leniency rules in the EU.

Methodology for the selection of cases

The following case selection includes the most relevant decisions of the Austrian Supreme Court in the field of antitrust damages. It does not attempt to be exhaustive. Decisions of lower courts in civil matters are usually not publicly available. In addition, we have included one decision of the Austrian Supreme Court in cartel matters, which contains important clarifications on the applications of the Directive 2014/104/EU in Austria.

List of Cases

All the case comments mentioned are available in the Concurrences e-Competitions Bulletin

Supreme Court

21/12/2022, Case 5 Ob 193/22a; *LKW Kartell*, e-Competitions Bulletin, Art. N° 116297
www.concurrences.com/116297
Andreas Traugott

22/05/2022, Case 16 Ok 1/22s; *Austrian Construction Cartel*, e-Competitions Bulletin, Art. N° 116296
www.concurrences.com/116296
Andreas Traugott

27/09/2016, Case 1 Ob 104/16z; *LIBOR*, e-Competitions Bulletin, Art. N° 111954
www.concurrences.com/111954
Stefanie Stegbauer

30/08/2016, Case 4 Ob 131/16t; *LIBOR*, e-Competitions Bulletin, Art. N° 111953
www.concurrences.com/111953
Stefanie Stegbauer

30/08/2016, Case 4 Ob 120/16z; *LIBOR*, e-Competitions Bulletin, Art. N° 111952
www.concurrences.com/111952
Stefanie Stegbauer

16/06/2015, Case 4 Ob 95/15x; *Aufzugskartell*, e-Competitions Bulletin, Art. N° 111951
www.concurrences.com/111951
Stefanie Stegbauer

29/10/2014, Case Eg: Case 7 Ob 121/14s; *Aufzugskartell, e-Competitions Bulletin, Art. N° 111950*
www.concurrences.com/111950
Stefanie Stegbauer

25/05/2014, Case 8 Ob 81/13i; *Aufzugskartell*, e-Competitions Bulletin, Art. N° 111949
www.concurrences.com/111949
Stefanie Stegbauer

15/05/2014, Case 6 Ob 47/14a; *Aufzugskartell*, e-Competitions Bulletin, Art. N° 111948
www.concurrences.com/111948
Stefanie Stegbauer

16/12/2013, Case 6 Ob 186/12i; *Aufzugskartell*, e-Competitions Bulletin, Art. N° 111947
www.concurrences.com/111947
Stefanie Stegbauer

12/02/2013, Case 4 Ob 168/12b; *Aufzugskartell*, e-Competitions Bulletin, Art. N° 111947
www.concurrences.com/111947
Stefanie Stegbauer

17/10/2012, Case 7 Ob 48/12b; *Aufzugskartell*, e-Competitions Bulletin, Art. N° 111945
www.concurrences.com/111945
Stefanie Stegbauer

14/08/2012, Case 5 Ob 39/11p; *Aufzugskartell*, e-Competitions Bulletin, Art. N° 111944 www.concurrences.com/111944
Stefanie Stegbauer

02/08/2012, Case 4 Ob 46/12m; *Bankomatvertrag*, e-Competitions Bulletin, Art. N° 111943 www.concurrences.com/111943
Stefanie Stegbauer

15/05/2012, Case 3 Ob 1/12m; *Aufzugskartell*, e-Competitions Bulletin, Art. N°111942 www.concurrences.com/111942
Stefanie Stegbauer

14/07/2010, Case 7 Ob 127/10t; *Aufzugskartell*, e-Competitions Bulletin, Art. N° 111941 www.concurrences.com/111941
Stefanie Stegbauer

BELGIUM

Gerrit Oosterhuis
Partner, Houthoff

Angela Ortega González
Professional Support Lawyer, Houthoff

Vincent Mussche
Partner, Liedekerke

In Belgium, private enforcement of competition law has been underdeveloped for a long time. The first relatively modern procedure was set out in the Law on Trade Practices of 14 July 1991[1] (Article 25). This procedure enabled claimants to obtain a cease-and-desist order against traders for acts of unfair competition. However, there was no specific legal basis for bringing actions for damages for breach of competition law. Damages claims were based on general provisions such as those for contractual claims for damages (Article 1142 and following of the Belgian Civil Code, "BCC") and claims on the basis of tort (Article 1382 BCC). Since the adoption of the Act on Actions for Damages for infringements of the competition law provisions of 6 June 2017 ("Belgian Damages Act"),[2] implementing Directive 2014/104/EU ("Damages Directive"), private enforcement of Belgian – and European – competition law before the Belgian national courts have become increasingly popular. The Belgian Damages Act entered into force on 22 June 2017 and introduced important changes to the Belgian system intended to encourage private enforcement actions. The Belgian Damages Act also contains a few rules that differ from the Damages Directive: (i) the voluntary compensation of damage by a cartel participant can be taken into account by the Belgian Competition Authority ("BCA") when calculating the cartel fine, and (ii) the definition of a cartel which also covers hub-and-spoke cartels.

1. Jurisdiction

Under the Belgian competition law system, infringements of national or European competition law are handled by the BCA, which is the relevant authority for public enforcement of competition law, whereas the national courts are in charge of private enforcement.

There are no specialised competition law courts. Accordingly, the courts of first instance or the commercial courts have jurisdiction, in accordance with the general rules of civil procedure. This does not apply to class actions, for which the Courts of Brussels have exclusive jurisdiction.[3]

2. Relevant legislation and legal grounds

In Belgium, natural or legal persons which have suffered harm as a result of a violation of competition law can claim damages before the national courts, on the basis of the general regime concerning contractual liability (Articles 1142 *et seq* BCC) and extra contractual liability (Articles 1382 *et seq* BCC).

To be valid, a claim for damages must be based both on an infringement of Belgian or European competition law (which constitutes irrefutable evidence of fault) as well as on the relevant tort law provisions. Under tort law, a person has to compensate for the

---

1 "Wet betreffende de handelspraktijken, de voorlichting en bescherming van de consument/Loi sur les pratiques du commerce et sur l'information et la protection du consommateur".

2 The Act was published in the Belgian Official Gazette on 12 June 2017, p. 63596.

3 Article XVII.35 of the Belgian Code of Economic Law (CEL).

damage caused by its fault (implying a tortious action) (Article 1382 BCC) or by its negligence (Article 1383 BCC). To obtain compensation, the claimant must demonstrate the existence of:

- a fault;
- a damage; and
- a causal link between the fault and the damage.

Fault is quite easy to demonstrate. Fault or negligence can lie (i) in the infringement of any statutory rule or (2) in not complying with a duty of care. An infringement of Belgian or European competition law constitutes accordingly irrefutable evidence of fault. However, it is in principle not necessary that the BCA (or the European Commission) has previously adopted a decision establishing an infringement for the claim to be admitted. This is different for class actions, which can only be follow-on actions.

Prior to the adoption of the Belgian Damages Act, victims of competition law infringements could also bring private damage claims as a tort claim on the basis of Article 1382 BCC, *i.e.* the general provisions of Belgian law on tort liability. With the entry into force of the Belgian Damages Act a number of new procedural and substantive rules regarding actions for damages for competition law breaches were introduced.[4] The main modifications include:

- a (rebuttable) presumption that cartels cause harm;
- the irrefutable establishment of infringement if such was held in a final decision of the BCA;
- *the prima facie* establishment of infringement if such was held in a final decision of other NCAs;
- new disclosure rules to facilitate access to evidence;
- the availability of passing-on defense;
- a rebuttable presumption of the passing-on of overcharges for indirect purchasers;
- the codification of joint and several liability and specific contribution rules; and
- a broader scope of the class actions regime.

These rules apply as a *lex specialis* to private enforcement actions. In a subsidiary order, the ordinary procedural rules on tort are applicable (Article XVII.71§2 Code of Economic Law: "CEL").

Both direct and indirect customers are entitled to bring private enforcement actions.

Temporal application

The substantive rules of the Belgian Damages Act (*i.e* regarding the presumption of harm and liability) apply to competition law infringements committed after 22 June 2017. The procedural rules (*i.e.* regarding the evidence and effect of decisions) apply to all actions introduced after 26 December 2014, even when they concern competition law infringements that occurred before 22 June 2017.

---

4 Title 3 "The action for damages for infringements of competition law" of Book XVII of the CEL

3. What types of anti-competitive conduct are damages actions available for?

Pursuant to Article I.22 CEL, the specific rules concerning private actions laid down in the Belgian Damages Act are applicable to private damages claims for infringements of the European antitrust provisions (*i.e.* articles 101 or 102 of the Treaty on the Functioning of the European Union ("TFEU") and their equivalent under Belgian law (namely, Articles IV.1 or IV.2 CEL). Nevertheless, taking into account the limited scope of application of the *lex specialis*, claimants can still bring damages actions for competition law infringements under the common provisions of Belgian law as well. In that case the regular procedural and substantial (tort) rules will apply.

4. What forms of relief may a private claimant seek?

According to the Belgian Damages Act, the purpose of damage actions is for the victims to obtain compensation. Exemplary or punitive damages are, thus, not available in Belgium and cannot be awarded by Belgian courts.

In accordance with Belgian tort rules, compensatory damages cover the actual loss, including lost profits, plus interest. In other words, the victims must be restored into the situation in which they were before the infringement occurred or into the situation that would have existed without the infringement.

In principle, except for the (rebuttable) presumption of harm applicable in cartel cases,[5] the extent of the loss has to be fully demonstrated by the applicant. This requires the application of theories of harm under competition law, such as the calculation of the "but-for prices". Article 962 of the Belgian Judicial Code allows the courts to appoint experts. The courts can do so *ex officio* or with the consent of the parties. The parties can also produce their own expert reports. It is common that experts are used in complex damage litigations. Moreover, the courts can ask the BCA for assistance in the quantification of the damages.[6] It still remains to be seen how keen the BCA will be to involve itself in disputes between private parties.

The fact that the infringers may have paid a fine in the context of public enforcement is not relevant to determine the damages. However, according to Article IV.70§1 CEL, introduced by the Belgian Damages Act, it is possible for the BCA to take into account financial compensation paid by an infringer in the context of a consensual settlement of private enforcement actions, as a mitigating circumstance in the calculation of the fine. In order to avoid abuse of this rule, such voluntary compensation should take place prior to the BCA's decision to impose a fine.

With respect to interests, Article XVII.72 CEL specifically entitles claimants to interest on the damages awarded in court. Compensatory interest accrues from the date the damages were incurred until the moment of final payment. As a general rule, courts

---

5 *Supra.*

6 Article IV.77 CEL juncto Article 962 Judicial Code.

apply the legal interest rate which is determined by governmental decree and published in the Belgian Official Gazette.[7]

Apart from damages actions, claimants can also seek the following remedies:

- Interim measures: a claimant may request the competent court to grant interim measures in summary proceedings when there is a risk of serious and irreparable damage. Such measure is temporary and is not binding on the court that will hear the case on the merits. The burden of proof is on the claimant, who must demonstrate that the requested interim measures are necessary, that he holds a *prima facie* claim and that the relief is appropriate in the situation at hand (articles 19§3 and 584 of the Judicial Code).
- Actions for a cease-and-desist order (Articles XVII.1 to XVII.13 and XVII.27 CEL). These rules deal with a specific procedure to obtain cease-and-desist orders from the president of the commercial court that has jurisdiction in cases relating to unfair trade practices. Under Belgian law, competition law infringements are considered unfair trade practices in the sense of Article VI.104 CEL.
- Nullity of contractual clauses (Article 1108 BCC). Under this provision, parties do no longer have to comply with the invalidated clauses or contract and will be entitled to damages from the other party.
- Declaratory judgment (Article 18 Belgian Judicial Code). This is a declaration that a given practice does not constitute a competition law infringement. The alleged infringer must establish that its rights are seriously jeopardised and that a declaratory judgment would eliminate the threat.

The general Belgian tort law rules provide that all persons that contributed to the wrongdoing and the harm caused by that wrongdoing, are jointly and severally liable. Article XVII.86§1 CEL as inserted by the Belgian Damages Act, reiterates this view. According to this provision, companies that have infringed competition law shall be jointly and severally liable for the harm caused, although two types of parties cannot be held jointly and severally liable:

- (Effective) immunity recipients (Article XVII.86§3 CEL).
- Small- and medium-sized enterprises (SMEs), which only have to pay damages for the harm caused to their own (direct or indirect) customers.
  SMEs must satisfy a number of (cumulative) conditions:
  - The SME had a market share below 5M(at any time during the infringement).
  - The application of the normal rules of joint and several liability would permanently jeopardise the economic viability of the SME and cause its assets to lose all their value.
  - The SME was not a leader or coercer of the anti-competitive activity and it is not a persistent offender (Article XVII.86§2 CEL).

Still, if a claimant is unable to obtain full compensation from the other infringers (for example, due to insolvency), the immunity recipient or SME will still be fully liable in accordance with Article XVII.86§2 and Article XVII.86§3 CEL.

---

7 In 2019 and 2018 the legal interest date was 2%.

5. Passing-on defence

The Belgian Damages Act introduced the passing-on defence in Articles XVII.83 *et seq* ELC. This principle accepts the defendant's right to demonstrate that the claimant has reduced its actual loss, by passing-on (in whole or in part) the overcharge[8] to subsequent clients. The burden of proving that the overcharge was passed on, will be on the defendant that invokes the defence. Article XVII.84 CEL clarifies that the passing-on defence can obviously not be invoked against end customer. In addition, the passing-on defence is not available in the context of class actions.

The Damages Act also introduces a rebuttable presumption that suppliers pass on overcharges – at least partially. Indirect purchasers can rely on this presumption if three conditions are met:

- The defendant infringed competition law.
- The infringement resulted in an overcharge for the direct purchaser.
- The indirect purchaser has purchased the goods or services that were the object of the infringement of competition law, or has purchased goods or services derived from or containing them.

As this presumption is rebuttable, the burden of proof shifts back to the indirect purchaser if the defendant brings credible evidence that the overcharge was not or was only partially passed on to the indirect purchaser (Article XVII.84 CEL).

6. Pre-trial discovery and disclosure, treatment of confidential information

Pre-trial discovery

Belgian procedural law does not provide for a specific discovery procedure for competition law cases. Hence, there is no pre-trial discovery process and the general rules of the judicial code apply.

Evidence held by other parties or third parties

Parties may request Belgian courts to order the production of documents (Articles 877 to 882-bis of the Judicial Code) at any stage of the proceedings. Under certain conditions, the courts may order a party to produce a document. To this end, the claimant must demonstrate:

- that a party to the proceedings or a third party is in possession of a document that could prove a fact that is decisive for the dispute or for the final decision.
- that there are serious, precise and concurring reasons to suspect that the third party in question has the document.

However, even if these conditions are fulfilled, the courts still have discretion to decide whether or not the document has to be produced. In this context, they have to find a

---

8 The overcharge is defined as the difference between the price actually paid and the price which would otherwise have been paid in the absence of the infringement of competition law (Article I.22, § 17, CEL).

balance between various factors, including the relevance of the evidence, the legality of a refusal based on confidentiality reasons and the arguments in favour of delivering an "order to produce evidence". In practice, courts apply the conditions to produce documents in a strict way in order to protect business confidentiality.

The Belgian Damages Act also offers the possibility for a court to order document production and specifies under which circumstances a private party could obtain access to evidence from another party. The requesting party must describe the (categories of) documents as precisely and narrowly as possible and the court must, then, balance the legitimate interests of the parties (including, for instance, the right to obtain compensation, the costs of disclosure or the existence of commercially sensitive information in the requested documents) (Article XVII.74 CEL).

Evidence held by the BCA

Finally, the Belgian Damages Act introduced the possibility to request and obtain evidence from the file of the BCA. This possibility is subject to two main conditions. First, courts must confirm that no (third) party is reasonably able to provide the requested evidence (Article XVII.77§2, juncto IV.45§2, Article IV.46 CEL) and secondly, that the request satisfies the proportionality principle. Regarding the latter, they must take into account:

- whether the disclosure request has been formulated specifically with regard to the nature, subject matter or contents of documents submitted to the competition authority or held in the file thereof.
- whether the disclosure request is related to an action for damages.
- the need to guarantee the effectiveness of public competition law enforcement (Article XVII.78§1 CEL).

Confidentiality of the evidence in the BCA's file

Certain categories of evidence from the BCA's file enjoy additional protection against discovery.

1) Belgian Courts may only order the disclosure of so-called "grey-list" information, after the BCA has issued a decision or alternatively, has terminated the proceedings. "Grey-list information" includes:
   - information that was prepared by a natural or legal person specifically for the proceedings of a competition authority;
   - information that the competition authority has drawn up and sent to the parties in the course of its proceedings; and
   - settlement submissions that have been withdrawn. (Article XVII.79§1 CEL, Belgian courts may only order the disclosure of this information). Such submissions may contain information that is useful for third parties that want to substantiate a claim for damages.
2) Belgian courts cannot order the disclosure of so-called "black-list information", namely:
   - leniency corporate statements; and
   - settlement submissions (Article XVII.79§2).

Evidence covered by the blacklist, obtained only through access to the file of the BCA, cannot be included in the file of an action for damages. Following a similar reasoning, evidence included in the grey list can only be used from the moment the BCA has closed its proceedings. If these rules are violated and such evidence is submitted, the documentation in question will be considered inadmissible (Article XVII.80§1 and Article XVII.80§2 CEL).

Evidence which is not covered by the black or the grey list but has been obtained solely through access to the file of a competition authority, can only be validly submitted in private damage claims by the person who succeeded in obtaining the evidence (Article XVII.80§3 CEL).

The disclosure of other categories of evidence is in principle allowed, although the national judge retains discretion and determines on a case-by-case basis whether a certain document has to be submitted.

Finally, from a more general perspective, under the Belgian Damages Act, courts are required to take appropriate measures to ensure the protection of confidential information (for instance by removing commercially sensitive passages in documents, restricting the persons allowed to get access to information and publishing summarised/non-confidential versions of decisions).

7. Limitation Periods

In Belgium, Articles 2262 *et seq* BCC set out the principles concerning limitation periods which apply before the national courts.

The BCC provides that claims in tort are time-barred:

- Five years after the day on which the claimant became (or should reasonably have become) aware of the damage and the identity of the person responsible for this damage (*i.e.* the relative limitation period).
- Twenty years after the date on which the fact, action or negligence that caused the damage occurred (*i.e.* the absolute limitation period).

Article XVII.90§1 CEL refers to the common limitation periods provided in the BCC and specifies that the relative limitation period of five years starts to run after the competition law violation has ceased and the claimant is aware (or should reasonably have been aware) of the infringement, the harm that was suffered and the identity of the party which caused the damage.

The limitation period is interrupted if the competition authority starts investigations or proceedings concerning the infringement in question. The interruption ends when the authority adopts a final infringement decision or terminates the investigations or proceedings in any other way the BCA (Article XVII.90§2 CEL).

The limitation period is suspended during any proceedings aiming at the amicable resolutions of disputes (excluding arbitration). This suspension applies to parties involved in the amicable dispute resolution. The suspension is limited to a maximum two-years period since the beginning of the proceedings (Article XVII.91 CEL).

8. Appeal

The judgment s of the court of first instance and of the commercial court in private enforcement actions can be appealed before the relevant Court of Appeal, on both factual and legal grounds, according to the general principles of procedural law. As a general principle, judgment s rendered in first instance are immediately enforceable.

Decisions of the Court of Appeal can be appealed on questions of law and formal requirements before the Supreme Court.

9. Class actions and collective representation

In Belgium, there are three types of collective proceedings:

- actions for collective redress (class actions);
- actions of collective interest; and
- collective (related) actions.

Actions for collective redress (class actions)

The possibility to bring an action for collective redress for a number of violations of Belgian and EU rules was introduced in March 2014 and entered into force on 1 September 2014. Actions for collective redress are only admitted for alleged infringements by a company of its contractual obligations or of specifically enumerated Belgian and European provisions (Article XVII.36§1 and Article XVII.37 CEL). The common element of these provisions is that they concern consumer protection. The list of contractual obligations includes provisions relating to *inter alia* credit services, (retail) market practices, product safety and intellectual property.

On 6 June 2017, the Belgian legislature extended the scope of application of actions for collective redress in order to cover violations of competition law (Article XVII.36.1° CEL juncto Article XVII.37.1° (a) and 33° CEL). On the basis of these provision, groups of consumers (and since 1 June 2018 also groups of SMEs) represented by non-profit organisations or public bodies, are entitled to bring class actions. In order to exercise this right, consumer associations and public interest groups have to comply with all legal conditions to act as a group representative (Article XVII.39 CEL). A group representative can be:

- an association for the defence of consumer interests that has legal personality and is represented on the Consumer Council; or
- an association of at least three years' standing which is approved by the Minister for the Economy and is not permanently operated for the purpose of financial gain; or
- the Consumer Mediation Service where it (the Mediation Service) is seeking to negotiate a collective redress agreement with the defendant businesses.

The group representative bringing the action must specify in the request for collective redress its choice for an opt-in or opt-out system and the reasons for this choice, within two months from the submission of the request (section 1, Article XVII.42 CEL). As a general rule, the courts take a decision on the admissibility of the action within two months from its submission and its decision will indicate whether the applicable system willl be "opt-in" or "opt-out", as well as the period within which consumers must exercise their option rights (from thirty days to three months) (section 2, Article XVII.43 CEL). However, opt-in systems are compulsory for:

- consumers who have no habitual residence in Belgium (section 2, Article XVII.48 CEL); and
- actions for physical or moral collective damage (section 2, Article XVII.43 CEL).

When an opt-out system has been admitted, claimants who have not exercised their right to opt-out can still opt-out of a settlement if they can demonstrate that they were tnott reasonably aware of the court's decision on the admissibility of the collective redress action as brought by the group representative (section 4, Article XVII.49 CEL).

Actions for collective redress are generally regulated by the same provisions of Book XVII, Title 3 CEL, as individual damage actions. There are, however, two exceptions:

- Defendants cannot invoke the passing-on defence.
- The usual rule that the court can suspend the proceedings for a period of two years in case the parties engage in consensual dispute resolution, is not applicable. (Article XVII.70 CEL juncto Articles XVII.83 and XVII.89 CEL).

Actions of collective interest

On the basis of specific legislation, an organisation or a group of people, may seek injunctive relief against practices that harm the general interests of consumers or of the members of such organisation. While these organisations cannot claim damages for their members, they may seek compensation for their own damage to the extent that their own personal interests were harmed.

Collective (related) actions

If different private enforcement actions are started by different claimants but concerning a comparable body of facts, the Belgian courts can join such individual claims in order to save resources. In other words, the related actions are handled by the court jointly, although formally they remain individual actions (Articles 30 and 701 of the Judicial Code).

Methodology for the selection of cases

In Belgium, the decisions and case law of the national courts are only published in legal journals. In addition, only selected cases are published. Therefore, there is a general lack of information as regards the use of damages claims in court, the amounts claimed, and main obstacles for a successful claims for damages for competition law infringements in Belgium.

The attached data was selected on the basis of a review of relevant legal journals.

List of Cases

All the case comments mentioned are available in the Concurrences e-Competitions Bulletin

Court of Appeal

15/02/2008, *Review Toepassingen van Communicatie BVBA / De Schepper J. and Raad voor de Mededinging*, e-Competitions Bulletin, Art. N° 111937
www.concurrences.com/111937
Gerrit Oosterhuis

Commercial Courts

29/04/2022, *A.J. Veurinck BV / DAF Trucks NV en Paccar Financial Holdings Europe BV (A/18/02226)*, e-Competitions Bulletin, Art. N° 116300
www.concurrences.com/116300
Vincent Mussche

23/03/2017, *Herman Verboven e.a. / Honda Motor Europe Logistics*, e-Competitions Bulletin, Art. N° 111940
www.concurrences.com/111940
Gerrit Oosterhuis

24/04/2015, *Belgische Staat/liftenproducenten*, e-Competitions Bulletin, Art. N° 111939
www.concurrences.com/111939
Gerrit Oosterhuis

24/11/2014, *Europese Commissie/Otis e.a. (A.R. A/08/06816)*, e-Competitions Bulletin, Art. N° 111938
www.concurrences.com/111938
Gerrit Oosterhuis

BRAZIL

Joyce Honda
Partner, Cescon Barrieu

Thales de Melo e Lemos
Senior Associate, Cescon Barrieu

José Gabriel Assis de Almeida
Partner, J.G. Assis de Almeida & Associados

Mickael Viglino
Partner, J.G. Assis de Almeida & Associados

In Brazil, private antitrust litigation is set forth in Law No. 12,529/2011 (the "Brazilian Antitrust Law") but is also based on general rules of tort liability provided in Law No. 10,406/2002 (the "Brazilian Civil Code"). Private enforcement of antitrust law has historically been limited, but there is a trend of expansion resulting from stronger public prosecution of cartels and broad diffusion of competition policy; new rules and guidance from government agencies and authorities; and especially from recent Law No. 14,470/2022 which entered into force in November 2022 and amended the Brazilian Antitrust Law to introduce specific procedural rules aimed at promoting private antitrust litigation.

1. Jurisdiction

The primary authority in charge of enforcing antitrust law in Brazil is the Administrative Council for Economic Defence ("CADE"). However, CADE is only in charge of public enforcement and not of private damages actions.

Therefore, victims of anti-competitive practices can seek compensation before civil state courts in the venue of their domicile, according to Article 53, V, of Law No. 13,105/2015 (the "Brazilian Code of Civil Procedure").

If the Brazilian Government, state-owned companies, government agencies – such as CADE, foundations, professional activity supervisory boards or even the Federal Public Prosecutor's Office – are parties, the jurisdiction will be of federal courts. In case such entities intervene in the process as interested third parties, the case records shall also be sent from the state courts to the federal courts.

2. Relevant legislation and legal grounds

Article 47 of the Brazilian Antitrust Law expressly states that parties directly or indirectly harmed by anti-competitive practices, as well as entities with a standing to propose collective actions in Brazil, may sue the infringers to obtain damages and the cessation of the practices, regardless of any inquiry or any on-going administrative process. This means that infringers can be sued even if no violation had been previously established by CADE.

The Brazilian Antitrust Law was recently amended by Law No. 14,470/2022 to provide further guidance regarding private antitrust litigation[1]. Article 47 of the Brazilian Antitrust Law, as amended, now provides that those harmed by collusive practices are entitled to double damages; that passing-on of overcharges will not be presumed; and that the statute of limitations will be paused during CADE's investigations, among other relevant changes.

---

1 In some cases, CADE may also issue non-binding guidance regarding the calculation of damages, to help potential claimants. CADE also issued a Resolution No. 21/2018, which regulates the procedure to access documents and information contained in its administrative proceedings. In addition, it establishes that CADE may consider, in the calculation of fines or settlements' values, eventual judicial or extrajudicial reparation of the damages caused.

That said, claimants must also resort to general rules of tort liability for matters not specifically covered by the Brazilian Antitrust Law, even after it was amended.

The general rule of tort liability in the Brazilian legal system is set forth by Article 927 of the Brazilian Civil Code, which establishes that any party that causes harm to others, by committing a wrongful act, is bound to repair it.

In addition, Article 186 of the Brazilian Civil Code sets forth that any party that violates rights and causes harm to another, by action, voluntary omission, negligence, or imprudence, commits a wrongful act. Abuse of rights is also a wrongful act, according to Article 187 of the Brazilian Civil Code. Therefore, the configuration of a wrongful act requires the violation of the legal system and consequent harm to another party.

This means that tort liability – and, therefore, antitrust damages actions in Brazil – is subject to the existence of four essential conditions: (i) wrongful act; (ii) fault or intent[2]; (iii) harm; and (iv) causal link between the wrongdoing and the harm, in accordance with Article 927, which requires wrongful act and harm, and Article 403, which requires causal link, both from the Brazilian Civil Code.

Any victim, whether they are direct or indirect customers, competitors, suppliers, etc., can seek compensation before the Brazilian courts, as long as they can prove they were harmed by the anti-competitive conduct. Parties have the right to employ all legal, as well as morally legitimate, means to prove the facts on which the claim is based, even if they are not specified in the Brazilian Code of Civil Procedure. Usual methods include documental and expert evidence.

As indicated above, it is not necessary that CADE, the Public Prosecutor or criminal courts have started an investigation or issued a decision finding an infringement for the action to be admitted, and therefore "stand-alone actions" are possible. However, to date, most antitrust damages actions in Brazil were based on decisions from CADE convicting companies for participating in cartels and can be characterised as "follow-on actions". Since Law No. 14,470/2022 established that the statute of limitations is paused during CADE's investigations, the proeminence of follow-on actions should persist.

Private antitrust damages actions will usually not be stayed as a result of ongoing investigations by CADE regarding the same conduct. However, defendants may seek the stay of a claim based on related pending decisions, such as the judicial review of CADE's decision in which the claim is based, in accordance with Article 313, V, "a", of the Brazilian Code of Civil Procedure. Some claims were stayed based on this provision[3].

---

2 The necessity to prove fault or intent in antitrust damages actions against companies is debatable, since the Brazilian Antitrust Law establishes strict liability for companies that take part in anti-competitive conducts. However, it can also be argued that mentioned strict liability only applies in the public enforcement and that demonstration of guilt or intent is fundamental to civil liability.

3 As an example, see Process No. 0004954-43.2013.8.21.0012 of the Dom Pedrito, Rio Grande do Sul, judicial district, involving the "cartel of medicinal gases".

3. What types of anti-competitive conduct are damages actions available for?

Antitrust damages actions can be brought against any kind of anti-competitive conduct, meaning any act that has the purpose or may produce any of the following effects, whether or not they succeed and regardless of fault: (i) limiting, adulterating, or in any way hindering free competition or free enterprise; (ii) controlling relevant markets of goods or services; (iii) arbitrarily increasing profits; and/or (iv) abusively dominating a market, in accordance with Article 36 of the Brazilian Antitrust Law.

As examples, the following conducts, mentioned in Article 36 of the Brazilian Antitrust Law, may be subject to antitrust damages actions: (i) agreements with competitors regarding prices, quantity of goods, allocation of shares or segments of markets, etc.; (ii) promotion or influence of uniformed or concerted business practices amongst competitors, aiming to standardize the agents' conducts (e.g. imposition of price lists for a given category, or by a class association); (iii) limiting or preventing the access of new entrants to the market; (iv) creating difficulties for the establishment, operation or development of competitors; and others, but mainly those listed in the Brazilian Antitrust Law.

4. What forms of relief may a private claimant seek?

In accordance with Article 47 of the Brazilian Antitrust Law, private claimants may seek: (i) the cessation of the anti-competitive conducts and (ii) compensation for losses and damages suffered.

This means a private claimant may seek pecuniary damages – including overcharges paid and any loss of profits – as well as pain and suffering damages (non-pecuniary losses). In the case of cartels, for instance, non-pecuniary losses could be claimed based on the reduction of welfare for consumers deprived of access to the affected products, either because of overcharges or reduction in supply. This may be the case, for example, in relation to a cartel that affects public health or essential goods.

As a rule, compensation is measured by the magnitude of the damages (Brazilian Civil Code, article 944), and damages must be assessed on a case-by-case basis.

Article 47 of the Brazilian Antitrust Law as amended by Law No. 14,470/2022 departs from this principle and provides that those harmed specifically by cartels or influence on the adoption of uniform conducts (e.g., price charts imposed by class associations) are entitled to double compensation. Only signatories of Leniency and Cease-and-Desist Agreements with CADE will not have to compensate in double.

Law No. 14,470/2022 entered into force in November 2022 and does not affect legal acts perfected and fully performed under the previous law (Decree-Law No. 4,657/1942, so-called "Introductory Law to the Rules of Brazilian Law").

The nature of this double compensation is at the origin of discussions around the entry into force of this provision of Law No. 14,470/2022. If it is a form of punitive damages, it tends to be applied to infringements committed after it became enforceable

(Federal Constitution, art. 5, 'XL'). If it is not punitive, but rather a stimulus to settlements with CADE, then it also applies to conducts practiced before it came into force. In any case, double compensation does not apply to infringements which were investigated in administrative proceedings concluded by CADE before Law No. 14,470/2022 entered into force. This matter will have to be settled by case law, which is still pending.

In principle, infringers may be considered jointly and severally liable for the damage caused by collective anti-competitive conducts, based on Article 942 of the Brazilian Civil Code. This means that victims can claim full compensation from any of them, who is then entitled to claim the co-debtors their respective share, in accordance with Articles 283 and 934 of the Brazilian Civil Code. Yet, joint and several civil liability for collective anti-competitive conducts is subject to discussions[4]. Law No. 14,470/2022 excludes the joint liability of signatories of Leniency and Cease-and-Desist Agreements with CADE, but does not provide anything regarding the other infringers in collective conducts, and case law is still pending.

Claimants may also seek an injunction to immediately cease the anti-competitive conduct – such as discriminatory practices or denying access to essential facilities, among others, in accordance with Article 47 of the Brazilian Antitrust Law and Articles 294 to 311 of the Brazilian Code of Civil Procedure[5].

The calculation of damages usually demands the production of expert evidence, which may be requested by the parties or *ex officio* by the judge, in accordance with Article 370 of the Brazilian Code of Civil Procedure.

As the calculation of civil damages in cases of anti-competitive practices may be an arduous task for the judiciary, decisions from CADE may sometimes include considerations and guidance for judges to set the amount to be paid to the victim in case the claim is received.[6] The Public Prosecutor's Office or the judge may also request CADE to provide information, including any estimation of damages it could have made in the course of the administrative investigation. In accordance with Article 118 of the Brazilian Antitrust Law and Article 138 of the Brazilian Code of Civil Procedure, CADE may also be notified to intervene as assistant or *amicus curiae* in claims involving Brazilian Antitrust Law.

Finally, the calculation of non-pecuniary losses caused by anti-competitive conducts is a complex and hardly predictable matter in Brazil, especially due to the lack of clear and settled parameters for such task. Usually, for cases involving non-pecuniary losses in general, courts consider the intensity of suffering and case law. In the case of antitrust damages claims, however, there is still not sufficient case law or guidance in Brazil, and non-pecuniary losses awarded so far are somewhat arbitrary.

---

4 See PASTORE, Ricardo Ferreira; MOTTA, Lucas Griebeler; IGNÁCIO, Renata Rossi. *Responsabilização solidária de cartelistas em ações indenizatórias: reflexões, limites e desafios*. In: A Livre Concorrência e os Tribunais Brasileiros: Análise crítica dos julgados no Poder Judiciário envolvendo matéria concorrencial. São Paulo: Singular, 2018.

5 As an example, see Process No. 332.865 (2013/0120915-8) – MG at the Brazilian Superior Court of Justice, involving the so called "cartel of medicinal gases".

6 For instance, CADE, administrative process No. 08700.002821/2014-09, Paulo Burnier da Silveira, 07 June 2017.

5. Passing-on defence

In the absence of express provisions by the law, Courts in Brazil have admitted the passing-on defence, at least in the first and second instances[7], based on Article 944 of the Brazilian Civil Code, which establishes that compensation is measured by the extension of the damages, and Article 884 of the Brazilian Civil Code, which prohibits unjust enrichment.

Article 47 of the Brazilian Antitrust Law as amended by Law No. 14,470/2022 now provides that the passing-on of overcharges is not presumed, and that the burden of proof is on the defendants, which settles an important controversy.

Nonetheless, for the purpose of proving the passing-on, the defendants may claim the disclosure of documents in possession of the claimants (Articles 396 to 404 of the Brazilian Code of Civil Procedure).

In addition, if claimants can more easily demonstrate that overcharges were not passed on to their own consumers, the judge may shift the burden of proof to the claimants, provided this is done in a reasoned decision. In that case, claimants must be given the opportunity to challenge the shifting of the burden of proof (Article 373, §1º of the Brazilian Code of Civil Procedure), *i.e.,* they may ask the judge to reconsider his/her decision to shift the burden of proof.

If the court supports the passing-on defence, indirect customers would still need to file a new lawsuit, subject to the same legal requirements and rules previously indicated.

6. Pre-trial discovery and disclosure, treatment of confidential information

There is no pre-trial discovery phase in Brazil. Unless provided otherwise by any specific legislation, such as what happens for the passing-on defence, the burden of proof falls on the claimant regarding the facts that constitute his rights, and on the defendant as to the existence of any fact that blocks, modifies or extinguishes the claimant's rights.

The judge may also assign the burden of proof differently, provided this is done in a reasoned decision, giving the assigned party the opportunity to argue against the shift of the burden of proof, as previously mentioned.

In addition, in accordance with Articles 381 to 383 of the Brazilian Code of Civil Procedure, a claimant may present a motion for the early production of evidence. The motion shall be admitted in cases in which: (i) there is reasonable fear that it may become impossible or very difficult to attest certain facts during the course of the suit; (ii) the evidence to be produced may render viable an amicable solution between the parties or facilitate a swift outcome through another adequate mean of dispute resolution; and (iii) prior knowledge of the facts may either justify or avoid the filing of the suit.

The claimant must precisely state the facts on which the evidence rests. The judge shall then determine the service of process upon parties who have interest in the production of

---

7 To date, there is no public decision from the superior/supreme courts yet.

evidence or in the fact to be proven. The interested parties may request the production of any piece of evidence in the same proceeding, provided it is related to the same fact, unless its joint production causes excessive delay – this should be assessed in each case, based on a proportionality analysis.

In those proceedings, the judge shall not render judgment on the occurrence or not of the fact, nor on the respective legal consequences.

Furthermore, during a lawsuit, a claimant may request the disclosure of documents or evidence in possession of defendants or third parties. This means that the judge may order the production of documents from the files of CADE or from criminal investigations.

CADE's Resolution No. 21 of 12 September 2018, regulates the procedure to access documents and information contained in administrative proceedings to impose sanctions for violations against the economic order. By standard, all documents and information are considered public, and even confidential records will be publicised after CADE's Tribunal final decision. However, there are exceptions that will be maintained confidential even after CADE's final decision, such as: (i) the anti-competitive conduct records elaborated based on self-accusatory documents and information voluntarily submitted during the negotiations of leniency agreements and settlements; (ii) documents that contain industrial secrets; (iii) documents related to business activity whose disclosure may represent competitive advantages to other economic agents; (iv) documents and information whose confidentiality is protected in specific legislation, such as tax and banking information, professional secrets, among others; (v) documents whose confidentiality was defined in judicial decisions; (vi) documents provided by a proponent during the negotiations of Leniency Agreement or Settlements subsequently frustrated; and others. Nevertheless, access to those documents and information may be granted by specific judicial decisions, keeping in mind the necessity to protect the national policies of leniency and settlements.

7. Limitation periods

Article 46-A of the Brazilian Antitrust Law, which was introduced by recent Law No. 14,470/2022, provides that the limitation period for antitrust damages actions is of five years, counted from the unequivocal knowledge about the infringement[8,9], which is presumed after the publication of CADE's final decision regarding the same conduct. This settles a historic controversy in case law regarding the starting point of the limitation period for antitrust damages claims, but leaves the discussion open regarding whether

8 The limitation period for individual antitrust damages actions used to be of three years, according to Article 206, § 3º, V of the Brazilian Civil Code. For collective actions, the limitation period was already considered to be five years, by analogy with Law No. 4717/1965, which sets forth the limitation period for collective claims ("*Ação Popular*"). The new limitation period established by Law No. 14,470/2022 will not be applicable to demands that were already time-barred, in accordance to Article 206, §3º, V, of the Brazilian Civil Code, at the time it became enforceable.

9 The limitation period for individual antitrust damages actions used to be of three years, according to Article 206, § 3º, V of the Brazilian Civil Code. For collective actions, the limitation period was already considered to be five years, by analogy with Law No. 4717/1965, which sets forth the limitation period for collective claims ("*Ação Popular*"). The new limitation period established by Law No. 14,470/2022 will not be applicable to demands that were already time-barred, in accordance to Article 206, §3º, V, of the Brazilian Civil Code, at the time it became enforceable.

any other event during such investigation may evidence such unequivocal knowledge (e.g., the public disclosure of the investigations). For stand-alone actions, courts will have to decide on a case-by-case basis.

Article 46-A of the Brazilian Antitrust Law also provides that the limitation period does not run during CADE's respective administrative inquiry or proceeding[10].

Parties potentially harmed by anti-competitive conducts may also seek motions to interrupt the limitation period running. Those consist of simple and non-adversarial proceedings, set forth in Article 202 of the Brazilian Civil Code and Article 726 of the Brazilian Code of Civil Procedure. They can be used to interrupt the limitation period once and retain the rights for future lawsuits.

8. Appeal

Rulings of civil courts must be appealed before the respective state or federal Court of Appeals, which has jurisdiction over matters of fact and law.

Rulings of the Court of Appeals may be appealed before the Brazilian Superior Court of Justice, which rules only on points of law related to the application of federal laws or treaties, and the Brazilian Supreme Court, which rules on points of law related to the Brazilian Constitution.

9. Class actions and collective representation

Under Brazilian Antitrust Law, antitrust damages actions may be proposed by entities listed in Article 82 of Law No. 8.078/1999 (the "Brazilian Consumer Protection Code") for the defence of homogeneous individual rights.

Furthermore, Law No. 7.347/1985 specifically regulates collective actions in Brazil for the recovery of damages caused by infractions against the economic order, in addition to the general provisions of the Brazilian Antitrust Law as amended by Law No. 14,470/2022.

In accordance with mentioned legislation, collective actions for the recovery of antitrust damages may be filed by: (i) the Public Prosecutor's Office; (ii) the Public Defender's Office; (iii) the Union, states, the federal district and municipalities; (iii) government agencies, state-owned companies, foundations and private companies controlled by the government; and (iv) associations that already existed for at least one year and that include in their institutional objectives the defence of consumers, competition or the economic order.

The majority of collective actions related to antitrust damages, in Brazil, were filed by the Public Prosecutor's Office, usually after CADE sent an official letter to the Public Prosecutor informing such Prosecutor of a recently issued infringement decision and suggesting that collective actions be initiated.

---

10 The administrative inquiry is a preliminary investigative procedure, when the authority understands that evidence is not sufficient to iniative an administrative proceeding. The administrative inquiry may be kept confidential in the benefit of the investigations, at the authority's discretion.

According to Article 103, III, of the Brazilian Consumer Protection Code, decisions in collective actions relating to antitrust damages give rise to *res judicata* and are binding upon everyone – benefiting all the victims and their successors – only if the claim is granted. This means that each individual party or their successors may proceed with the liquidation and execution of the decision for their part of the damages. However, if the claim is not granted, interested parties that did not act as co-claimants may file individual lawsuits.

Collective actions do not operate as *lis pendens* to individual lawsuits, but the positive *res judicata* will not benefit the individual claimants if they do not request the suspension of their individual claims within 30 days, counted from the knowledge that the collective action exists.

10. Key issues

Law No. 14,470/2022, which entered into force in November 2022, modified the Brazilian Antitrust Law with the purpose of promoting antitrust damages claims and settling several matters which were object of controversy in Brazilian courts, such as the applicable limitation period and its starting point and the burden of proof regarding passing-on defence.

Nonetheless, important discussions remain, including: (i) the starting point for the limitation period in stand-alone actions; (ii) if unequivocal knowledge about an infringement can happen before the publication of CADE's final decision; (iii) if double compensation is applicable to infringements that took place before Law No. 14,470/2022 entered into force; and (iv) how defendants will be able to prove the passing-on, since they probably do not have access to the claimants' pricing strategies.

In addition, the calculation of antitrust damages is still an arduous task for the claimants and the judiciary. This step usually demands the production of expert evidence and, even so, may stumble in the lack of familiarity of Brazilian courts with antitrust matters, lack of documents to base the calculation and difficulties to reach legal standards. The consulted case law shows that the liquidation phase in antitrust damages actions is surrounded with uncertainties, as very often, in the past, the damages awarded were estimated or arbitrated by courts in a merely discretionary manner (*i.e* with no actual link between the harm and the award).

Decisions from CADE may sometimes include considerations and guidance for judges, and CADE may be requested to provide information or to intervene in claims. However, additional changes in the Brazilian legislation, joined by the specialisation of Brazilian courts in antitrust matters, would be helpful.

Finally, the access, by claimants in antitrust damages actions, to confidential documents from CADE's investigations, is still an issue. CADE's Resolution No. 21 of 12 September 2018 regulates such procedure and provides some guidance, but there is still no settled case law regarding the cases in which such acess shall be granted and to what extent.

Methodology for the selection of cases

The attached database includes cases found through research of case law from the various state, federal and higher courts in Brazil, based on the terms "cartel" and

"Law 12.529/2011" (the Brazilian Antitrust Law), and on Article 47 thereof (which provides for private antitrust damage claims). We selected cases in which decisions on the merits are publicly available. In addition, we listed cases that represent different types of actions (e.g., individual claims, class actions, public-interest civil actions), as well as cases that bring different requests and results.

List of Cases

All the case comments mentioned are available in the Concurrences e-Competitions Bulletin

Federal Supreme Court

02/10/1997, "Process No. 964.306 (Extraordinary Appeal), e-Competitions Bulletin, Art. N° 111932
www.concurrences.com/111932
Joyce Honda, Thales Lemos

Superior Court of Justice

Process No. 7099345-90.2009.8.13.0024 (civil lawsuit); Interlocutory Appeal in Special Appeal nº 332865-MG, e-Competitions Bulletin, Art. N° 111936
www.concurrences.com/111936
Joyce Honda, Thales Lemos

Federal District Appellate court

07/08/2013, Process No. 0036211-12.2013.8.07.0001 (Civil Appeal), e-Competitions Bulletin, Art. N° 111929
www.concurrences.com/111929
José Gabriel Assis de Almeida, Mickael Viglino

Regional Federal Appellate Courts

26/08/2017, Process No. 1050035-45.2017.8.26.0100 (Civil Appeal); Process No. 1076834-28.2017.8.26.0100 (Civil Appeal); Process No. 1076386-55.2017.8.26.0100 (Civil Lawsuit); Process No. 1076640-28.2017.8.26.0100 (Civil Lawsuit); Process No. 1076741-65.2017.8.26.0100 (Civil Lawsuit); and others, e-Competitions Bulletin, Art. N° 111930
www.concurrences.com/111930
Joyce Honda, Thales Lemos

16/12/2013, Process No. 0004954-43.2013.8.21.0012 (civil lawsuit), e-Competitions Bulletin, Art. N° 111935
www.concurrences.com/111935
Joyce Honda, Thales Lemos

03/10/2006, Process No. 70068906171 (Civil Appeal), e-Competitions Bulletin, Art. N° 111933
www.concurrences.com/111933
Joyce Honda, Thales Lemos

26/08/2005, Process No. 3002976-90.2005.8.26.0506 (Civil Appeal), e-Competitions Bulletin, Art. N° 111928
www.concurrences.com/111928
José Gabriel Assis de Almeida, Mickael Viglino

05/04/1999, Process No. 0012334-56.1999.4.05.8300 (Civil Appeal), e-Competitions Bulletin, Art. N° 111934
www.concurrences.com/111934
Joyce Honda, Thales Lemos

03/04/1995, Process No. 0051034-04.1995.4.03.6100 (Civil Appeal), e-Competitions Bulletin, Art. N° 111931
www.concurrences.com/111931
Joyce Honda, Thales Lemos

CHILE

Benjamin Grebe
Partner, Prieto Abogados

Andrea Von Chrismar
Counsel, Prieto Abogados

Historically, Chile has used a system that has privileged the actions of the National Economic Prosecutor's Office ("FNE") to prosecute the conducts contemplated in the Competition Law (Decree-law no. 211 of 1973) without leaving much room for private enforcement. Before the modification of the law, the Chilean system provided an action for damages that had to be initiated after a condemnatory judgment issued by the Competition Court and that could only be brought before the competent Civil Court according to the general procedural rules. Before such Civil Court, only the loss and the causality had to be proved, since the facts and the legal qualification had been clearly established by the Competition Court Decision. However, the law also provided for another option to victims of anti-competitive practice, who could also go directly to Civil Courts, without a final judgment of the Competition Court, in which case, damages, causality, and the existence of the anti-competitive conduct had to be proven.

With Law No. 20,945 published in August 2016, a series of modifications were introduced, including a new system of compensation for damages for attacks against competition. In this regard, the reform contemplates two actions:

- first, an individual action incorporated in the new Article 30 of Competition Law; and
- second, a collective action in the new Article 51 of Law No. 19,496 on the Protection of Consumer Rights (both Articles modified as a result of the reform of the year 2016).

This increased the incentives for private parties to participate in proceedings before the Competition Court, and also the deterrent and corrective power of its resolutions, since in addition to the fines imposed by this authority, compensation for damages will also apply.

1. Jurisdiction

The Competition Court ("*Tribunal de Defensa de la Libre Competencia*") has exclusive jurisdiction to resolve antitrust matters in Chile and to decide on public and private disputes.

Article 30 of Competition Law establishes that the damages actions arising from a final judgment of the Competition Court shall be filed before this Court. Thus, it is understood that currently there are no damages actions if there is no judgment issued by the Competition Court. Moreover, the only competent court to hear damages actions will be the Competition Court itself. Accordingly, the legislator sought both to contribute to the procedural economy and to allow the damage caused to be determined by the same specialised tribunal that established the facts serving as antecedents. While stand-alone actions are possible according to general rules of non-contractual liability, in such cases all the elements of the liability must be proven. Therefore, the burden of proof and procedures have higher complexities than the process before the Competition Court.

Finally, it should be noted that the final paragraph of Article 30 provides that the Competition Court shall also be competent to rule civil actions arising from the criminal procedure contemplated in Title V of the law (these are collusion, or agreements or concerted practices involving competitors).

2. Relevant legislation and legal grounds

In the first place, the damages actions must comply with the general requirements established by the Chilean legislation, jurisprudence and doctrine, constructed principally from Article 2,314 of the Chilean Civil Code, and which would be the following:

- existence of fraudulent or culpable conduct;
- existence of damage;
- causal relationship between the conduct and the damage; and
- absence of liability exonerators.

Considering specific terms, the only norm regarding damages actions for anti-competitive conducts is found in Article 30 of Competition Law (without prejudice to Article 51 of Law No. 19.496, which enshrines the special procedure for the protection of the collective or diffuse interest of consumers).

The Competition Court shall base its decision on the facts established in its previous judgment about the anti-competitive conduct that caused the damage. Furthermore, the Court will evaluate the evidence according to Sound Criticism Rules.[1]

The compensation for the anti-competitive damages shall include all damages caused during the period in which the infringement has been extended.

Article 30 establishes the procedure to be followed in the individual compensation actions filed before Competition Court, which is known in the legislation as the "summary procedure", consists of a shorter and more efficient mechanism for obtaining compensation. According to Article 680 of the Chilean Code of Civil Procedure, the summary procedure will apply in all cases where "the action filed requires, by its nature, expeditious processing to be effective". As it is a shorter procedure than the ordinary one, it allows to the victim to reduce costs. In general, in the Chilean system, the summary procedure is applied in cases that requires speed of processing for effective results. On the other hand, Article 51 of the Law No. 19.936, which provides actions for protection of the collective of diffuse interes of consumer, states the procedure to be followed in such actions shall be the special procedure provided for in the same law, even if they are brought before the Competition Court.

3. What types of anti-competitive conduct are damages actions available for?

The damages action is not limited to any anti-competitive agreements or abuses of dominant position. An enforceable judgment issued by the Competition Court is sufficient. In other words, a final ruling issued by the Competition Court condemning any antitrust conduct is enough. This judgment is the only but necessary antecedent to file an action for compensation for damages without being limited to any particular anticompetitive conduct.

---

1 According to Sound Criticism Rules, the judge is free to appreciate the evidence, but always respecting the principles of logic, the maxims of experience, and scientifically sound knowledge. This system is different from the Legal or Assessed Evidence one, where it is the law that gives each evidence submitted a predetermined value or weighting, mandatory for the judge. In Chilean legislation, it is the legislator who establishes whether Sound Criticism Rules or Legal Evidence will apply in the procedure.

4. What forms of relief may a private claimant seek?

The law is clear in stating that damages actions "shall include all damages caused during the period in which the infringement has been extended," without making distinctions as to consequential damages, lost profits or moral damages. However, as a general rule in the Chilean legal system, the only damages that can be compensated are the direct and not the indirect ones.

The damages included in the compensation will be analysed below in paragraph 9.

5. Standard of proof

Article 30 also establishes that the proof appreciation within this procedure will be evaluated in accordance with the Sound Criticism Rules. This proof appreciation, which is more flexible than the one regulated by law, is consistent with the legislator's idea of granting competence in damages actions to a specialised court, which has greater flexibility in the analysis and weighting of evidence with respect to such technical and complex matters.

There has been no precedent to date as regards passing-on defence.

6. Confidentiality, discovery, exhibition, leniency

In the trial before Competition Court, all documents and other records are public, with some exceptions established in the same Competition Law, such as commercially sensitive data of the companies. Nevertheless, other parties, and third parties such as consumers could review all non-confidential data to fund a damage action.

Furthermore, claimants for damages could ask the Court to order companies to exhibit some documents, including those provided in the trial for anti-competitive infringement.

Regarding leniency, the Chilean system does not include any benefit related to damages actions for anti-competitive infringements. The benefits of leniency are limited to the penalty of a fine and imprisonment. The publicity of the information and records – with the above-mentioned exceptions – are one of the deterrents for potential leniency applicants, given the fact that mostly all information will be publicly available for civil claimants.

7. Limitation periods

Regarding the individual action contemplated in Article 30 of Competition Law, the final paragraph of Article 20 of Competition Law states that civil actions arising from an antitrust conduct shall be exercised up to four years from the date on which the final judgment serving as antecedent to the civil action is found to be final and enforceable.

In the absence of an express provision, regarding the collective action contemplated in Article 51 of Law No. 19,496, the general rules established in Article 2514 of the Chilean Civil Code shall apply, which establishes that ordinary actions may be exercised within a five years term[2], starting from the date when the obligation became enforceable (which,

---

[2] Ordinary actions have a different term than the executive ones, which shall be exercised within a three years' term.

in the case of damage claims, occurs once the final judgment serving as antecedent to the civil action is found to be final and enforceable).

Likewise, according to the general rules, the period for exercising the actions are naturally interrupted when the debtor recognises the obligation, either expressly or tacitly, and are civilly interrupted by the interposition of the lawsuit (Article 2518 of the Civil Code).

8. Appeal

Article 30 sets that the final judgment issued by the Competition Court, can only be subject to an appeal before the Supreme Court, that can review and reverse with broad powers on the merits of the case.

9. Class actions and collective representation

Class actions, under Chilean law, are contemplated in law No. 19,496, as a mean to protect the interest of the consumers. The class action is only for consumers matters and have no application in other areas. To file a claim for collective damages, the law requires the coordination of at least 50 people affected by the same illicit behavior, or the representation of the National Consumer's Service ("SERNAC") or consumers associations.

This action, in antitrust matters is found in Article 51 of Law No. 19,496. The first paragraph of said Article states the procedure "shall apply when the collective or diffuse interest of consumers is affected. This special procedure shall be subject to the following procedural rules. All the submitted evidence must be appraised in accordance with the sound criticism rules".

The foregoing without prejudice to what is stated in No. 2 of Article 51 of Law No. 19,496: "The compensations determined in this procedure may not be extended to moral damages suffered by the claimants". As a general rule in the Chilean system, the only damages that can be compensated are the direct and not the indirect ones.

According to this Article, in the event of harm to the collective or diffuse interest of consumers through an anti-competitive conduct, the lawsuit may be processed in accordance with the previous special procedure before the Competition Court. This may be the case where, for example, collusion has led to an increase in the price passed on to consumers. Thus, it is possible to conclude that the Competition Court may hear individual claims through the summary procedure, and class actions through the special procedure contemplated in Article 51 of Law No. 19.496.

For example, the Competition Court established that even if the lawsuit is filed jointly, the damages are individual, so that each of the claimants must prove the respective damage suffered and there is not a kind joint and several liability among the defendants.

On the other hand, and since the law does not distinguish between individual and collective actions, it has been understood that the jurisdiction of the Competition Court to hear damages actions may be extended to the collective actions contemplated in Article 51 of Law No. 19.496 on the Protection of Consumer Rights (which contemplates a special procedure for the protection of the collective or diffuse interest of consumers). Such Article states that, "notwithstanding the provisions of Article 30 of Competition

Law, and without prejudice to the appropriate individual actions, the damages actions filed before the Competition Court (on the occasion of violations of Competition Law), declared by a final enforceable judgment , may be processed through the procedure established in this paragraph when the collective or diffuse interest of consumers is affected."

This change in legislation is very recent, so there is no precedent for its application, where compensation for damage for collective interest has been awarded. Notwithstanding this, it has been said by the chilean Supreme Court (in just one case at the moment) that Article 51 is an alternative procedure to Article 30 of the competition law, which will be applicable in cases of collective actions, with jurisdiction of the Competition Court.

Methodology for the selection of cases

To date, ten lawsuits have been filed under this new modality before the Competition Court, seven of them correspond to class actions (all seven for cartel cases, five of them for the supermarkets case, one for the poultry case and one for the Ro-Ro transport case). Two cases (one private action and one class action) initiated by lawsuits have ended with a settlement, without a final decision of the Court. In one of the settlements, the agreement was to compensate through the payment to non-profits organizations (*Cy-pres* or *fluid recovery* doctrine). While there are no more cases of compensation for damages in Chilean case law with a final judgment, it is possible to extract some trends laid down by the Competition Court from the aforementioned cases.

List of Cases

All the case comments mentioned are available
in the Concurrences e-Competitions Bulletin

Competition Court

21/04/2020 (Date of admission), *Demanda de Papelera Cerrillos S.A. contra CMPC Tissue S.A. y otra*, CIP-3-2020, e-Competitions Bulletin, Art. N° 111927
www.concurrences.com/111927
Benjamín Grebe, Daniella Ibaceta

25/06/2019 (Date of admission), CIP- 3- 2019, e-Competitions Bulletin, Art. N° 111926
www.concurrences.com/111926
Benjamín Grebe, Daniella Ibaceta

14/12/2017 (Date of admission), *Demanda de Sandra Fuentes Salazar y otros contra Empresa de Transportes Rurales Limitada y otros*, CIP-1-2017, e-Competitions Bulletin, Art. N° 111925
www.concurrences.com/111925
Benjamín Grebe, Manuela Barros

FRANCE

Sergio Sorinas
Partner, Herbert Smith Freehills LLP

Marie Louvet
Of Counsel, Herbert Smith Freehills LLP

In France, private antitrust litigation has been based on general rules of civil contractual and tort liability. First milestone decisions date back to the early 2010s. Private enforcement of antitrust law has historically been limited but the implementation of Directive 2014/104/EU into French law by Ordinance No. 2017-303 ("Ordinance") and Decree No. 2017-305 ("Decree") of 9 March 2017, which have introduced specific procedural rules for private antitrust actions (Articles L.481-1 et seq. of the French Commercial Code), has facilitated antitrust damages actions.

1. Jurisdiction

The primary authority in charge of enforcing competition law in France is the French Competition Authority ("FCA"). However, the FCA is only competent for public enforcement and not for private damages actions.

Victims of anti-competitive practices can seek compensation either on the basis of a prior decision from the FCA or another competition authority finding an infringement of competition law (follow-on action) or absent any prior decision, on a stand-alone basis (stand-alone action). However, in case a public enforcement procedure is ongoing, stand-alone actions for damages may be stayed until the competition authority has decided on the case.

French courts have jurisdiction insofar as (i) the defendant's residence or place of business is in France, (ii) the anti-competitive practice occurred in France, or (iii) the damage was suffered in France. Claimants can bring their action before one of the eight civil or eight commercial courts specialised in competition law, spread across the French territory. Collective actions, however, can be brought before any civil court in France.

First instance rulings can only be appealed before the Paris Court of Appeal, which has exclusive jurisdiction.

Administrative courts have jurisdiction when the alleged damage relates to an administrative contract. Criminal courts have jurisdiction when the claim is based on criminal liability (which, under French law, may arise in respect of certain anti-competitive conducts such as e.g., bid rigging). The rules applicable to administrative and criminal actions are not covered in this overview.

The jurisdictional clause included in an agreement may also be applicable provided that the alleged anti-competitive practices materialise in the contractual relations between the parties and/or by means of contractual terms.

2. Relevant legislation and legal grounds

In order to be valid, a claim for damages must be based both:

(i) on civil liability legislation:
- either general civil liability:
  - Tortious liability: Articles 1240 et seq. of the French Civil Code; or

 - Contractual liability (when the alleged harm results from contractual relationships between the parties, e.g., for an abuse of dominance): Articles 1103 et seq. of the French Civil Code;
- And/or the new framework introduced by the Ordinance and the Decree which provide specific procedural rules relating to the liability of infringers of competition law: Articles L.481-1 et seq. of the French Commercial Code ("FCCom");

(ii) and the relevant French and/or EU antitrust legislation: private antitrust actions can be based on any violation of French (Articles L.420-1, L.420-2, L.420-2-1, L.420-2-2 and L.420-5 FCCom) or EU (Articles 101 and 102 TFEU) competition law.

Any victim, whether they are direct or indirect customers, competitors, suppliers, or other victims, can seek compensation before French courts provided that they satisfy the general conditions set out by civil liability rules, such as standing and interest in the case. A claimant must show that it has a legitimate, direct and personal interest in the action for damages. In practice, competitors (which were not part of the anti-competitive practices), direct and indirect customers, as well as end consumers, may have standing, provided they have suffered harm from such practices.

To date, most cases have been based on the general tortious liability regime, which is still applicable to any actions for damages based on an infringement of competition law arising before 11 March 2017 (Article 1240 of the French Civil Code). It requires the claimant to bring evidence of (i) a fault – e.g., an anti-competitive behaviour, (ii) damage, and (iii) causation between the two. The burden of proof of the three above-mentioned elements falls on the claimant, and has traditionally be considered as limiting the development of private enforcement in France.

The Ordinance and the Decree have made it easier for claimants to establish those three elements, in particular for follow-on actions:

- Article L.481-2 FCCom provides that a decision of the FCA finding an infringement of competition law which can no longer be appealed on such findings constitutes irrefutable evidence of a fault. This does not apply to decisions of inadmissibility, dismissal, or commitment decisions of the FCA, since there is no finding of an infringement, but still applies to settlement decisions. French courts may still use commitment decisions, in which the FCA raises only competition concerns on the basis of a preliminary assessment of the competitive situation, as *prima facie* evidence of the fault. In the *PMU/Betclic* case, the Paris Court of Appeal considered that the commitment decision might still provide sufficient elements to establish the undertaking's liability.[1]

  As regards decisions by the European Commission, French courts are bound by final decisions of the European Commission enforcing Articles 101 and 102 TFEU as their decisions cannot be contrary to the Commission's findings. However, decisions of national competition authorities in the EU only have evidential value (e.g., they are taken into account as a piece of evidence, but the court is not bound by the decision).

[1] Paris Court of Appeal, 12 September 2018, n° 18/04914, *PMU / Betclic.*

Parties, which have been granted immunity from fine under a leniency programme, are not exempt from civil liability. However, they benefit from some protection as regards access to the file and cannot be found jointly and severally liable for damages with other parties to the infringement (except in specific circumstances as detailed below).

- Article L.481-7 FCCom provides for a presumption that anti-competitive agreements cause damage. This presumption alleviates the claimant's burden of proof in establishing causation between the anti-competitive practice and the damage suffered. It does not apply for abuses of dominance.
- Article L.481-4 FCCom has introduced a rebuttable presumption that the purchaser has not passed on the additional costs incurred as a result of the anti-competitive practice to its own customers.

Rationae temporis application of the Ordinance

Pursuant to the principle of non-retroactivity of the law, the new substantial provisions of the Ordinance, and in particular the above-mentioned presumptions, are only applicable to facts causing liability that have arisen after 11 March 2017.

However,

- procedural rules regarding the production of evidence[2] apply to all claims lodged since 26 December 2014 (as provided in Article 22 of the Directive);
- provisions regarding the limitation period apply when the limitation period had not expired at the date of entry into force of the Ordinance. In such case, account must be taken of the period that has already elapsed.

For the time being, most actions remain subject to the previous substantive provisions. That being said, while refusing to apply any of the above-mentioned presumptions to facts pre-dating the Ordinance, French case-law has ruled under the general tortious liability regime that:

- decisions of the FCA or the European Commission finding an infringement of competition law by the defendant are sufficient to establish a fault;[3]
- in cartel cases, the limitation period only starts once the competition authority has issued its decision, considering that it is only at such point in time that the victim is aware of all of: the practices, the fact that they are anti-competitive, that they caused harm, and the identity of the infringing party(ies).[4]

What types of anti-competitive conduct are damages actions available for?

Damages actions are not limited to anti-competitive agreements and abuses of dominant position. They are also available for damage resulting from abuses of economic dependency (Article L.420-2, 2° FCCom), allocation of exclusive import rights in French overseas

---

2 Articles L. 483-1 to L. 483-4, L. 483-6, L. 483-7, L. 483-9 and the first four paragraphs of articles L.483-7 and L.483-10, and Article L.462-3 FCCom.

3 French Supreme Court, 1 March 2023, n° 20-18.356, *Digicel*.

4 Paris Court of Appeal, section 5-4, 5 January 2022, n° 19/22293, *Vania / Carrefour France*.

territories (Article L.420-2-1 FCCom), agreements or practices relating to transportation (Article L.420-2-2 FCCom) and abusively low retail prices (Article L.420-5 FCCom).

What forms of relief may a private claimant seek?

Punitive damages are not available under French law.

The sole purpose of damages actions is to compensate the victim for the damage suffered. Causation between the fault and the damage must be direct, which means that the claimant must prove that the damage it suffers results entirely from the anti-competitive behaviour.

Article L.481-3 FCCom provides that damage caused by anti-competitive practices includes (i) the overcharge paid, (ii) loss of profits, (iii) loss of opportunity and (iv) moral prejudice. As mentioned above, Article L.481-7 FCCom has introduced a presumption that anti-competitive agreements and concerted practices cause damage.

Claimants may (i) request pecuniary compensation, but also (ii) ask the court to declare their agreement with the defendant null and void, or (iii) issue an injunction requiring the defendant to grant access to an essential facility or to resume business relationships for example.[5]

Undertakings that have infringed competition law are jointly and severally liable for the damage caused by the infringement to the claimant. This means that a victim can claim full compensation from any of them until fully compensated. Infringing undertakings contribute to the payment of damages in proportion of their relative responsibility in the harm caused (so that they are able to recover a contribution from any other undertaking if they have to pay the victim in full).

However, infringing undertakings that have been granted immunity from fine by the FCA are not jointly and severally liable towards other victims than those with whom they have direct or indirect contractual relationships, unless the said victims are unable to obtain compensation from the other infringers (Article L.481-11 FCCom).

3. Passing-on defence

The burden of proof of causation between fault and damage falls on the claimant.

Pursuant to the previous regime, before the entry into force of the Ordinance, it was on the purchaser to demonstrate that it has not passed on the overcharge resulting from the anti-competitive practices to its own customers.

Article L.481-4 FCCom has reversed the presumption underlying the "passing-on defence" and provides that a direct or indirect purchaser is deemed not to have passed on the overcharge to its own customers. It is now for the defendant to prove that the purchaser has done so. In a 2017 decision, the Paris Court of Appeal applied this new presumption in a case that was subject to the previous regime and confirmed the loss by finding that the defendants failed to show that the overcharge had been passed on

---

5 For an example of injunction to resume business relationships, see the judgment of the Paris commercial court of 10 February 2021 in the *Google/Oxone* case.

to the claimant's own customers.[6] However, more recently, French courts seem to have become more strict and refused to apply such presumption when the facts at stake predated the entry into force of the Ordinance on 11 March 2017.[7]

4. Pre-trial discovery and disclosure, treatment of confidential information

There is no discovery procedure in France: the burden of proof falls on the claimant and the defendant has no disclosure obligation. However, the claimant is entitled to request the disclosure of documents held by the defendeant that are considered necessary to prove the alleged facts (Article L.481-3 FCCom).

The judge may also order the production of documents from the file of the FCA, the European Commission or a national competition authority within the EU, but only after the public enforcement proceedings have come to an end. However, under Article L.483-5 FCCom, the judge cannot order the disclosure of documents pertaining to the parties' (i) leniency applications and (ii) settlement submissions.[8]

In addition, prior to bringing claim, any party can ask the court to order pre-trial investigation measures or document disclosure to access evidence that is deemed necessary for the resolution of the dispute (Article 145 of the French Code of Civil Procedure).

Law No. 2018-670 of 30 July 2018 provides for a specific regime protecting business secrets in proceedings before the French civil and commercial jurisdictions. The judge may for instance decide that only a non-confidential version of certain documents will be provided, that the pleadings will be held *in camera*, or that only a non-confidential version of the decision will be available online. In practice, the judge may design innovative solutions in order to find the right balance between protecting confidential information and disclosing relevant documents to the parties such as data rooms with a confidentiality obligation for the requesting party.[9] This law has replaced previous similar provisions, which initially only applied to private antitrust actions for damages.

5. Limitation periods

Under the general civil liability regime, the limitation period is five years from the date when the victim becomes or should have become aware of, cumulatively, (i) the litigious behaviour and the fact that it was anti-competitive, (ii) the harm that it caused to the victim and (iii) the identity of the infringer(s) (Article 2224 of the French Civil Code).

Where the competition law infringement at stake is a "continuous infringement", the limitation period does not start to run until the infringement has ceased (this has been confirmed by Article L.482-1 FCCom).

---

6 Paris Court of Appeal, 20 September 2017, n° 12/04441, *JCB Services*.

7 See e.g. Paris commercial court, 20 February 2020, No. 420491, *Provera et. al.*.

8 Previous legislation already provided that documents prepared by an infringing undertaking with a view to apply for leniency or collected by the FCA in the context of a leniency application could not be disclosed to civil courts.

9 T. com. Paris, 25 September 2017, *Carrefour*.

The starting point of the limitation period has been much debated by the case-law. For follow-on cartel cases, as mentioned above, it is now established that, irrespective of the applicable regime (general tortious liability or provisions of Article L.481-1 *et seq.* FCCom), the limitation period does not start until the competition authority has issued its decision finding an infringement of competition law. Case-law is not as established for abuse of dominance cases, where courts have adopted a stricter approach in certain instances where the claimant already was a plaintiff before the FCA.[10]

In addition, the starting point of the limitation period for damages actions introduced against an infringing undertaking that has been granted immunity, or a reduction of fine, is postponed until the claimant is able to act against the other infringing undertakings (in case they appeal the competition authority decision) (Article L.482-1 FCCom).

The start of a procedure by the FCA, the European Commission or a national competition authority in the EU, as well as any act of investigation relating to an infringement of competition law, interrupts the limitation period as long as the competition authority decision can be appealed (this captures any ordinary form of appeal and therefore excludes an appeal before the French Supreme Court, which is limited to points of law) (Article L.462-7 FCCom).

6. Appeal

Rulings of commercial and civil courts can be appealed before the Paris Court of Appeal, which has exclusive jurisdiction in competition matters (Articles L.420-7 and R.420-5 FCCom).

Rulings of the Paris Court of Appeal may be appealed before the French Supreme Court, which rules only on points of law, and not on the facts.

Class actions and collective representation

French Law No. 2014-344 of 17 March 2014 ("Hamon Law") introduced an "opt-in" class action into French law, whereby consumers that are victims of an infringement of competition law by the same undertaking(s) may file a single claim. An authorised consumer association must introduce the claim on behalf of consumers affected by the infringement that have opted in. This can only be a follow-on action.

As a first step, the judge hearing the class action shall rule on the defendant's liability in the case presented by the association, determine the category of consumers who can join the action and identify the amount of damages or the method to determine this amount. The judge orders public notice of this judgment to make consumers aware that they can join the class action and thereby seek compensation.

Once informed of the decision, consumers may choose to join the action and therefore receive compensation in the terms of the judgment, or not.

To date, very few class actions have been introduced before the French jurisdictions and, to the best of our knowledge, none in antitrust matters.

---

[10] Paris Court of Appeal, 9 February 2022, n° 19/19969, *CNAMTS / Sanofi*.

7. Key issues

Calculation of damages

More than five years after the transposition of Directive 2014/104/EU, most claims for damages are now subject to the Ordinance.
Previous questions such as the starting point of the limitation period or the passing on defence, have now been clarified.
The most recent case law is focusing on the assessment of the harm suffered by the victims of competition law infringement. This remains a complex task for judges considering the French tort law principle of full compensation. A significant part of the dispute is now relying on economic expert's reports and analyses.

Third-party funding

Third-party funding is when a company which is not victim of the practices at stake provides funds for the potential victim or victims' legal fees and expenses incurred in the litigation, in exchange for an agreed return. Third-party funding is not new but had not emerged in France until recently.

This is changing. Following the trend of neighbouring countries (*e.g.*, the United Kingdom and Germany), the press has recently reported that French restaurants, supported by third-party funding entities, were considering the introduction of collective actions for damages against meal voucher issuers following the FCA decision fining them for anti-competitive practices in 2019 (Decision 19-D-25 of 17 December 2019). Two entities are orchestrating these actions: one is a platform specialising in the management of damage claims, the other is a French fiduciary law firm offering to act as a trustee.

Methodology for the selection of cases

The following cases are the most relevant ones in the French case-law for both follow-on and stand-alone proceedings. This selection does not attempt to be exhaustive.

First instance judgments are included only to the extent that they are of particular relevance. In cases where the initial judgment has been appealed, only the last decision is being referred to.

List of Cases

All the case comments mentioned are available in the Concurrences e-Competitions Bulletin

Supreme Courts

01/03/2023, French Supreme Judiciary Court, n° 20-18.356, e-Competitions Bulletin, Art. N° 116314
www.concurrences.com/116314
Marie Louvet, Agathe Esch

19/10/2022, French Supreme Judiciary Court, n° 21-19197, e-Competitions Bulletin, Art. N° 116325
www.concurrences.com/116325
Marie Louvet, Agathe Esch

28/09/2022, French Supreme Judiciary Court, n° 21-20.731, e-Competitions Bulletin, Art. N° 116327
www.concurrences.com/116327
Marie Louvet, Agathe Esch

17/06/2022, French Supreme Judiciary Court, n° 454189, e-Competitions Bulletin, Art. N° 116331
www.concurrences.com/116331
Marie Louvet, Agathe Esch

Courts of Appeal

17/02/2023, Paris Administrative Court of Appeal, n° 14PA02419, e-Competitions Bulletin, Art. N° 116315
www.concurrences.com/116315
Marie Louvet, Agathe Esch

14/09/2022, Paris Court of Appeal, sections 5-4, n° 20/17560, e-Competitions Bulletin, Art. N° 116329
www.concurrences.com/116329
Marie Louvet, Agathe Esch

23/02/2022, Paris Court of Appeal, sections 5-4, n° 19-19239, e-Competitions Bulletin, Art. N° 116334
www.concurrences.com/116334
Marie Louvet, Agathe Esch

09/02/2022, Paris Court of Appeal, n° 19/19969, e-Competitions Bulletin, Art. N° 116336
www.concurrences.com/116336
Marie Louvet, Agathe Esch

05/01/2022, Paris Court of Appeal, sections 5-4, n° 19/22293, e-Competitions Bulletin, Art. N° 116340
www.concurrences.com/116340
Marie Louvet, Agathe Esch

24/11/2021, Paris Court of Appeal, sections 5-4, n° 20/04265, e-Competitions Bulletin, Art. N° 116341
www.concurrences.com/116341
Marie Louvet, Agathe Esch

24/09/2021, Paris Court of Appeal, sections 5-11, n° 20/14416, e-Competitions Bulletin, Art. N° 116342
www.concurrences.com/116342
Marie Louvet, Agathe Esch

23/06/2021, Paris Court of Appeal, sections 5-4, n° 17/04101, e-Competitions Bulletin, Art. N° 116344
www.concurrences.com/116344
Marie Louvet, Agathe Esch

06/03/2019, Paris Court of Appeal, Pôle 5 Ch. 4, n° 17/21261, e-Competitions Bulletin, Art. N° 111849
www.concurrences.com/111849
Marie Louvet

12/09/2018, Paris Court of Appeal, pôle 5, ch.4, n° 18/04914, e-Competitions Bulletin, Art. N° 111850
www.concurrences.com/111850
Marie Louvet

27/05/2015, Paris Court of Appeal, ch.5-4, n° 14/14758, e-Competitions Bulletin, Art. N° 111852
www.concurrences.com/111852
Marie Louvet

20/12/2017, Paris Court of Appeal, pôle 5, ch.4, n° 15/07266, e-Competitions Bulletin, Art. N° 111853
www.concurrences.com/111853
Marie Louvet

20/09/2017, Paris Court of Appeal, n° 12/04441, e-Competitions Bulletin, Art. N° 111854
www.concurrences.com/111854
Marie Louvet

05/07/2017, Paris Court of Appeal, n° 15/12365, e-Competitions Bulletin, Art. N° 111855
www.concurrences.com/111855
Marie Louvet

10/05/2017, Paris Court of Appeal, pôle 5, ch.4, n° 15/05918, e-Competitions Bulletin, Art. N° 111858
www.concurrences.com/111858
Marie Louvet

14/12/2016, Paris Court of Appeal, Pôle 5, ch.4, n° 13/08975, e-Competitions Bulletin, Art. N° 111859
www.concurrences.com/111859
Marie Louvet

07/12/2016, Paris Court of Appeal, ch.5-4, RG 14/01036, e-Competitions Bulletin, Art. N° 111860
www.concurrences.com/111860
Marie Louvet

13/04/2016, Paris Court of Appeal, Pôle 5, ch.4, n° 13/24840, e-Competitions Bulletin, Art. N° 111861
www.concurrences.com/111861
Marie Louvet

25/11/2015, Paris Court of Appeal, Pôle 5, ch.4, n° 12/02931, e-Competitions Bulletin, Art. N° 111862
ww.concurrences.com/111862
Marie Louvet

22/10/2015, Paris Court of Appeal, ch.5-4, RG 14/03665, e-Competitions Bulletin, Art. N° 111863
www.concurrences.com/111863
Marie Louvet

02/10/2015, Paris Court of Appeal, pôle 5, ch.11, n° 14/15779, e-Competitions Bulletin, Art. N° 111864
www.concurrences.com/111864
Marie Louvet

02/07/2015, Paris Court of Appeal, Pôle 5, ch.5, n° 13/22609, e-Competitions Bulletin, Art. N° 111865
www.concurrences.com/111865
Marie Louvet

27/06/2012, Paris Court of Appeal, Pôle 5, ch. 4, n° 10/04245, e-Competitions Bulletin, Art. N° 111869
www.concurrences.com/111869
Marie Louvet

24/06/2004, Versailles Court of Appeal, 12e ch.2, n° 2002-07434, e-Competitions Bulletin, Art. N° 111871
www.concurrences.com/111871
Marie Louvet

Commercial Courts

27/10/2022, Lyon Commercial Court, n° 2018J191, e-Competitions Bulletin, Art. N° 116324
www.concurrences.com/116324
Marie Louvet, Agathe Esch

09/03/2023, Paris Commercial Court, n° 2019063474, e-Competitions Bulletin, Art. N° 116313
www.concurrences.com/116313
Marie Louvet, Agathe Esch

23/01/2023, Paris Commercial Court, n° 2021037634, e-Competitions Bulletin, Art. N° 116316
www.concurrences.com/116316
Marie Louvet, Agathe Esch

10/02/2021, Paris Commercial Court, 10 February 2021, n° 2020035242, e-Competitions Bulletin, Art. N° 116345
www.concurrences.com/116345
Marie Louvet, Agathe Esch

20/02/2020, Paris Commercial Court, 3e ch., n° 2017021571, e-Competitions Bulletin, Art. N° 111847
www.concurrences.com/111847
Marie Louvet

30/03/2011, Paris Commercial Court, 6e ch., n° 2009-073089, e-Competitions Bulletin, Art. N° 111870
www.concurrences.com/111870
Marie Louvet

Tribunal of First Instance

06/06/2017, Lille Tribunal of First Instance, n° 15/10938, e-Competitions Bulletin, Art. N° 111856
www.concurrences.com/111856
Marie Louvet

GERMANY

Christian Ritz
Partner, Hogan Lovells International LLP

Carolin Marx
Partner, Hogan Lovells International LLP

With the support of Dr. Judith Solzbach, Senior Associate,
and Hanna Weber, Senior Associate, Hogan Lovells International LLP

Germany has a dedicated set of rules that govern the recovery of (and defence against) antitrust damages claims. Equally, German courts have been dealing with respective cases for years and can rely on a breadth of experience and case law. In recent years, the number of antitrust damages actions has increased with the result that several cases have now also reached Germany's highest civil court – the *Bundesgerichtshof* (the Federal Court of Justice or "FCJ"). The resulting judgments continue to provide clarity for both claimants and defendants. Combined with Germany's relatively low court fees, efficient court proceedings and Germany's internationally well-respected *Bundeskartellamt* (the Federal Cartel Office or "FCO"), Germany is among the preferred jurisdictions for antitrust damages actions in Europe.

1. Jurisdiction

The FCO is competent to issue administrative decisions in relation to infringements of competition law. Private enforcement, however, is in the hands of the individual victims affected by the infringement.

Germany's competent civil courts of first instance for private antitrust damages actions are the *Landgerichte* (Regional Courts) as per Section 87 of the German Act against Restraints of Competition (*Gesetz gegen Wettbewerbsbeschränkungen* – "GWB"). In Germany, there is a total of 115 Regional Courts, but the legislator encouraged individual federal states to designate one or more centrally and exclusively competent courts per state to hear private antitrust cases (Section 89 GWB). Several states have made use of this opportunity. Claimants must consider such centrally competent courts when determining jurisdiction.

Specialised antitrust chambers within these individual courts often deal with these cases. The existence of such expert judicial bodies has contributed to the high quality of judgments in Germany regarding antitrust damages actions over the years.

2. Relevant Legislation and Legal Grounds

The key legal provision granting individuals a claim for damages as the consequence of an intentional or negligent violation of European Union ("EU") and/or German competition law is Section 33a (1) GWB. In its current form, this provision was adopted through the 9th amendment to the GWB in June 2017, which implemented the EU Antitrust Damages Directive ("Damages Directive") of 2014 and transposed it into German law. Whereas previously there were only basic rules on antitrust damages to be found in the GWB, now there are extensive and detailed provisions (Section 33 – Section 33h GWB).

In principle, antitrust damages claims are governed by the substantive law applicable at the time when the damage occurred, such as at the time of delivery of cartelised goods – unless otherwise determined by transitional provisions. For example, the Damages Directive and its German implementation in the GWB are generally applicable to claims that have arisen after 26 December 2016.

While Section 33a GWB is the basis for antitrust damages claims in Germany, Section 33 (1) GWB also grants affected parties a claim for injunction and rectification – *e.g.,* they can request that the infringer ceases the current infringement and desists from future infringements.

Right to bring an action

Any affected person – competitor or other market participant – who is impaired by the infringement can seek compensation under German law. This is in line with the Court of Justice of the European Union ("CJEU") according to which the principle of effectiveness (*effet utile*) requires that any individual must be able to claim compensation for any damages caused by competition law infringements.[1]

This includes not only direct, but also indirect victims who purchased cartelised goods from direct customers of the infringers (Section 33c GWB). In addition to this, even customers who did not purchase goods or services from cartel participants may be considered affected by a cartel where it can be demonstrated that the general market price level has increased as a result of a cartel (also known as "umbrella pricing").

Even more, according to a CJEU ruling, even those who are not part of a supply chain trading the cartelised product in question can, nevertheless, claim damages.[2] This CJEU ruling brought about a change in German case law: previously courts required claimants to demonstrate that a cartel infringement had an impact on specific transactions. However, a recent judgment issued by the German Federal Court of Justice in January 2020 (*Schienenkartell II*) revisited this consideration. The Court clarified that this previous hurdle, named "cartel impact" (*Kartellbetroffenheit*), has been lowered to a rather abstract standard: in pre-Damages Directive cases it is now sufficient that the claimant demonstrates that the infringement is generally suitable to cause direct or indirect harm to the claimant.

Under the new rules implementing the Damages Directive (Section 33a (2) GWB) a reversal of the burden of proof is, in fact, already put in place on this point – e.g., the claimant will be able to rely on a rebuttable presumption that a cartel causes harm.

Proof of a competition law infringement and binding effect of authority decisions

Generally, the claimant bears the burden of proof regarding the existence of a competition law infringement.

In case the claimant bases its action on facts that have not previously been the subject of a competition authority's decision or facts outside the scope of such decision (a "Stand-alone action"), this burden of proof may be particularly burdensome.

However German law also allows for so-called "Follow-on actions". Pursuant to Section 33b GWB, courts shall be bound by a finding of an infringement as established

---

1 CJEU, Case C-199/11, 6 November 2012, *Otis*, para. 41.

2 CJEU, Case C-199/11, 6 November 2012, *Otis*, para. 41.

in a final decision by (i) the FCO, (ii) the European Commission, or (iii) another national competition authority in another EU Member State. "Decision" also covers fining decisions following a settlement procedure with the European Commission or the FCO. The binding effect covers not only the operative part of the decision, but also the factual and legal grounds on which the finding of the cartel infringement is based.

Commitment decisions by the FCO (Section 32b GWB), the European Commission (Article 9 VO 1/2003) or other relevant competition authorities do not have the same binding effect pursuant to Section 33b GWB. This does not mean, however, that a court faced with an antitrust damages action will ignore such commitment decisions. In the context of actions following a commitment decision, the findings of the respective competition authority regarding the infringement may be considered by courts as an indication, or even *prima facie* evidence (*Anscheinsbeweis*), of an infringement.[3]

Proof of causation

Generally, the claimant also bears the burden of proof regarding causation and quantum of the damages claimed.

Regarding causation, claimants can rely on certain relaxations of the burden of proof. Previously claimants could rely on the concept of prima facie evidence, which can be considered the "next best thing" after a full reversal of the burden of proof. While the German Federal Court of Justice abrogated this practice through its judgment dated 11 December 2018 (*Schienenkartell I*), it did emphasise that there is a strong factual presumption regarding causation on individual transactions where they fall within the scope of the cartel agreement in terms of content, time and geographical scope. This is known as the "principle of experience", but it is only an indication that is capable of being rebutted.[4]

Similarly, the Higher Regional Court of Frankfurt am Main ruled in a recent judgment that *prima facie* evidence does not apply in cases of exchange of information between competitors.[5]

In any event, courts may rely on Section 287 German Code of Civil Procedure (*Zivilprozessordnung* – "ZPO") when assessing causation and quantum, which allows courts to estimate damages (Section 33a (3) GWB).

Economists are regularly employed in German antitrust damages cases. Parties will often submit party expert opinions in order to assert and defend against damage theories. According to a ruling by the Higher Regional Court of Stuttgart[6], these expert opinions must be able to be reviewed by the court in order to be conclusive. For this, the parties would have to disclose the underlying assumptions and methods as well as the data used. Court-appointed experts may additionally serve in assisting the court in forming its opinion. The German Federal Court of Justice in its *Schienenkartell II* judgment

---

3 CJEU, Case C-547/16, 23 November 2017, *Gasorba*, para. 29.

4 FCJ, Case KZR 35/19, 23 September 2020, *Truck Cartel*.

5 Higher Regional Court of Frankfurt a. M., Case 11 U 98/18, 12 May 2020, *Drogeriekartell*.

6 Higher Regional Court of Stuttgart, Case 2 U 101/18, 9 December 2021, *Truck Cartel*.

however clarified that an expert opinion, whether by a party or court-appointed expert, does not replace the court's own judicial assessment of evidence.

Defendant and concept of an undertaking

Antitrust damages claims can be directed against any company responsible for the anti-competitive conduct that infringed competition law. Several infringers acting together may be held jointly and severally liable (Section 33d (1) GWB). There are certain limitations regarding this joint and severable liability for leniency applicants (Section 33e GWB), small- and medium-sized enterprises (Section 33d (3), (4) GWB) and infringers who have reached a settlement with an injured party (Section 33f GWB).

In accordance with EU competition law the concept of an "undertaking" covers any entity engaged in an economic activity, irrespective of its legal status and financing. However, pursuant to general principles of German corporate law, only the acting legal entity is generally liable for a breach of law. In its recent ruling in *Skanska*, the CJEU however confirmed that the concept of "undertaking" with regard to the imposition of fines should be similarly applied to antitrust damages actions.[7] This broad interpretation in certain cases at least leads to liability of legal successors. Whether the case law would lead to an even more extensive liability of companies for infringements of competition law by any affiliated entity was the subject of numerous discussions, especially in Germany. In its ruling in *Sumal*[8], the CJEU now confirmed that follow-on damages actions can be brought against any group entity that is part of the same "economic unit" as the infringing entity. Multiple group entities form a single economic unit, irrespective of legal status, where there is (1) an economic, organisational and legal link between the subsidiary and the parent company and (2) a specific link between the economic activities of the subsidiary and the parent company. The "undertaking" responsible for an infringement of competition law, therefore, is the economic unit, not the individual group entity. One direct consequence of this ruling is that subsidiaries can be liable for breaches of competition law that occurred within the parent company ("top-down" or "downward liability"). From the claimants' perspective, *Sumal* opens up the freedom to decide against which entity and, hence, in which jurisdiction to bring damages claims.

3. What types of anti-competitive conduct are damages actions available for?

In Germany, antitrust damages actions are available for all infringements of EU and German competition law. This includes:

- multilateral anti-competitive conduct, such as cartel agreements and illicit exchange of competitively sensitive information (Article 101 TFEU and Section 1 GWB); and
- unilateral conduct, such as the abuse of a dominant position (Article 102 TFEU and Section 18, 19 GWB) as well as – specifically in Germany – abuse of a strong market position with regard to undertakings with relative or superior market power (Section 20 GWB).

---

7 CJEU, Case C-724/17, 14 March 2019, *Skanska Industrial Solutions Oy*, para. 43-47.

8 CJEU, Case C-882/19, 6 October 2012, *Sumal*, para. 41-52.

Damages actions are also available following violations of decisions taken by a competition authority (Section 33 (1) GWB). A violation of the prohibition on gun-jumping under merger control law may also be considered as relevant anti-competitive conduct. In this context, a decision taken by a "competition authority" refers in general to German authorities, in particular to the FCO, the Federal Ministry of Economics and the German federal state cartel authorities. Although decisions of the European Commission may not be covered by the mere wording, they can be argued to be equivalent in order to ensure that the effectiveness of civil enforcement of decisions of the European Commission does not fall behind the German cartel authorities. Furthermore, it is essential that the decision of the competent competition authority is binding.

4. What forms of relief may a private claimant seek?

To remedy the immediate effects of an infringement, claimants may enforce their claim for injunction and rectification – *e.g.,* can request that the court orders the infringer to cease the current infringement and desist from future infringements (Section 33 (1) GWB). Such actions may also take the form of interim injunctions.

To remedy damages caused by an infringement, claimants can seek relief in the form of damages (Section 33a (1) GWB).

Pursuant to Section 249 of the German Civil Code (*Bürgerliches Gesetzbuch* – "BGB"), the claim for damages constitutes *in rem* restitution – *e.g.,* the restoration of the economic situation that would have existed but for the damaging event. If the competition law infringement is, for example, the unjustified refusal to deal (such as the refusal to conclude a contract), the claim for damages can be directed towards the conclusion of such a contract. If *in rem* restitution is not possible or only possible at disproportionate expense, the claim for damages aims at monetary compensation pursuant to Section 251 BGB, including loss of profit (see also Section 252 BGB).

5. Passing-on defence

German law acknowledges the so-called "passing-on defence", meaning defendants can argue that, in the event a claimant resold the cartelised products or services (and has passed-on any price-increase induced by the infringer to a third party), the claimant would not, in fact, have suffered any (or at least only partial) damage (Section 33c (1) s. 2 GWB). In German law, the passing-on defence is in line with the general doctrine of setting off any benefits obtained by the claimant – a loss that has been passed on does not need to be compensated.

However, the mere fact that the claimant resold the product or service does not initially preclude the claimant from having a claim (Section 33c (1) s. 1 GWB). Whether and to what extent pass-on occurred will then have to be examined by the court – likely with the help of economists. The burden to substantiate and to prove the existence and extent of any pass-on effects lies with the defendant. To do so, German case law requires defendants to demonstrate that pass-on is particularly plausible under general market conditions with reference to the price elasticity of demand, the price development and the product characteristics.[9] Furthermore, the defendant is required to show that even if the overcharge itself was in fact passed on, the claimant did not incur other disadvantages from the overcharge, such as a decline in demand (so-called volume effects).

Moreover, in its judgment of May 2020 the German Federal Court of Justice[10] stated that there is no benefit sharing if the third party to whom the claimant is said to have passed on his damage has assigned to the claimant any claims in this regard against the defendant cartel participant, the claimant has notified the cartel participant of such assignment and there is no possibility of passing-on the damage to further customers or service levels downstream from the third party.

In this ruling the Federal Court of Justice clarified also that a secondary burden of proof on the part of the cartel injured party with regard to the more detailed circumstances of its price calculation is generally out of the question if two conditions are met: (i) In the case of a passing-on of damages, at most marginal effects on the offer prices of the downstream market are to be expected, which can hardly be reliably determined and only with great effort and (ii) there is a risk of an unfair relief of the injured party due to the lack of enforcement of possible claims for damages of the customers at the downstream market level.

The other side of the coin regarding pass-on naturally is the right of indirect customers to sue for antitrust damages (Section 33c (2) and (3) GWB).

6. Pre-trial discovery and disclosure, treatment of confidential information

As there is a typical information asymmetry between claimants and defendants in competition litigation cases, the Damages Directive required Member States to implement rules on disclosure of evidence. Germany has met this by incorporating such rules as part of the 9th amendment to the GWB in 2017.

So far there is scant case law on the rules on disclosure of evidence pursuant to the new regime incorporated in Section 33g GWB. Existing case law merely covers the question of intertemporal applicability of the framework implemented by the German legislator in 2017 with the 9th amendment to the GWB. Before the 9th amendment to the GWB entered into force, courts were very reluctant to apply general civil procedural rules ordering a production of documents, such as Section 142 German Civil Code of Procedure (*Zivilprozessordnung* – "ZPO"), in competition litigation cases.

With the new rules set out in Section 33g GWB, claimants and defendants can seek disclosure of evidence required to establish or defend a claim, *e.g.*, information or documents that are not available[11] to the claimant due to a structural information deficit inherent in

---

9 FCJ, Case KZR 75/10, 28 June 2011, *ORWI*; FCJ, Case KZR 19/20, 13 April 2021, *LKW-Kartell*; Higher Regional Court of Karlsruhe, Case 6 U 204/15 Kart (2), 9 November 2016, *Grauzementkartell*; District Court of Frankfurt a. M., Case 2-06 O 358/14, 30 March 2016, *Schienenfreunde*; District Court of Hannover, Case 18 O 418/14, 31 May 2016.

10 FCJ, Case KZR 8/18, 19 May 2020, *Schienenkartell IV.*

11 District Court of Munich, Case 37/ 0 18471/18, 27 March 2020, *Stufenklage bei LKW-Kartell.*

the claim. Whereas claimants can choose to request such disclosure of evidence already in a pre-trial stage, defendants can only do so once a damage claim is pending against them.

In German law, the party seeking disclosure is obliged to reimburse the other party for the reasonable costs which it incurred in surrendering evidence (Section 33 (7) GWB).

As required by the Damages Directive, German law limits the disclosure of evidence on the basis of proportionality (Section 33g (3) GWB). Further, exceptions apply to evidence included in the file of a competition authority – *e.g.*, leniency statements and settlement submissions (Section 33 (4), (5) GWB). If a party intentionally or with gross negligence discloses incorrect or incomplete information, this party is liable for any resulting damages under German law (Section 33g (8) GWB).

The discovery tool set out in Section 33g GWB is partly applicable in injunction proceedings: in case a decision of the competition authority has binding effect pursuant to Section 33b GWB, the defendant can be ordered by way of preliminary injunction to surrender this decision to the claimant (Section 89b (5) GWB).

The issue of protecting confidential information is dealt with under the requirement of proportionality (Section 33g (3) no. 3 GWB). Therefore, courts can dismiss a motion seeking disclosure of evidence if confidentiality issues would lead to a disproportionate outcome. Courts can also take other measures required to safeguard the protection of confidential information (Section 87 (7) GWB). However, the legislator did not further specify which measures can be taken. Practical solutions that were developed in IP law cases might, therefore, be applied accordingly to competition litigation cases in the upcoming years when disclosure of information will be applied more frequently in practice by German courts.

7. Limitation periods

The limitation period of antitrust damage claims is governed by Section 33h GWB which implements the Damages Directive.

According to Section 33h (1), (2) GWB, the basic limitation period is five years and begins at the end of the year during which: (i) the claim arose; (ii) the claimant first obtained or should have obtained knowledge of the facts giving rise to the claim and the identity of the infringer, and (iii) the infringement was brought to an end.

There are two cut-off limitation periods.

- First, under Section 33h (3) GWB, claims will be time-barred after ten years, regardless of any knowledge by the claimant, calculated from the year-end of the year during which (i) the claim arose and (ii) the infringement ended.
- Second, there is a thirty-years cut-off limitation period beginning at the time of the competition law infringement (Section 33h (4) GWB).

Limitation is suspended during (and one year after) competition authority proceedings (Section 33h (6) No. 1, 2 GWB). Limitation is also suspended by bringing a claim for discovery (Section 33h (6) No. 3 GWB).

The limitation period regime under Section 33h GWB applies to claims arising after 26 December 2016 and to claims having arisen prior to 27 December 2016 unless they were already time-barred on 9 June 2017 (Section 186 (3) s.2 GWB). Where claimants cannot (yet) rely on the new rules on limitation, they will generally face the previously applicable three-years limitation period.

In a decision from August 2022, the German Federal Court of Justice[12] clarified that, according to Section 852 BGB, the enrichment obtained through the tortious act – the cartel infringement – can still be claimed after the expiry of the limitation period for claims for damages. This claim is subject to a limitation period of ten years from its creation or thirty years from the commission of the act of infringement or the other event triggering the damage. Although the claims are limited to the enrichment gained, this can still be significant, especially in proceedings in which the infringements occurred long ago.

8. Appeal

Judgments by the *Landgerichte* (Regional Courts) can be appealed before the *Oberlandesgerichte* (Higher Regional Courts). Again, German federal states have the opportunity to designate one or more centrally and exclusively competent Higher Regional Court per state which will hear private antitrust actions (Section 92 GWB). Within each Higher Regional Court competent to hear antitrust damages cases, there will be a specialised antitrust division (Section 91 GWB). The judgments by the Higher Regional Courts can be appealed on points of law before the German Federal Court of Justice. At the German Federal Court of Justice, there also is a specialist antitrust panel (Section 94 GWB).

9. Class actions and collective representation

Germany does not provide for US- or UK-style class actions. There are, however, several measures under German law that address the need for a large number of potentially affected claimants to bundle their claims and benefit from collective efforts.

Currently, the most common approach in Germany is the assignment model. Individuals assign their claims to entities that will then bring a complaint in their own name. In practice, this will either be an intra-company entity that bundles claims within a group of companies, or the second option is the assignment to an external, special purpose vehicle ("SPV"). Generally, those SPVs must have sufficient funding to be able to cover the costs in the event the SPV does not prevail in court. They must also be registered in the official registry for legal services as per Section 10 Legal Services Act (*Rechtsdienstleistungsgesetz* – "RDG"). The Federal Court of Justice expressly declared this assignment model permissible in 2021[13] and clarified in another ruling from June 2022[14] that this applies irrespective of the number of assigned claims and with the result that even the "mass" assignment is effective.

---

12 FCJ, Case KZR 111/18, 8 August 2022, *VBL-Gegenwert III.*

13 FCJ, Case II ZR 84/20, 13 July 2021, *AirDeal.*

14 FCJ, Case VIa ZR 418/21, 13 June 2022, *financialright.*

As these rulings were not issued in the context of cartel damages, it is still controversial within the courts of instance whether cartel damages claims can also be asserted in this way. The majority of the courts of instance are of the opinion that competition law exceeds the competence of legal services providers due to its complexity and the economic questions that are to be decided and reject corresponding actions by SPVs as inadmissible for lack of active legitimacy.[15]

However, in the absence of other equally suitable alternatives for the enforcement of antitrust damages claims, this view could constitute a violation of the European law principle of effectiveness, which may soon have to be decided by the CJEU following a referral by the Regional Court of Dortmund[16]. Until then – or a clarifying ruling of the FCJ – legal uncertainty remains in this area.

With the various assignment models under scrutiny, claimants may consider making use of the Model Declaratory Action (*Musterfeststellungsklage*) established in 2018. While individual claimants still have to enforce their claims after a successful Model Declaratory Action, it may be a first step in bundling claims with more legal certainty.

Methodology for the selection of cases

The attached case database covers the most important judgments of German courts in the field of competition litigation, both in follow-on cases and stand-alone cases. Cases have been chosen on the basis of their relevance, but the database does not seek to be exhaustive. The cases presented in the database originate from all three possible instances (Regional Courts, Higher Regional Courts and the Federal Court of Justice).

In general, in cases where a judgment of a lower court has been appealed, only the last judgment was included in the database. If there were additional findings of the lower court exceeding the last judgment's findings, the lower court's judgment is included in the database as well.

---

15 Regional Court of Stuttgart, Case 53 O 260/21, 10 January 2022; Regional Court of Stuttgart, Case 30 O 176/19, 20 January 2022; Regional Court of Dortmund, Case 8 O 7/20 (Kart), 08 June 2022; Regional Court of Mainz, Case 9 O 125/20, 07 October 2022.

16 Regional Court of Dortmund, Case 8 O 7/20 (Kart), 08 June 2022.

List of Cases

All the case comments mentioned are available in the Concurrences e-Competitions Bulletin

Federal Court of Justice

08/08/2022, *VBL-Gegenwert III*, KZR 111/18, e-Competitions Bulletin, Art. N° 116264
www.concurrences.com/116264
Christian Ritz, Carolin Marx, Dr. Judith Solzbach, Hanna Weber

28/06/2022, *Stahl-Strahlmittel*, KZR 46/20, e-Competitions Bulletin, Art. N° 116263
www.concurrences.com/116263
Christian Ritz, Carolin Marx, Dr. Judith Solzbach, Hanna Weber

13/06/2022, *Financialright VIa*, ZR 418/21, e-Competitions Bulletin, Art. N° 116246
www.concurrences.com/116246
Christian Ritz, Carolin Marx, Dr. Judith Solzbach, Hanna Weber

13/07/2022, *Air Deal II*, ZR 84/20, e-Competitions Bulletin, Art. N° 116364
www.concurrences.com/116364
Christian Ritz, Carolin Marx, Dr. Judith Solzbach, Hanna Weber

13/04/2021, *Truck Cartel*, KZR 19/20, e-Competitions Bulletin, Art. N° 116363
www.concurrences.com/116363
Christian Ritz, Carolin Marx, Dr. Judith Solzbach, Hanna Weber

10/02/2021, *Schienenkartell VI*, KZR 63/18, e-Competitions Bulletin, Art. N° 116362
www.concurrences.com/116362
Christian Ritz, Carolin Marx, Dr. Judith Solzbach, Hanna Weber

23/09/2020, *Schienenkartell V*, KZR 4/19, e-Competitions Bulletin, Art. N° 116360
www.concurrences.com/116360
Christian Ritz, Carolin Marx, Dr. Judith Solzbach, Hanna Weber

23/09/2020, *Truck Cartel*, KZR 35/19, e-Competitions Bulletin, Art. N° 116359
www.concurrences.com/116359
Christian Ritz, Carolin Marx, Dr. Judith Solzbach, Hanna Weber

19/05/2020, *Schienenkartell III*, KZR 70/17, e-Competitions Bulletin, Art. N° 116357
www.concurrences.com/116357
Christian Ritz, Carolin Marx, Dr. Judith Solzbach, Hanna Weber

19/05/2020, *Schienenkartell IV*, KZR 8/18, e-Competitions Bulletin, Art. N° 116358
www.concurrences.com/116358
Christian Ritz, Carolin Marx, Dr. Judith Solzbach, Hanna Weber

28/01/2020, *Schienenkartell II*, KZR 24/17, e-Competitions Bulletin, Art. N° 111839
www.concurrences.com/111839
Christian Ritz, Carolin Marx, Dr. Judith Solzbach, Hanna Weber

29/10/2019, *Berufungszuständigkeit II*, KZR 60/18, e-Competitions Bulletin, Art. N° 111835
www.concurrences.com/111835
Christian Ritz, Carolin Marx, Dr. Judith Solzbach, Hanna Weber

11/12/2018, *Schienenkartell I*, KZR 26/17, e-Competitions Bulletin, Art. N° 111825
www.concurrences.com/111825
Christian Ritz, Carolin Marx, Dr. Judith Solzbach, Hanna Weber

27/11/2018, *Zuckerkartell X*, ARZ 321/18, e-Competitions Bulletin, Art. N° 111824
www.concurrences.com/111824
Christian Ritz, Carolin Marx, Dr. Judith Solzbach, Hanna Weber

12/06/2018, *Grauzementkartell II*, KZR 56/16, e-Competitions Bulletin, Art. N° 111817
www.concurrences.com/111817
Christian Ritz, Carolin Marx, Dr. Judith Solzbach, Hanna Weber

12/07/2016, *Lottoblock II*, KZR 25/14, e-Competitions Bulletin, Art. N° 111813
www.concurrences.com/111813
Christian Ritz, Carolin Marx, Dr. Judith Solzbach, Hanna Weber

14/07/2015, *Trinkwasserpreise*, KVR 55/14, e-Competitions Bulletin, Art. N° 111812
www.concurrences.com/111812
Christian Ritz, Carolin Marx, Dr. Judith Solzbach, Hanna Weber

18/11/2014, *Calciumcarbid-Kartell II*, KZR 15/12, e-Competitions Bulletin, Art. N° 111810
www.concurrences.com/111810
Christian Ritz, Carolin Marx, Dr. Judith Solzbach, Hanna Weber

28/06/2011, *ORWI*, KZR 75/10, e-Competitions Bulletin, Art. N° 111809
www.concurrences.com/111809
Christian Ritz, Carolin Marx, Dr. Judith Solzbach, Hanna Weber

Higher Regional Courts

24/02/2022, Truck Cartel 2 U 64/20, e-Competitions Bulletin, Art. N° 116227
www.concurrences.com/116227
Christian Ritz, Carolin Marx, Dr. Judith Solzbach, Hanna Weber

16/12/2021, Truck Cartel 2 U 4/20, e-Competitions Bulletin, Art. N° 116215
www.concurrences.com/116215
Christian Ritz, Carolin Marx, Dr. Judith Solzbach, Hanna Weber

17/11/2021, Sugar Cartel 6 U 56/20 Kart, e-Competitions Bulletin, Art. N° 116366
www.concurrences.com/116366
Christian Ritz, Carolin Marx, Dr. Judith Solzbach, Hanna Weber

10/02/2021, HDF-Platten U (Kart) 8/19, e-Competitions Bulletin, Art. N° 116361
www.concurrences.com/116361
Christian Ritz, Carolin Marx, Dr. Judith Solzbach, Hanna Weber

12/05/2020, Drogeriekartell 11 U 98/18, e-Competitions Bulletin, Art. N° 111844
www.concurrences.com/111844
Christian Ritz, Carolin Marx, Dr. Judith Solzbach, Hanna Weber

09/01/2020, Truck Kartell 29 W 1380/19 Kart, e-Competitions Bulletin, Art. N° 111837
www.concurrences.com/111837
Christian Ritz, Carolin Marx, Dr. Judith Solzbach, Hanna Weber

14/10/2019, HEMA-Vertriebskreis II 3 U 1876/18, e-Competitions Bulletin, Art. N° 111834
www.concurrences.com/111834
Christian Ritz, Carolin Marx, Dr. Judith Solzbach, Hanna Weber

08/05/2019, Schienenkartell III VI-U (Kart) 11/18, e-Competitions Bulletin, Art. N° 111830
www.concurrences.com/111830
Christian Ritz, Carolin Marx, Dr. Judith Solzbach, Hanna Weber

23/01/2019, Schienenkartell I VI-U (Kart) 18/17, e-Competitions Bulletin, Art. N° 111826
www.concurrences.com/111826
Christian Ritz, Carolin Marx, Dr. Judith Solzbach, Hanna Weber

28/06/2018, Schienenkartell; 2 U 13/14 Kart , e-Competitions Bulletin, Art. N° 111820
www.concurrences.com/111820
Christian Ritz, Carolin Marx, Dr. Judith Solzbach, Hanna Weber

28/06/2018, Weichenkartell; 29 U 2644/17 Kart, e-Competitions Bulletin, Art. N° 111822
www.concurrences.com/111822
Christian Ritz, Carolin Marx, Dr. Judith Solzbach, Hanna Weber

26/09/2018, Verkürzter Versorgungsweg VI-U (Kart) 24/17, e-Competitions Bulletin, Art. N° 111823
www.concurrences.com/111823
Christian Ritz, Carolin Marx, Dr. Judith Solzbach, Hanna Weber

03/04/2018, Herausgabe von Beweismitteln II; VI-W (Kart) 2/18, e-Competitions Bulletin, Art. N° 111816
www.concurrences.com/111816
Christian Ritz, Carolin Marx, Dr. Judith Solzbach, Hanna Weber

06/07/2017, Zuckerkartell; 18 AR 7/17, e-Competitions Bulletin, Art. N° 111814
www.concurrences.com/111814
Christian Ritz, Carolin Marx, Dr. Judith Solzbach, Hanna Weber

18/02/2015, CDC; VI-U (Kart) 3/14, e-Competitions Bulletin, Art. N° 111811
www.concurrences.com/111811
Christian Ritz, Carolin Marx, Dr. Judith Solzbach, Hanna Weber

28/01/2004, Vitamin Kartell; 6 U 183/03, e-Competitions Bulletin, Art. N° 111808
www.concurrences.com/111808
Christian Ritz, Carolin Marx, Dr. Judith Solzbach, Hanna Weber

Regional Courts

04/05/2020, Zuckerkartell 18 O 50/16, e-Competitions Bulletin, Art. N° 111842
www.concurrences.com/111842
Christian Ritz, Carolin Marx, Dr. Judith Solzbach, Hanna Weber

05/03/2020, Truck Kartell – Nigeria-Exportfahrzeuge 30 O 261/17, e-Competitions Bulletin, Art. N° 111841
www.concurrences.com/111841
Christian Ritz, Carolin Marx, Dr. Judith Solzbach, Hanna Weber

07/02/2020, Truck Kartell 37 O 18934/17, e-Competitions Bulletin, Art. N° 111840
www.concurrences.com/111840
Christian Ritz, Carolin Marx, Dr. Judith Solzbach, Hanna Weber

19/12/2019, Truck Kartell 30 O 8/18, e-Competitions Bulletin, Art. N° 111836
www.concurrences.com/111836
Christian Ritz, Carolin Marx, Dr. Judith Solzbach, Hanna Weber

25/09/2019, Schienenkartell 2-06 O 649/12, e-Competitions Bulletin, Art. N° 111833
www.concurrences.com/111833
Christian Ritz, Carolin Marx, Dr. Judith Solzbach, Hanna Weber

07/06/2019, Löschfahrzeug-Kartell 37 O 6039/18, e-Competitions Bulletin, Art. N° 111832
www.concurrences.com/111832
Christian Ritz, Carolin Marx, Dr. Judith Solzbach, Hanna Weber

24/04/2019, Truck Kartell 14 O 117/18 Kart, e-Competitions Bulletin, Art. N° 111829
www.concurrences.com/111829
Christian Ritz, Carolin Marx, Dr. Judith Solzbach, Hanna Weber

14/03/2019, Truck Kartell 30 O 234/17, e-Competitions Bulletin, Art. N° 111828
www.concurrences.com/111828
Christian Ritz, Carolin Marx, Dr. Judith Solzbach, Hanna Weber

23/01/2019, Zuckerkartell 14 O 110/18 Kart, e-Competitions Bulletin, Art. N° 111827
www.concurrences.com/111827
Christian Ritz, Carolin Marx, Dr. Judith Solzbach, Hanna Weber

03/08/2018, Truck Cartel; 9 O 49/18, e-Competitions Bulletin, Art. N° 111821
www.concurrences.com/111821
Christian Ritz, Carolin Marx, Dr. Judith Solzbach, Hanna Weber

27/06/2018, Truck Kartell; 8 O 13/17 [Kart], e-Competitions Bulletin, Art. N° 111819
www.concurrences.com/111819
Christian Ritz, Carolin Marx, Dr. Judith Solzbach, Hanna Weber

18/06/2018, HEMA-Vertriebskreis; 19 O 9571/14, e-Competitions Bulletin, Art. N° 111818
www.concurrences.com/111818
Christian Ritz, Carolin Marx, Dr. Judith Solzbach, Hanna Weber

13/09/2017, Schienenkartell; 8 O 30/16 [Kart], e-Competitions Bulletin, Art. N° 111815
www.concurrences.com/111815
Christian Ritz, Carolin Marx, Dr. Judith Solzbach, Hanna Weber

ITALY

Guido Carducci
Attorney-at-Law, Carducci Arbitration

Irene de Angelis
Head of Antitrust Affairs, Intesa Sanpaolo

Jacques Moscianese
Head of Institutional Affairs, Intesa Sanpaolo

Pietro Merlino
Partner, Orrick, Herrington & Sutcliffe

Veronica Pinotti
Partner, White & Case

Italy has implemented Directive no. 104/2014 of 26 November 2014 on actions for damages for infringements of EU and national competition law (the "Directive") by the Legislative Decree no. 3/2017 (the "Decree"). The Decree entered into force on 3 February 2017, and later on, Article 1 of the Decree which is related to scope was amended on 19 November 2020. However, scope remains unaffected in its essence and the Decree continues to govern actions for damages for infringements of EU and national competition law.

1. Jurisdiction

The authority primarily in charge of enforcing competition law in Italy is the Italian Competition Authority (*Autorità garante della concorrenza*, the "ICA"). However, the ICA is only competent for public enforcement and not for private damages actions. Final infringement decisions of the ICA may be appealed before administrative courts. Such courts, in case of appeal, have no jurisdiction to rule on actions for damages for infringement of antitrust law.

In Italian competition law ordinary courts have jurisdiction as to claims for damages for infringements of EU and national competition law under the Decree.

Specialized commercial courts of Milan, Rome, and Naples have the exclusive jurisdiction as to such claims. The parties may not contract out this jurisdiction.

Seeking damages for infringement of competition law may take the form of, either stand-alone action, brought before the competent national court regardless of a preliminary procedure initiated before a competition authority, or as a follow-on action, brought before the competent national court but based on an earlier decision of a competition authority confirming the infringement. Alternative Dispute Resolution ("ADR") is possible. Nevertheless, courts have jurisdiction if the parties do not reach a consensual solution to their dispute.

2. Relevant legislation and legal grounds

Since its entry into force (3 February 2017) the Decree is self-sufficient within its scope of application and its procedural or substantive provisions. Nevertheless, and unsurprisingly for a decree implementing an EU Directive on liability, the Decree requires the application of ordinary Italian law as to the issues it does not govern directly.

Before the Decree these actions for damages were subject to tort law in the Italian Civil Code (the "ICC"), where compensation is due for any harm caused by others intentionally or by negligence.

Given the recent entry into force of the Decree (3 February 2017) and its non-retroactive application, most of the Italian court judgments provided in this database relate to claims that originate in facts having occurred before, and only some judgments are issued after, the entry into force of the Decree. Court judgments issued before remaining of interest at present, indirectly for the consideration they granted to the Directive (in its making or after its adoption, but before its implementation in Italian law by the Decree), directly as to the issues that the Directive and then the Decree do not directly govern. Such issues, for instance the scope and quantification of damages, remain governed by "ordinary" Italian law.

3. What types of anti-competitive conduct are damages actions available for?

The Decree applies to claims for damages by an infringement of competition law committed by a company or an association of companies. If the infringement and the harm alleged are confirmed, claimant is entitled to receive full compensation covering the damage, the loss of profit and the applicable interests.

Relevant infringements of EU or national competition law for the application of the Decree are anti-competitive agreements and concerted practices or abuse of dominant position, pursuant to Articles 101 or 102 TFEU or, in Italian law, Articles 2, 3, and 4 of Law no. 287/1990. The Decree also covers infringement of national competition law provisions of other Member States that pursue mainly the same objectives as Articles 101 and 102 TFEU. Needless to say, such infringements of foreign competition law are unfrequently raised before Italian courts.

In view of the joint and several liability of the corporations having co-infringed competition law, claimant(s) can seek full compensation from any of them until the loss is fully compensated. However, a derogatory regime concerns small- and medium-sized ("SME") corporations (as defined by the EU Recommendation 2063/361) to the extent that they are subject to joint and several liability only with regard to their own direct and indirect purchasers if each corporation had 5% or less of the market share during the period of infringement and if a joint liability would cause an irreparable prejudice to the corporations' economic stability. Such a derogatory regime does not apply, and the principle of joint liability applies, if parties having suffered harm, other than the SME's direct and indirect purchasers, are not in the position to obtain full compensation, or if the SME had a leading role in the infringement.

4. What form of relief may claimant seek

First, punitive damages are not an option under Italian law.

Second, the relief for the harm suffered in direct causation from an infringement of competition law is financial compensation. Damages are quantified including actual loss (*damnum emergens*) and loss of profit (or *lucrum cessans*), plus the applicable interests. Overcompensation is not allowed. Should it be impossible to prove the actual extent of the damage, the court may decide to grant compensation on an equitable basis.[1]

To obtain full compensation the claimant shall prove:

- in stand-alone actions: (i) the competition law infringement, (ii) the existence of the harm and its amount, (iii) the causal link between the competition law infringement and the harm;
- in follow-on actions: the harm and causation (see below).

---

[1] In greater detail, see articles 1223, 1226, 1227 of the ICC, Article 10 of the Decree.

The Decree goes further than ordinary Italian law by setting the rebuttable presumption of actionable damage as soon as an infringement of competition law is due to a cartel.

5. Passing-on defence

Compensation for harm caused by infringement of competition law is due whether the claimant is a direct or indirect purchaser. Defendant may invoke the passing-on defence but carries the burden of proof to demonstrate that the claimants passed on to purchasers or customers the whole or part of the overcharge arising from the infringement thus avoiding that loss which therefore cannot be claimed.

Beyond the obvious burden of proof, the Decree establishes the rebuttable presumption of pass-on overcharge where the indirect purchaser is able to prove that (i) the defendant has committed an infringement of competition law; (ii) this infringement has led to a surcharge for the defendant's direct purchaser; and (iii) it has purchased goods or services relating to the infringement.

6. Pre-trial evidence and disclosure, treatment of confidential information

Italian courts may order disclosure of evidence by a party and third parties, upon a reasoned request submitted by one of the parties, in principle claimant. Article 3 of the Decree introduced into the Italian procedural system the possibility for a party to seek such disclosure by a court exhibition order to the other party, and the order is to identify the specific items or categories of the requested evidence by its "constitutive elements", such as nature, the timeframe concerned, subject matter and content. Courts' disclosure orders must be strictly proportionate to the decision to be adopted, in the light of the likelihood that the infringement occurred, the scope and the cost of exhibition and the rights of the disclosing party. If confidential information is involved in the request for disclosure, the judge shall adopt appropriate measures. The Decree clarifies that its disclosure rules do not affect legal privilege.

This disclosure procedure applies only to antitrust damages action. The ordinary regime (Article 210 of the Italian Code of Civil Procedure) requirs the judge, before issuing a disclosure order, to assess whether the evidence is necessary.

Where the parties or third parties are not reasonably in the position to provide the evidence contained in the file instructed by the ICA then Article 4 of the Decree entitles national courts to order the disclosure of such evidence provided the disclosure be proportionate and the request for disclosure be specific as to, documents submitted to the ICA, the damages claim, the interest in pursuing a public law competition objective. Italian courts may not issue a disclosure order concerning leniency applications (as to the attached documents) and settlement submissions.

Pursuant to Article 7 of the Decree, final decisions (*res iudicata*, no longer subject to challenges) issued by the ICA or by an administrative court upon its review of a ICA's decision, with regard to the existence (or absence) of an infringement of competition law constitute the final determination on such infringement with regard to respondent for the damages action before an Italian court. This final determination is limited to the factual analysis of the infringement of competition law, including the nature of infringement and its scope (material, personal, temporal and territorial). Inversely, if there is no final determination, the court has jurisdiction to decide about the existence of the harm, its quantification or the causation between the harm and the infringement of competition law. The same rule applies to a final decision from a National Competition Authority, or a court, of another EU Member State though with a significant difference: before the Italian court the evidence the decision provides as to the existence and scope of the infringement may be evaluated also in light of other evidence.

Under the pre-Decree regime, a final finding of infringement by the ICA constituted *privileged evidence* only as to the existence of such infringement as well as to its nature and scope. Such final finding by the ICA did not bind the court having jurisdiction on the damages claim, it was regarded as particularly strong evidence in that respect although it could be overcome (For instance, in the *Pfizer* decision, Commercial Court of Rome, 24 July 2017, No. 15020, *Ministry of Health and Ministry of Economy and Finance / Pfizer Italia S.r.l.*)

7. Limitation period

Article 8 of the Decree sets out a limitation period of five years for damages actions stemming from an antitrust infringement. As to the time when the limitation period starts to run the Decree is further detailed than the ordinary regime in Italian law (Article 2935 ICC) and requires the limitation period not to run until the infringement of competition law has ceased and the claimant knows, or can reasonably be presumed to know, the following elements: (i) the conduct and the awareness it constitutes an infringement; (ii) the infringement has caused him a harm; and (iii) the identity of the infringer.

Moreover, the five-years time limitation period shall be suspended when the ICA or the EU Commission opens an investigation or a procedure on the same infringement of competition law covered by the claim for damages. Suspension will last until a year after such investigation or procedure is concluded.

8. Appeal

The judgments of the specialized commercial courts of Milan, Rome and Naples may be appealed before the competent Courts of Appeal, whose judgment are appealable, on matters of law only, before the Italian Supreme Court.

9. Class actions and collective representation

Under the Decree, not only individual private actions are admitted, but also class actions by two or more consumers and users that are in a contractual, as well as non-contractual, relationship to companies, producers, and that are affected by anti-competitive or commercial unfair practices. They can file the class action, also without legal representation, before the ordinary court.

10. Key issues

The Decree entered into force on 3 February 2017 and does not yet apply to most antitrust damages actions brought at present in Italy. Nevertheless, as mentioned above, some of the judgments included in the database show what can be fairly described as an anticipated application of the key provisions of the Directive, to the benefit of claimants as to circumstances not covered by the Decree since its entry into force. Evidence of infringement is crucial for claimants and the key provision concerning the binding effect of the ICA's final findings of infringement of competition law was not part of Italian pre-Decree law.

Methodology for the selection of cases

The database for Italy includes the most relevant Italian antitrust damages cases, both follow-on and stand-alone. It does not attempt to be exhaustive. The judgments have been selected based on their relevance. If a judgment has been appealed references to the final judgment and indications as to its output are included in the database whenever possible.

List of Cases

All the case comments mentioned are available in the Concurrences e-Competitions Bulletin

Supreme Court of Cassation

16/12/2015, S.F. / Alleanza Toro Assicurazioni S.p.A., No. 25323, e-Competitions Bulletin, Art. N° 111791
www.concurrences.com/111791
Jacques Moscianese, Irene de Angelis

25/11/2015, S.F. / Milano Assicurazioni S.p.A., No. 24114, e-Competitions Bulletin, Art. N° 111792
www.concurrences.com/111792
Jacques Moscianese, Irene de Angelis

11/09/2015, S.D. /. Reale Mutua Assicurazioni S.p.A., No. 17996, e-Competitions Bulletin, Art. N° 111793
www.concurrences.com/111793
Jacques Moscianese, Irene de Angelis

06/07/2015, L.L. / Fondiaria – Sai S.p.A., No. 13890, e-Competitions Bulletin, Art. N° 111795
www.concurrences.com/111795
Jacques Moscianese, Irene de Angelis

04/06/2015, Comi S.r.l. et al. / Cargest S.r.l., No. 11564, e-Competitions Bulletin, Art. N° 111796
www.concurrences.com/111796
Pietro Merlino, Tommaso Olivieri, Giulia Scrivanti

Courts of Appeal

15/10/2021, Agroservizi srl in liquidazione, cerved group spa, italservice sipca srl, italservice cgc srl, its novum Srl in liquidazione c. agenzia dell'entrate. Number General Registry. 2194/2020, e-Competitions Bulletin, Art. N° 116276
www.concurrences.com/116276
Guido Carducci

21/09/2021, Digital World Television S.R.L., c. Sky Italia – S.r.l., Number General Registry 3949/2019, e-Competitions Bulletin, Art. N° 116277
www.concurrences.com/116277
Guido Carducci

18/06/2021, Eutelia S.p.A. / Vodafone Omnitel N.V. S.p.A., No. 1919, e-Competitions Bulletin, Art. N° 116278
www.concurrences.com/116278
Veronica Pinotti, Patrizia Pedretti, Michela Francavilla

06/04/2021, Alicargo and others / SEA Società esercizi aeroportuali S.p.A., No. 1097, e-Competitions Bulletin, Art. N° 116281
www.concurrences.com/116281
Veronica Pinotti, Patrizia Pedretti, Michela Francavilla

21/05/2020, Società Esercizi Aeroportuali S.E.A. S.p.A. / Qatar Airways – Linee Aeree Del Qatar No. 1242/2020 (General Registry: 3798/2018), e-Competitions Bulletin, Art. N° 116282
www.concurrences.com/116282
Pietro Merlino, Tommaso Olivieri, Giulia Scrivanti

21/01/2020, Iveco S.p.A./Cave Marmi Vallestrona S.r.l., No. 188/2020 (General Registry: 4525/2018), e-Competitions Bulletin, Art. N° 116372
www.concurrences.com/116372
Pietro Merlino, Tommaso Olivieri, Giulia Scrivanti

Commercial Courts

25/10/2022, Coprem – Costruzione prefabbricati modulari S.r.l. / Bonna Sabla S.A., No. 8365, e-Competitions Bulletin, Art. N° 116266
www.concurrences.com/116266
Jacques Moscianese, Irene de Angelis

21/10/2022, Nippon Cargo Airlines Co., Ltd. / SEA S.p.A., No. 8292, e-Competitions Bulletin, Art. N° 116270
www.concurrences.com/116270
Jacques Moscianese, Irene de Angelis

20/10/2022, G.V. / Intesa Sanpaolo S.p.A., No. 8267, e-Competitions Bulletin, Art. N° 116272
www.concurrences.com/116272
Jacques Moscianese, Irene de Angelis

27/09/2022, Codacons / Rolex Italia S.p.A., No. 7389, e-Competitions Bulletin, Art. N° 116274
www.concurrences.com/116274
Jacques Moscianese, Irene de Angelis

20/04/2022, Fallimento RS Italia S.r.l. / Gruppo Inox S.r.l., No. 3458, e-Competitions Bulletin, Art. N° 116275
www.concurrences.com/116275
Jacques Moscianese, Irene de Angelis

30/05/2019, D.F. S.r.l. / I.C.E. S.p.A. and P.C.A. S.p.A., General Registry No. 56090, e-Competitions Bulletin, Art. N° 111781
www.concurrences.com/111781
Guido Carducci

15/03/2018, Brussels Airlines SA/NV, American Airlines Inc. and Aegean Airlines SA / SEA S.p.A., No. 3011, e-Competitions Bulletin, Art. N° 111783
www.concurrences.com/111783
Pietro Merlino, Tommaso Olivieri, Giulia Scrivanti

24/07/2017, Ministry of Health and Ministry of Economy and Finance / Pfizer Italia S.r.l., No. 15020, e-Competitions Bulletin, Art. N° 111784
www.concurrences.com/111784
Pietro Merlino, Tommaso Olivieri, Giulia Scrivanti

24/06/2016, Alpina Società Immobiliare S.r.l., Arno S.r.l., Enrico Belloti / Banco di Brescia Sanpaolo Cab S.p.A., Banca Popolare Commercio e Industria S.p.A., No. 7884, e-Competitions Bulletin, Art. N° 111787
www.concurrences.com/111787
Jacques Moscianese, Irene de Angelis

23/06/2016, Franco Bartolomei / Banco Popolare soc. coop., No. 7796, e-Competitions Bulletin, Art. N° 111789
www.concurrences.com/111789
Jacques Moscianese, Irene de Angelis

28/07/2015, BT Italia S.p.A. / Vodafone Omnitel N.V., No. 9109, e-Competitions Bulletin, Art. N° 111794
www.concurrences.com/111794
Pietro Merlino, Tommaso Olivieri, Giulia Scrivanti

15/07/2015, Best Office S.p.A. / Intesa Sanpaolo S.p.A., No. 8720, e-Competitions Bulletin, Art. N° 111797
www.concurrences.com/111797
Jacques Moscianese, Irene de Angelis

14/04/2014, Airline Logistic S.r.l., Globe Air Cargo S.r.l., Swissport Cargo Services Italia S.r.l., Worldair S.r.l., Sasco S.r.l. / SEA S.p.A., No. 3324, e-Competitions Bulletin, Art. N° 111799
www.concurrences.com/111799
Pietro Merlino, Tommaso Olivieri, Giulia Scrivanti

Court of Milan

24/05/2021, A.B.E. S.N.C and others/Iveco S.p.A and others, No. 4491, e-Competitions Bulletin, Art. N° 116280
www.concurrences.com/116280
Veronica Pinotti, Patrizia Pedretti, Michela Francavilla

04/10/2018, Cave Marmi Vallestrona/Iveco, No. 9759, e-Competitions Bulletin, Art. N° 111782
www.concurrences.com/111782
Veronica Pinotti, Patrizia Pedretti

27/06/2016, Swiss International Airline S.p.A. / SEA Società esercizi aeroportuali S.p.A., No. 7970, e-Competitions Bulletin, Art. N° 111785
www.concurrences.com/111785
Veronica Pinotti, Patrizia Pedretti

21/06/2016, Teleunit S.p.A. / Telecom Italia S.p.A. No. 8008, General Registry 76561/2008, e-Competitions Bulletin, Art. N° 111786
www.concurrences.com/111786
Guido Carducci

05/04/2016, Eutelia S.p.A. / Vodafone Omnitel N.V. S.p.A., No. 4255, e-Competitions Bulletin, Art. N° 111788
www.concurrences.com/111788
Jacques Moscianese, Irene de Angelis

24/12/2015, Arslogica Sistemi S.r.l./ IBM Italia S.p.A., No. 4620, e-Competitions Bulletin, Art. N° 111790
www.concurrences.com/111790
Veronica Pinotti, Patrizia Pedretti

14/05/2014, Intermatica S.p.A. / Telecom Italia S.p.A. No. 6621, General Registry 8025/2009, e-Competitions Bulletin, Art. N° 111798
www.concurrences.com/111798
Guido Carducci

27/12/2013, Brennercom S.p.A /Telecom Italia S.p.A., No. 16319, General Registry 22423/2010, e-Competitions Bulletin, Art. N° 111804
www.concurrences.com/111804
Guido Carducci

04/06/2013, Viaggiare s.r.l. / Ryanair Ltd., No. 7825, e-Competitions Bulletin, Art. N° 111805
www.concurrences.com/111805
Guido Carducci

13/02/2013, OKCom S.p.A / Telecom Italia S.p.A, No. 2159, General Registry 76568/2008, e-Competitions Bulletin, Art. N° 111806
www.concurrences.com/111806
Guido Carducci

KOREA

Cecil Saehoon Chung
Head of International Antitrust, Yulchon LLC

Woo Yul Lee
Partner, Yulchon LLC

Tae Yong Kim
Counsel, Yulchon LLC

Private antitrust enforcement in South Korea has not been very vigorous compared to other jurisdictions. This is because Korean antitrust enforcement has largely relied on the initiative of the Korea Fair Trade Commission ("KFTC"), which has served as the primary enforcer of Korean antitrust law including the Monopoly Regulation and Fair-Trade Act ("MRFTA"), the basic Korean antitrust statute. With its legislative intent of promoting private as well as public antitrust enforcement, the MRFTA currently provides for a lesser burden of proof in a damages action arising from a violation of the MRFTA. In practice, however, this provision has yet to be fully adopted by Korean courts because there have been relatively few antitrust damages actions in Korea, whether initiated in the aftermath of relevant KFTC proceedings or otherwise, and because antitrust damages actions essentially remain "civil" in nature.

Under Korean civil law, neither punitive damages nor a class action is generally available. However, this long-standing characteristic of the Korean legal regime has been undergoing major changes, particularly in the antitrust sphere. For instance, a quasi-treble damages provision was introduced with the 2011 amendment of the Korean subcontracting statute[1], which is also enforced by the KFTC.[2] A similar treble damages-like provision was added to the MRFTA in September 2018 and became effective in September 2019. In addition, comprehensive amendments to the MRFTA, which came into effect on December 30, 2021 ("2021 Amendments to the MRFTA"), introduced, among other provisions, private injunctive relief from unfair trade practices (excluding unfair support to affiliates).[3] Although there was also in-depth discussion on introducing antitrust class actions, they were ultimately not adopted in the 2021 Amendments to the MRFTA. The developments in general bode well for invigorated private antitrust litigation in Korea.

1. Jurisdiction

Because the MRFTA does not address jurisdiction over private antitrust litigation including damages actions, the Civil Procedure Act applies. Under the latter statute, a claimant alleging an antitrust injury may bring an action before the district court that has jurisdiction over (i) the defendant's domicile or (ii) the *locus* of the defendant's conduct at issue (Articles 2 through 6 and 18 of the Civil Procedure Act).[4] Korean law does not provide for a court with specific jurisdiction to hear competition law cases.

1 Article 35 (2) of the Fair Transactions in Subcontract Ac provides that "If a person is injured or incurs loss as a result of conduct by a principal contractor in violation of Article 4, 8(1), 10, 11(1) or (2), or 12-3(3) of this Act, the principal contractor shall be liable for the injury or loss to the extent not exceeding three times the injury or loss; provided that the foregoing provision shall not apply where the principal contractor proves the absence of intention or negligence regarding the injury or loss." In other words, the amount of damages is not automatically trebled but simply may be increased up to three times the actual damages.

2 However, a damages claim in Korea can be decided only by a Korean court, rather than the KFTC, which may only issue administrative sanctions.

3 Article 108 of the MRFTA. See below for the text and discussion of Article 108.

4 The *locus* could be any of the following: the place of decision; the place of implementation, and the place of effect.

2. Relevant legislation and legal grounds

To be valid, an antitrust damages claim must be based on one of the two provisions below:

(i) Article 109 of the MRFTA (antitrust provision):

"Where a person suffers harm due to any violation of this Act by a business entity or trade association, the business entity or trade association is liable for the ensuing damages; provided that the foregoing shall not apply where the business entity or trade association proves the absence of intention or negligence regarding the violation."

(ii) Article 750 of the Civil Code (tort provision):

"Any person who causes loss to or inflicts injury on another by unlawful conduct, whether intentionally or negligently, shall be held liable for the ensuing damages."

These two provisions serve as elective jurisdictional grounds for private antitrust litigation, including damages actions. Before its 2004 amendment, the MRFTA contained a provision explicitly stating that a claim based on the MRFTA did not preclude an identical claim under the Civil Code. Even though that provision was repealed through the 2004 amendment, it has been consistently recognised that a claimant alleging an antitrust injury may rely on either Article 109 of the MRFTA or Article 750 of the Civil Code as the jurisdictional grounds for the antitrust claim at issue.

From a claimant's perspective, Article 109 of the MRFTA is more advantageous since, unlike Article 750 of the Civil Code, it shifts to the defendant the burden of proof for the absence of the defendant's wilfulness or negligence. The 2021 Amendments to the MRFTA also introduced a provision allowing a party to a damages action alleging unfair concerted conduct or unfair trade practice (excluding unfair support of affiliates) to request that the opposing party is ordered to produce material needed to prove or determine the damages.[5] However, there is one important caveat: under Article 109 of the MRFTA, a claimant may file a damages action only against a business entity or trade association. In contrast, Article 750 of the Civil Code allows for the filing of a damages action against individuals as well as business entities.

Irrespective of the choice of jurisdictional grounds, a claimant may initiate a private antitrust action in Korea even before the commencement of any KFTC proceedings against any defendant in the private action. Such "stand-alone" action, however, rarely takes place due to the difficulty in satisfying the burden of proof, particularly for the very first element of any private antitrust action: the presence of an antitrust violation by the defendant(s).

3. What types of anti-competitive conduct are damages actions available for?

In Korea, any antitrust violation may serve as the substantive grounds for an antitrust damages action. Thus, such an action may allege a violation ranging anywhere from

---

[5] Under Article 111 of the MRFTA, at a party's request, the court may order the opposing party to produce material to prove or determine the damages in a damages action (excluding material concerning a leniency application under Article 44(4)) alleging a violation of Article 40(1), Article 45(1) (excluding subparagraph 9), or Article 51(1)(1) of the MRFTA, unless the latter party has valid grounds for refusing to comply with the order.

cartel activity (Article 40 of the MRFTA) and abuse of dominance (Article 5 of the MRFTA) to unfair trade practice (Article 45 of the MRFTA), improperly benefitting a specially related party (Article 47 of the MRFTA), retaliatory measure (Article 48 of the MRFTA) and resale price maintenance (Article 46 of the MRFTA).

4. What forms of reliev may a private claimant seek ?

Until recently, the only relief available was compensatory damages with the notable exception of up to three times the actual damages for certain violations of the Korean subcontracting statute. On September 19, 2019, however, the following treble damages-like provision of the MRFTA (in other words, no automatic trebling of the actual damages amount but the maximum amount could be up to three times the actual damages) went into effect:

Article 109 (2): "*Notwithstanding paragraph (1), where a person sustains loss because of conduct by a business entity or an organization of business entities in violation of Article 40 (prohibition of cartel activity), Article 48 (prohibition of retaliatory measure) or Article 51(1)(i) (prohibition of unfair restraint on competition by an organization of business entities), the business entity or the organization is liable to the extent not exceeding three times the damages; provided that the foregoing shall not apply where the business entity or the organization proves the absence of intention or negligence regarding the violation.*"

Further, the 2021 Amendments to the MRFTA, effective December 30, 2021, introduced private injunctive relief from unfair trade practices (excluding unfair support to affiliates) by a business entity or business association.[6]

Article 108 (1): "*A person who has suffered or is likely to suffer damages from a violation of Article 45(1) (excluding subparagraph 9) and Article 51(1)(4) (limited to the provisions related to unfair trade practices under Article 45(1) (excluding subparagraph 9)) may request the prohibition or prevention of the violating act against a business entity or business association that has committed or is likely to commit the violation.*"

5. Burden of proof

Any party injured by a violation of the MRFTA – whether a direct or indirect customer, a competitor, a supplier, or otherwise – is entitled to damages if the party proves (i) the violation of the MRFTA, *i.e.* the anti-competitive conduct; (ii) the presence and extent of injury, *i.e.* the damages; and (iii) causation between the anti-competitive conduct and the injury. Here, causation must be direct; hence, the claimant must prove that the injury at issue was caused, in its entirety, by the anti-competitive conduct at issue. As for the extent of injury, where it is practically impossible to determine the damages even though the claimant has satisfied the other two elements, the court may at its discretion award a reasonable amount of damages based on the available evidence (Article 115 of the

---

6 Thus, covered "unfair trade practices" woudl inlude practices such as unfairly rejecting a transaction or unfairly discriminating against the other party to a transaction. On the other hand, the coverage would not include the "unfair support to affiliates" category, which is unfairly favoring one's affiliates to the detriment of others.

MRFTA). In this regard, the Korean Supreme Court, while not explicitly recognizing the passing-on defence in principle, held that costs passed on to the claimant's customers after a price increase resulting from the defendant's cartel activity may be considered in limiting the damages awarded to the claimant[7].

With respect to the burden of proof, the Korean Supreme Court held that even where the KFTC's corrective measure against a violation was judicially affirmed, the facts ascertained by the KFTC with respect to the violation are not binding in a damages action but may simply constitute strong evidence of the violation. Thus, they have the effect of being deemed to be presumptive facts[8].

Once the claimant satisfies the requisite burden of proof in a private action jurisdictionally based on antitrust grounds, the defendant is liable for the damages unless it proves that the violation at issue was neither intentional nor negligent (Article 109 (1) of the MRFTA).[9] In contrast, if the claimant initiates a damages action on tort grounds (Article 750 of the Civil Code), it must also affirmatively prove the defendant's intention or negligence.

6. Pre-trial discovery and disclosure, treatment of confidential information

Under Korean civil procedure, there is no U.S. style pre-trial discovery. Whereas discovery is allowed to a limited extent (through a document production order as explained below), depositions are prohibited. The burden of proof falls on the parties, none of whom have a general disclosure obligation. If a party seeks a document possessed by the opposing party or a third party, it may request a court order for document production pursuant to Articles 344 through 353 of the Civil Procedure Act.

However, as noted above, the facts ascertained by the KFTC are deemed to be presumptive facts in a private action. Therefore, the claimant in a private action can more easily satisfy the requisite burden of proof by citing the facts ascertained by the KFTC in its investigation and decision. Furthermore, in a damages action on antitrust grounds (Article 109 (1) of the MRFTA), the court may compel the KFTC to provide the record of the relevant case, including interview reports, expert witness reports, the stenographic record, and any other evidence (Article 110 of the MRFTA). On the other hand, under Article 95, the KFTC may refuse to provide such documents to damages claimants and third parties on grounds of Article 44(4), which prohibit the KFTC from disclosing information concerning a leniency application unless (i) the leniency applicant consented to disclosure, or (ii) disclosure is required for purposes of bringing a related lawsuit or carrying out related official duties.

Documents presented by the parties during the court proceedings are not available to the general public. In addition, confidential information contained in a court submission may be protected through redaction when a third-party requests access to litigation record, subject to the court's review and ruling (Article 163 of the Civil Procedure Act). The court may also decide to examine certain evidence "*in-camera*" since a court hearing in Korea

---

7 Korean Supreme Court Case No. 2010*Da*93790, decided November 29, 2012.

8 Korean Supreme Court Civil Case No. 89Daka29075, decided April 10, 1990.

9 However, there is no known instance in which this defence succeeded.

is generally open to the public (Article 347(4) of the Civil Procedure Act). Such decision, however, is seldom made. However, once any information, including business secrets, is submitted to the court, the opposing party may access it. On the other hand, a party may refuse to submit certain information to the court on grounds that it constitutes business secrets (Article 344(1)(3) and Article 315(1)(2) of Civil Procedure Act).

7. Limitation periods

The MRFTA itself does not provide for the statute of limitations period governing private damages claims. Since the liability for damages under the MRFTA is categorized as tortious liability (Article 109 of the MRFTA), Article 766 of the Civil Code is applicable.[10] Under that provision, the limitation period is three years from the date on which the injured party became aware of or should reasonably have become aware of (i) the injury and (ii) the identity of the infringer.

Specifically addressing private antitrust damages actions, the Korean Supreme Court held that even where an injured party becomes aware of a corrective order issued by the KFTC, the three-years limitation period does not begin to run until the order is confirmed by a final judgment issued by the Seoul High Court or the Korean Supreme Court in an appeal from a Seoul High Court decision.[11] However, if at least ten years have passed from the date of the violation, a damages action based on the violation is time-barred regardless of whether the three-years limitation period has passed.

8. Appeal

An appeal from a district court decision is heard by a high court unless the district court proceedings were before a single judge, in which case the ensuing appeal is heard by an appellate panel of the district court (Article 28 of the Court Organization Act). The proceedings of an intermediate appeal are similar to trial proceedings, and the parties are granted opportunities to raise new allegations and to produce new evidence. An intermediate appellate decision may be appealed to the Korean Supreme Court, the court of last resort (Article 14 of the Court Organization Act), which only decides issues of law and does not engage in any fact-finding (Article 432 of the Civil Procedure Act).

9. Class Actions and Collective Representation

At present, a class action is not available for claimants alleging antitrust injury. Claimants with claims based on essentially the same factual and legal grounds can however jointly file actions in the form of a joinder of named claimants. Under this joinder procedure, such claimants may select one or more among them as their representatives (Article 53 of the Civil Procedure Act). Once this option is exercised, any judgment issued to the representative claimants are also binding with respect to the claimants who exercised the option.

---

10 Article 766 of the Civil Code: (1) The right to claim damages resulting from an unlawful act shall lapse by prescription if not exercised within three years commencing on the date when the injured party or his/her legal representative becomes aware of the injury and of the identity of the person who caused the injury. (2) The provision of paragraph (1) shall also apply if ten years have elapsed from the time that the unlawful act took place.

11 Korean Supreme Court Civil Case No. 2013Da215843, decided September 4, 2014.

10. Key Issues

Calculation of damages

Assessing the harm suffered by the victims of an MRFTA infringement is always a complex task in light of the Korean Supreme Court's adoption of the "difference-between-two-prices" theory. That is to say, the total amount of damages due to an illegal action is the difference between (i) the hypothetical financial status the victims would have been in but for the illegal conduct and (ii) their actual financial status after the illegal conduct. For example, in case of collusion, the difference between the but-for price (*i.e.* the hypothetical price but for the collusion) and the actual price (the price resulting from the collusion) is the amount of damages due to the collusion. The parties or the court usually appoints an economic expert to conduct analysis under various economic models and to calculate the but-for price.

Methodology for the selection of cases

The attached data base includes the most relevant and notable Korean Supreme Court cases with respect to antitrust damages actions in Korea.

List of Cases

All the case comments mentioned are available in the Concurrences e-Competitions Bulletin

Supreme Court

29/08/2019, Case No. 2017Da276679, Republic of Korea v. SK Engineering & Construction co., Ltd. and et al, e-Competitions Bulletin, Art. N° 116299
www.concurrences.com/116299
Cecil Chung

12/10/2018, Case No. 2016Da243115, Korea Electric Power Corporation v. Daehan Cable & Solution Co., Ltd. et al, e-Competitions Bulletin, Art. N° 116301
www.concurrences.com/116301
Cecil Chung

MEXICO

Ivan Szymanski Curiel
Associate, Santamarina y Steta, S.C.

Fernando Ruiz Alva
Independent consultant

Private antitrust litigation is still in an early stage of development in Mexico. Based on the concept of civil liability, private antitrust litigation is regulated under the Federal Civil Code ("FCC") and the Federal Code of Civil Procedures ("FCCP"). As of today, only two claims have been filed in Federal Courts. However, recent developments may enhance this practice: (i) the 2012 reform to civil legislation (FCC and FCCP) introduced and regulated class actions, and (ii) the issuance in 2014 of a new Federal Law on Economic Competition included, for the first time, provisions related to the claim of damages arising from anti-competitive conducts.

1. Jurisdiction

In 2013, the Federal Government decided to conduct a full revision of the constitutional, legal and institutional framework of the Mexican antitrust system. A completely new antitrust legal and regulatory framework was developed in 2014, and the following pieces of legislation entered into force:

a) amendments to Article 28 of the Federal Political Constitution of the United Mexican States ("Mexican Constitution") regarding monopolies and monopolistic practices, which, among others, ordered the creation of two new constitutionally autonomous regulatory and enforcing agencies: (i) the Federal Economic Competition Commission ("COFECE") for all antitrust issues, except for telecommunications and broadcasting, and (ii) the Federal Institute of Telecommunications ("IFT") for all issues relating to telecommunications and broadcasting in Mexico (the "Antitrust Agencies");

b) the issuance of the new Federal Law on Economic Competition ("FLEC");

c) the issuance of a new Federal Law on Telecommunications and Broadcasting;

d) the issuance of new sets of Regulatory Provisions of the FLEC and non-binding explanatory guidelines; and

e) amendments to Article 94 of the Mexican Constitution, ordering the creation Circuit Collegiate Tribunals and District Courts specialised in Economic Competition, Broadcasting Services and Telecommunications matters were create (together, the "Specialized Federal Courts").

As a result of the amendments to Article 94 of the Mexican Constitution, the Board of the Federal Judicial Council issued a decree which led to the creation of two Circuit Collegiate Tribunals (constitutional amparo trial court) and two District Courts (first instance), with exclusive authority to receive and resolve the claims on Economic Competition, Broadcasting Services and Telecommunications, including jurisdiction over amparo claims (*i.e.* constitutional appeals) versus the Antitrust Agencies resolutions. In 2018, the Board of the Federal Judicial Council also issued a decree creating two Circuit Unitary Tribunals in Civil, Administrative and Specialized in Economic Competition, Telecommunications and Broadcasting (second instance) with exclusive jurisdiction on hear and resolve appeals to the resolutions issued by the District Courts on **private parties claims for damages**.

Under Mexican legislation, civil actions for damages arising from anti-competitive conducts can only be filed after a resolution by an Antitrust Agency finding liability has been issued and such resolution has been declared final and conclusive.

2. Relevant legislation and legal grounds

As previously mentioned, the concept of damages in Mexico is based on civil liability principles. According to the FCC, individuals and undertakings are entitled to pursue direct damages actions based on contractual and non-contractual liability.

Article 134 of the FLEC confirms forth the possibility of private parties looking redress for the damages they suffered as a result of the anti-competitive conducts committed by third parties:

"Individuals that may have suffered damages or losses deriving from a monopolistic practice or an illicit concentration have the right to file judicial actions in defence of their rights before the specialised courts in matters of economic competition, broadcasting and telecommunications, once the Commission's resolution is final and conclusive.

The statute of limitations for lodging damages claims shall be stayed by the decision to initiate an investigation.

The Economic Agent's illegal actions shall be proven with the final resolution issued under the trial-like procedure, for the effects of lodging damages claims."

3. What types of anti-competitive conduct are damages available for?

Article 134 of the FLEC sets forth that damages actions are available for those who have suffered damages as a result of either a monopolistic practice or an illicit concentration.

The FLEC differentiates between two different kinds of monopolistic practices:

- absolute Monopolistic Practices (similar to the "*per se*" conducts or hardcore cartel practices); and
- relative Monopolistic Practices (conducts to be evaluated under a "rule of reason analysis").

Absolute monopolistic practices consist of contracts, agreements, arrangements or combinations amongst competing Economic Agents, which have as their purpose or effect any of the following: fixing prices, market allocation, output restrictions, bid-rigging and exchanging of information with the purpose or effect of any of the previously mentioned conducts.

Relative monopolistic practices are defined by the FLEC as those acts, contracts, agreements or combinations, carried on by one or more economic agents, that severally or jointly have substantial market power in the market affected by the relative monopolistic and which aim or effect is to (i) substantially impede the access, or (ii) to establish exclusive advantages in favour of one or several economic agents, improperly impeding or displacing, in this way, other economic agents in such a market. In Mexico, relative monopolistic practices relate almost exclusively to vertical restraints.

The illicit concentrations are those concentrations that did not request or received prior authorisation from the FECC and that have the purpose or the effect of obstructing, diminishing, harming or impeding free market access and economic competition.

4. What forms of relief may a private claimant seek?

The FCC sets forth that those who were harmed or injured because of the illicit acts of another, the perpetrator is obliged to repair it, unless it proves that the damage occurred as a result of guilt or inexcusable negligence of the victim.

The prior finding of infringement by the Antitrust Authorities is a condition precedent for bringing a damages action.

Therefore, damages actions in Mexico are only intended to repair the direct damage caused by the anti-competitive conduct. Additionally, in case of contractual relationships, claimants may also seek to declare the contract or specific clauses of a determined contract null and void directly in courts without the necessity of having to wait for the resolution of the Antitrust Agencies.

Damages actions on antitrust issues can be pursued either as private actions or as class actions (described below). A private claimant seeking damages may rely on the Antitrust Authorities' finding of infringement to establish the defendant's liability but must prove beyond reasonable doubt that a causal link exists between the infringement and the loss suffered, as well as the extent of the loss itself, as general rule the burden of proof rests on the claimant.

Moreover, any evidence relevant to proving loss is admissible, such as accounts showing a decrease in income. However, losses resulting from infringements of competition law are often very difficult to quantify. Specialized Federal Courts are entitled to ask the Antitrust Authorities for an opinion to estimate the loss caused by the infringement. However, the Specialized Federal Courts are not obliged to ask for the estimate nor are they bound to accept it if provided by the Antitrust Authorities.

However, some of the latest court-issued criteria in Mexico contemplate a new form of interpretation of the concept of damages: "punitive damages", under which it has been considered that the compensation to the victim is not only intended to repair the direct damage suffered in its assets, property, feelings, emotions, beliefs, honour, reputation, private life, physical appearance, or the consideration that others have of the victim, but also to punish the misconduct or neglect of duty of care which the liable person has incurred.

In other words, the Mexican Courts set also that the defendant should not only be ordered to compensate the actual damage caused to the claimant but shall also be punished for his carelessness when he has a duty of care.

5. Passing-on defence

Under Mexican legislation, the defendant will be considered liable only in relation to those damages that are the immediate and direct consequence of its anti-competitive conduct. Thus, it might be raised since the claimant can only be indemnified for the damage that he or she actually suffered.

Therefore, 'passing-on' defence looks reasonable in relation to civil and competition law, given that if the FCC establishes for there to be an indemnity, there shall be a direct damage if the claimant 'passed-on' that damage to its own purchasers, the claimant did not suffer any damage. As a result, there is no causation between the anti-competitive practice and the damage claimed and the claimant should not be entitled to an indemnity from the defendant. Consequently, the "passing-on defence" has not yet been formally recognised in Mexico.

6. Pre-trial discovery and disclosure, treatment of confidential information

In Mexico, there is very limited access to information since there are no rules or rights to carry out a pre-trial discovery; the only sources of information available are the non-confidential documents of the administrative proceeding before the Antitrust Agencies.

However, there are two exceptions to this rule: (i) once the damages proceeding has begun, the Specialized Federal Courts may issue an order requesting either the respective Antitrust Agency or the defendant to disclose certain information; and/or, (ii) if there is a substantial risk that the other party might destroy or modify a document that is relevant to be used as evidence, the Specialized Federal Courts may order the defendant to provide all relevant evidence or to produce any piece of documentation.

All confidential information given by/obtained from the investigated agents during the investigation carried on by the Antitrust Authorities will be kept as confidential. The Court will only disclose the information that is strictly necessary for bringing the claim or establishing the damage.

7. Limitation periods

The statute limitation period for bringing a civil action (the individual actions) for damages is two years from the date on which the damage was caused. But as established by Article 134 of the FLEC, the statute of limitations could be suspended by the decision to initiate an investigation.

In class actions, the limitation period is three and a half years from the date on which the damage was caused (Article 584 of the FCCP).

8. Appeal

COFECE decisions may only be challenged by way of a constitutional bi-instance trial (*amparo indirecto*).

Resolutions of District Courts (first instance), which would rule on any action for damages, can be challenged or appealed before the Unitary Tribunals (second instance). The resolution rendered in the appeal may in turn be challenged through a constitutional single instance trial (*amparo directo*) before a Circuit Collegiate Tribunal, on grounds that fundamental rights of the parties have been breached.

9. Class action and collective representation

The procedure, requirements and formalities of class actions are regulated in the Federal Code of Civil Procedures; the three different types of class actions that the FCCP considers are the following:

- diffuse actions: Restitution of things to the state where they were prior to the affectation or the substitute compliance in their case to be determined by the judge.
- collectively in the strict sense actions: the repair of the damage caused by the conduct of an action or refrain from doing so, as well as to cover the damage for each of those affected.
- individual actions: they are individuals grouped based on common circumstances, whose objective is the judicial claim of a third party of the forced fulfilment of a contract or its termination with its consequences and effects, but they have the same interest as the collectivity.

In order to start and certify a class action, the following requirements shall be met:

- acts that harm consumers or users of public or private goods or services or the environment or acts that have harmed the consumer due to the existence of illicit concentrations or monopolistic practices declared a final resolution issued by the Antitrust Agencies.
- that there are at least 30 members in the collectivity to be considered a class action and it would be up to them to demonstrate the actual damages and losses originated by the defendant.
- reasonable doubt that a causal link exists between the infringement and the loss suffered.
- that the damages suffered have not yet been analysed in previous processes.

As of 2020, a few class actions have been started in Mexico and only one of them was related to cartel infringements in the health market in the State of Jalisco (started in 2019). This is why there are no legal precedents available to fully understand how private antitrust litigation will develop in this regard and what the criteria will be applied by the judiciary to quantify the damages.

NETHERLANDS

Gerjanne te Winkel
Partner, Jones Day

Niels van Loon
Counsel, Jones Day

Due to its efficient and reliable judiciary, the Netherlands is an attractive jurisdiction for private antitrust litigation and damages actions. Dutch procedural law is characterised by pragmatism and cost-effectiveness. Courts fees are low, and judgments are automatically enforceable in all EU Member States.

In the Netherlands, private antitrust litigation is mainly based on (i) general rules of tort liability set out in the Dutch Civil Code (*Burgerlijk Wetboek*, "DCC"), (ii) the Dutch Code of Civil Procedure (*Wetboek van Burgerlijke Rechtsvordering,* "DCCP"), (iii) competition law provisions set out in the Dutch Competition Act (*Mededingingswet*, "DCA"), (iv) competition law provisions set out in the Treaty on the Functioning of the European Union ("TFEU"), (v) in the various other EU legislative acts adopted on the basis of the TFEU, and (vi) in the EU soft law tools regarding private enforcement.

Directive 2014/104/EU of the European Parliament and of the Council of 26 November 2014 on certain rules governing actions for damages under national law for infringements of the competition law provisions of the Member States and of the European Union ("Damages Directive") was implemented into Dutch law by means of a new act (Implementing Act Directive Private Enforcement of Competition law of 25 January 2017, Bulletin of Acts and Decrees (*Staatsblad*) 2017, 28, "Implementing Act"). The Implementing Act introduced a number of new provisions in the DCC and the DCCP. Thus far, substantive and procedural changes in Dutch law has had a relatively limited impact because many provisions of the Damages Directive are largely in line with the principles of liability and compensation applicable under Dutch law.

1. Jurisdiction

In the Netherlands, the Consumer & Market Authority (*Autoriteit Consument & Markt,* "ACM") is responsible for the public enforcement of competition law. Article 2 of the DCA assigns responsibility for the implementation and enforcement of the DCA to the ACM.

The ACM enforces the prohibition on restrictive agreements and the abuse of a dominant position. The ACM is also tasked with the merger control review. The ACM's duties include (i) processing complaints about alleged violations of the DCA (or the corresponding provisions of the TFEU), (ii) monitoring compliance with the DCA, (iii) detecting and investigating the possible formation of cartels and abuses of dominant positions, (iv) assessing proposed concentrations, and (v) terminating as well as imposing administrative sanctions for violations. The ACM however has no jurisdiction in relation to the private enforcement of competition law and cannot grant civil damages for violations of competition law.

Antitrust damages claims must be brought before the Dutch civil courts. The jurisdiction of the Dutch civil courts is mainly governed by the DCCP and Regulation (EU) No. 1215/2012 ("Brussel I recast"). In general, Dutch civil courts accept jurisdiction to hear antitrust damages cases:

1) if the claims are brought against legal or natural persons domiciled in the Netherlands (Article 4 Brussel I recast; and Article 2 Brussel I (old) for proceedings initiated before 10 January 2015);

2) if a claim is sufficiently closely connected with another claim that is submitted against a defendant that is domiciled in the Netherlands ('anchor defendant') (Article 8(1) Brussel I recast); or
3) if the harmful event resulting of the unlawful conduct occurred, or may occur, in the Netherlands. This may be the case, for example, if the practice has been active in, or focused on, the Netherlands (Article 6(e) of the DCCP or Article 5(3) of Brussel I (old)). Infringements of national competition law only are not governed by the new statutory provisions of the Implementing Act yet but are expected to be included in the scope of the Implementing Act at a later stage.

Damages claims can be brought before the Dutch civil courts following a decision of a competition authority establishing an infringement of competition law (follow-on actions) or, irrespective of a public enforcement procedure or decision, based on an alleged infringement of competition law to be determined by the civil court (stand-alone actions). In civil proceedings where a party pursuant to Article 6:193k(a) DCC claims damages for an infringement of competition law, Article 161a DCCP provides that an irrevocable ACM decision establishing that infringement of competition law will form irrefutable evidence.

2. Relevant legislation and legal grounds

The legal framework for antitrust damages claims is comprised of provisions of the DCC, the DCCP, specific provisions of the DCA and the TFEU. Antitrust damages claims are generally based on tortious liability (Article 6:162 DCC): the claimant must demonstrate that (i) the defendant committed a wrongful act, (ii) the wrongful act committed is imputable to the defendant, (iii) the claimant suffered damage, and (iv) there is a causal link between the wrongful act committed and the damage suffered.

The Implementing Act created a new section in Title 3 of Book 6 of DCC establishing a specific (but non-exclusive) statutory basis for damages actions arising out of infringements of EU competition law (Articles 6:193k through 6:193t). With a few exceptions in accordance with the Damages Directive, Article 6:193m DCC provides a statutory basis for joint and several liability for undertakings involved in the EU competition law infringement.

3. What types of anti-competitive conducts are damages actions available for?

Under Dutch law, damages may be claimed for damage suffered as a result of all types of anti-competitive agreements, concerted practices or unilateral conduct, including abuse of a dominant position, provided that the claimant can demonstrate that the conditions of Article 6:162 (wrongful act) are met. An infringement of Article 101 TFEU (prohibition on anti-competitive agreements and cartels) and/or Article 102 TFEU (prohibition on the abuse of a dominant position) constitutes a violation of an obligation imposed by law and is therefore a wrongful act.

4. What forms of relief may a private party seek?

Article 6:193l DCC creates the legal presumption that an antitrust infringement causes damages. The starting point under Dutch law is full compensation for damage suffered as a result of the wrongful act or negligence by another party. In this sense, Dutch private competition enforcement is fully in line with the Damages Directive which aims at achieving full compensation. A claimant may claim actual loss, loss of profits, reasonable costs incurred by the claimant to prevent or reduce the damage suffered and the statutory interest over the amount of damages claimed (Article 6:99 DCC).

Compensation may not lead to overcompensation, whether punitive, multiple or any other form of compensation. Furthermore, any profits gained by the claimant as a result of the wrongful act will be reasonably deducted from any compensation.

5. Passing-on defence

Pursuant to Article 6:193p DCC, defendants have a right to invoke a passing-on defence, arguing that a claimant has not suffered any damages because it passed the price increase on within the supply chain. Defendants asserting the passing-on defence carry the burden of proof.

In a 2016 ruling, the Dutch Supreme Court confirmed that passing-on is a valid defence under Dutch law.[1] On the other hand, Dutch case law shows that Dutch courts are willing to reject a passing-on defence if it can be shown (i) that the claimant's end-user base is generally widespread, (ii) that the claims of these individual end-users are relatively minor, and (iii) that for reasons of evidentiary complexity and procedural cost effectiveness these individual end-users are unlikely to file civil damages claims proceedings of their own.

That same Dutch case law confirms that, in the event that a passing-on defence is rejected by the court and individual end-users subsequently file a civil damages claim of their own against the defendant, the defendant always retains the possibility to implead the previously successful claimant for compensation already paid to that claimant in as far as that compensation covers the new claims of the individual end-users.[2] A successful impleader would result in the defendant being able to deduct the end-consumers' damages from what the defendant previously owed to the successful claimant.

6. Pre-trial discovery and disclosure, treatment of confidential information

In the Netherlands, there is no extensive pre-trial discovery system. Parties can, however, request the disclosure of information judicially and extra-judicially. The extra judicial method for obtaining disclosure of documents is for the claimant to request the competition authority ACM to disclose certain documents pursuant to the Open Government Act (*Wet Open Overheid,* "OGA"), which replaced the Government Information Act (*Wet Openbaarheid Bestuur*, "GIA") as of 1 May 2022.[3] On the basis of the OGA,

---

1 Dutch Supreme Court, 8 July 2016, ECLI:NL:HR:2016:1483 (*TenneT/ABB*).

2 District Court of Gelderland, 29 March 2017, ECLI:NL:RBGEL:2017:1724 (*Tennet/ABB*) and District Court of Gelderland, 10 June 2015, ECLI:NL:RBGEL:2015:3713 (*Tennet/Alstom*).

3 Although the GIA is replaced by the OGA, any jurisprudence concerning the GIA remains of importance for the applicability of the OGA.

any member of the public may request disclosure of information contained in files of public authorities. Although the ACM is not required to disclose any documents obtained by it within the framework of its investigation, the files of the ACM itself do fall within the scope of the OGA.

However, articles 5 of the OGA provide several exceptions, *inter alia* for business secrets, on the basis of which the ACM can deny certain requests for the disclosure of information. In addition, the Rotterdam District Court ruled in a 2015 decision that, with the exception of certain circumstances, Article 7 of the Establishment Act of the Netherlands Authority for Consumers and Markets ("Establishment Act"), pursuant to which the ACM is prohibited from disclosing any information in the performance of its statutory task, prevails over the OGA.[4] In appeal, the Administrative Court for Trade and Industry (*College van Beroep voor het Bedrijfsleven*) upheld the decision of the District Court of Rotterdam and furthermore ruled that the documents requested may contain information which is not covered by Article 7 of the Establishment Act. Therefore, for each document requested, the ACM must determine which information contained therein is covered by article 7 of the Establishment Act.[5]

Another method for obtaining (limited) disclosure is for a party to conduct a preliminary examination of a witness or expert. This method is often used by a party to assess the merits of its case up front. Furthermore, it is possible to seize evidence through the filing of an *ex parte* writ with the court for that purpose. However, it must be noted that a successful seizure of evidence does not provide any legal right to inspect or take copies of such evidence. This requires filing a separate claim for disclosure on the basis of Article 843a DCCP.

Pursuant to Article 843a DCCP – a claim on the basis of which can be filed as a motion in ongoing legal proceedings or in separate legal proceedings – parties can request specific (written or digital) information from any person who is in possession of such documents. In order to be successful, the claimant must have a legitimate interest in the disclosure. Dutch Courts will deny requests for the disclosure of documents if there are compelling interests to refuse such disclosure or if the requested information is not relevant. In accordance with Chapter II of the Damages Directive, the newly enacted Articles 844-850 DCCP provide for certain deviations from, and additions to, Article 843a DCCP (e.g. in relation to leniency and settlement applications). These provisions are applicable to actions for damages of which the Dutch courts were seized after 26 December 2014.

7. Limitation Periods

Article 6:193s DCC contains two statute of limitations periods for infringements of EU competition law:

- a five-years limitation period, which will start to run from the day following the day on which the infringement has ceased and the claimant has become aware,

---

[4] District court of Rotterdam, 13 May 2015, ECLI:NL:RBROT:2015:3381.

[5] Administrative court of Trade and Industry, 17 June 2016, ECLI:NL:CBB:2016:169.

or can reasonably be expected to have become aware, of the infringement, the fact that the infringement caused harm to it and the identity of the infringer; and
- a twenty-years limitation period, which will start to run from the day following the day on which the infringement has ceased.

This provision does not substantially differ from, and is in accordance with, the provision included in Article 3:310 DCC, and which concerns general limitation of damages claims. Article 3:310 DC stipulates that an action for compensation of damages lapses twenty years after the event that caused the damage. It remains relevant because Article 6:193s DCC has no retroactive effect.

In principle, the limitation period for follow-on actions begins to run when the European Commission or another competition authority has issued an infringement decision or a decision imposing a fine for an infringement.[6]

Under Dutch law, it is relatively easy to interrupt and extend the limitation period by sending a letter in which a claimant unequivocally reserves its rights in relation to the claim. Furthermore, Article 6:193t DCC provides two grounds for extending the limitation period.

- The limitation period may be extended in case of non-judicial dispute resolution for the duration of the resolution process. In case of mediation, the extension will end when a party or the mediator informs the other party in writing of the termination of the mediation, or when no actions have been taken for six months during the mediation process.
- In addition, the limitation period will be extended if a competition authority takes action for the purpose of an investigation or proceedings in relation to the infringement to which the action for damages relates. The duration of the extension is one year after the infringement decision has become final or after the proceedings are otherwise terminated.

8. Appeal

Final decisions in Dutch civil cases may be appealed on the basis of Article 322 DCCP. The case is heard by the Court of Appeal that has territorial jurisdiction. In case the lower court renders an interim decision or a decision in interim relief proceedings, appeal against such a decision is only possible with leave from the lower court. The Court of Appeal will conduct a full review of the merits of the case (i.e. factual and/or points of law).

A decision of the competent Court of Appeal may be appealed before the Dutch Supreme Court. However, the appeal to the Supreme Court is limited to points of law and insufficient reasoning concerning the decision of the Court of Appeal.

---

6 District Court of East Netherlands 16 January 2013, ECLI:NL:RBONE:2013:BZ0403 (*TenneT/ABB*).

9. Class actions and collective representation

Claimants have the option of initiating individual civil proceedings and collective proceedings. Following the entry into force of the Act on Collective Settlement of Mass Damages (*Wet Afwikkeling Massaschade in Collectieve Actie*, "WAMCA") on 1 January 2020, the position of claimants seeking redress has improved. It has become easier for claimants to claim monetary damages in collective actions that relate to events on or after 15 November 2016. Class actions under the WAMCA can also be brought before the Netherlands Commercial Court ("NCC"), a international commercial court in the Netherlands allowing parties to resolve large and complex international commercial disputes where proceedings are conducted in English. As a result of the new act, which provides a U.S.- style class action, the number of representative collective actions is increasing, putting the Netherlands at the forefront in Europe with respect to collective actions.

Under the WAMCA, class actions proceedings are subject to strict admissibility requirements in order to prevent to prevent a compensation culture. Third party litigation is possible in the Netherlands and is not regulated.

The action must have a sufficiently close connection with the Dutch jurisdiction which is presumed if any of the following requirements are met: (i) if the majority of the claimants reside in the Netherlands; (ii) if the defendant resides in the Netherlands; or (iii) if the event(s) which the class action is based on took place in the Netherlands.

Any claim organization that represents the interest of claimants will be assessed at an early stage of the proceedings (comparable to the US motion to dismiss) and must be admissible. Claim organizations must meet additional requirements in the field of representation, governance, and funding. A claim organization is only authorized to commence a class action if it has, by virtue of its articles of association, full legal capacity to protect similar interests of the claimants which it represents. In addition, claim organizations, inter alia, need to appoint a supervisory board and must operate as a non-profit.

Once all the admissibility requirements have been met, the claim organization needs to file its claim and must publish the claim in a dedicated class actions register. If there is more than one claim organization wishing to bring an action in relation to the same subject matter, the different actions will be joined and the court will appoint an Exclusive Representative to represent the interests of all the aggrieved parties in the action.

Following the appointment of the Exclusive Representative, the parties will be given the opportunity to reach a settlement. If the parties reach a settlement, the settlement agreement must be submitted to the court for approval. Members of the class will, in principle, have the opportunity to opt out within one month after publication in the class action register. Foreign claimants who are not domiciled in the Netherlands will have to opt in. If they do, they become members of the class. The WAMCA creates a potentially powerful tool for claimants to use all types of action.

On 11 April 2018, the European Commission introduced the directive COM(2018)184 on representative claims for the protection of consumers' collective interests (Directive). The Directive requires all Member States to establish a consumer collective redress action and a list of representative entities that can bring cross-border consumer collective actions.

Only representative entities on the list can commence collective actions for consumers in another Member State.

As a result of the Directive, the WAMCA will be amended and aligned with the Directive per 25 June 2023, albeit the amendments are minimal because the WAMCA is already largely in line with the Directive. The amendments relate to the admissibility and representativeness requirements of claim organizations.

Methodology for the selection of cases

The database includes cases in which the Dutch courts either awarded damages in relation to antitrust damages claims, or where the Dutch courts rejected the entire antitrust damages claims. The selection therefore does not cover cases that (i) were settled between the parties or (ii) are still pending before the Dutch courts. Moreover, interim judgments – mainly on procedural issues – have been excluded.

List of Cases

All the case comments mentioned are available in the Concurrences e-Competitions Bulletin

Supreme Court

08/07/2016, Case ECLI:NL:HR:2016:1483, e-Competitions Bulletin, Art. N° 111732
www.concurrences.com/111732
Gerjanne te Winkel, Niels van Loon

Courts of Appeal

10/03/2020, Cases ECLI:NL:GHAMS:2020:714 and ECLI:NL:GHAMS:2020:713, e-Competitions Bulletin, Art. N° 111730
www.concurrences.com/111730
Gerjanne te Winkel, Niels van Loon

26/11/2019, Case ECLI:NL: GHARL:2019:10165, e-Competitions Bulletin, Art. N° 111738
www.concurrences.com/111738
Gerjanne te Winkel, Niels van Loon

05/02/2019, Case ECLI:NL:RBMNE:2016:4284, e-Competitions Bulletin, Art. N° 111737
www.concurrences.com/111737
Gerjanne te Winkel, Niels van Loon

02/09/2014, Case ECLI:NL: GHARL:2014:6766, e-Competitions Bulletin, Art. N° 111730
www.concurrences.com/111730
Gerjanne te Winkel, Niels van Loon

District Courts

26/09/2018, Case ECLI:NL:RBROT:2018:8001, e-Competitions Bulletin, Art. N° 111736
www.concurrences.com/111736
Gerjanne te Winkel, Niels van Loon

20/07/2017, Case ECLI:NL:RBMNE:2016:4284, e-Competitions Bulletin, Art. N° 111735
www.concurrences.com/111735
Gerjanne te Winkel, Niels van Loon

29/03/2017, Case ECLI:NL:RBGEL:2017:1724, e-Competitions Bulletin, Art. N° 111734
www.concurrences.com/111734
Gerjanne te Winkel, Niels van Loon

16/11/2016, Case ECLI:NL:RBLIM:2016:9897 and ECLI:NL:RBLIM:2015:1791, e-Competitions Bulletin, Art. N° 111733
www.concurrences.com/111733
Gerjanne te Winkel, Niels van Loon

10/06/2015, Case ECLI:NL:RBGEL:2015:3713, e-Competitions Bulletin, Art. N° 111731
www.concurrences.com/111731
Gerjanne te Winkel, Niels van Loon

16/01/2013, Case ECLI:NL: RBONE:2013:BZ0403, e-Competitions Bulletin, Art. N° 111729
www.concurrences.com/111729
Gerjanne te Winkel, Niels van Loon

POLAND

Marcin Trepka
Partner, Baker McKenzie Krzyżowski Wspólnicy sp.k.
Elżbieta Buczkowska
Counsel, Baker McKenzie Krzyżowski Wspólnicy sp.k.

Private antitrust litigation is still a relatively new concept in Poland. While in the past private enforcement was legally possible under general civil law rules, it was not exercised at all. This was due mainly to the difficulty in proving the extent of the damage (quantum) and the causal link between the damage and the breach of competition law, which is a prerequisite for obtaining compensation. On 21 April 2017, following the implementation of the Damages Directive 2014/104/EU (the "Directive"), the act on claims for compensation for damage caused by competition law infringements (hereinafter referred to as the "Act")[1] was adopted. The Act aims to regulate the legal rules of private antitrust litigation in line with European Union law. After the adoption of the Act, the first private enforcement litigations were launched. However, all of them are still pending to date.

1. Jurisdiction

The main Polish authority in charge of enforcing competition law is the Office of Competition and Consumer Protection ("OCCP"). Polish law also provides for specialised competition district judiciary. However, the OCCP and the specialised judiciary are only competent for public enforcement and not for private damages actions.

Private antitrust damages actions can be brought before the Polish district civil courts under the general provisions of Polish civil law and the Act. Thus, private enforcement competition cases are decided by the same civil courts which have jurisdiction over standard civil cases. Local courts depend on the seat of the defendant or the location of the damage. There are no dedicated divisions or sections which specialise in hearing such cases[2].

Antitrust damages actions can be brought before the competent national court both as a stand-alone action, regardless of a preliminary procedure before the OCCP, or as a follow-on action, based on a decision retaining an infringement and issued by the OCCP. It is questionable whether the civil courts may halt a stand-alone action for damages until the competition authority has issued a decision.

2. Relevant legislation and legal grounds

Under the Act, anyone (whether they are direct or indirect customers, competitors, suppliers, and so forth) who has suffered harm caused by an infringement of competition law committed by a company or an association of companies, has the right to receive full compensation for the harm, the loss of profit, and the applicable interests.

As mentioned above, it is not necessary for the OCCP or the European Commission to have issued a prior decision establishing that an infringement has occurred in order for the action to be admitted. This applies to either individual or class actions.

---

1 *Ustawa z dnia 21 kwietnia 2017 r. o roszczeniach o naprawienie szkody wyrządzonej przez naruszenie prawa konkurencji.*

2 There has been a recent trend to refer these cases to intellectual property courts, but it is still too early to judge whether this will be the rule.

In Poland, an action for breach of competition law can be brought on the basis of competition law infringements defined in Articles 101 or 102 of the Treaty on the Functioning of the European Union (hereinafter defined as "TFEU") as well as Articles 6 and 9 of the Act of 16 February 2007 on the Protection of Competition and Consumers (which echoes Articles 101 and 102 of the TFEU in the domestic context).

The claim may rely on Article 3 of the Act (under the previous regime the claim could rely on the general provisions of civil law, *i.e.* Article 405 of Polish Civil Law, regulating claims related to unjust enrichment, or Article 415 of Polish Civil Law, regulating liability for torts). The provision of Article 3 of the Act not only establishes a new type of tort but sets its own principles of liability. The provision requires the claimant to prove: (i) the infringement of competition law, therefore proving the unlawfulness of the infringer's behaviour, (ii) damage and (iii) causation between the two.

The Act has made it much easier for claimants to establish these three elements:

- Article 3 of the Act introduced a presumption of fault of the infringer of competition law. This means that in order to be released from liability, the defendant would have to prove that its conduct did not amount to a breach of competition law.
- Article 7 of the Act applied a presumption that any infringement of competition law causes damage. In this respect the Polish regulation goes beyond the Directive, which requires such presumption only for cartels.
- Article 30 of the Act provides that findings regarding an infringement of competition law contained in a final decision delivered by the OCCP or a final ruling of a specialised judiciary issued in proceedings launched by the appeal against such OCCP's decision (*i.e.* a decision or ruling which can no longer be appealed against/challenged under national law) are binding for the civil court in the relevant proceeding. The same goes for the European Commission's final decisions enforcing Articles 101 and 102 TFEU. As regards decisions taken in another Member State, they have the same probative value as Polish official documents (Article 1138 of Code of Civil Procedure) and can be recognised by the Polish court as evidence of an infringement on the basis of a presumption of the facts (Article 231 of Code of Civil Procedure) (*i.e.* they are taken into account as a piece of evidence but the court is not formally bound by the findings made in such decisions as to whether competition law has been infringed).
- Article 30 of the Act does not apply to decisions of inadmissibility, dismissal, or commitment decisions of the OCCP, since such decisions do not contain findings of an infringement. However, such decisions can still have some evidential value.
- Parties which have been granted immunity from fines under a leniency programme are not exempted from civil liability. However, they benefit from a privileged position as they will only be found jointly and severally liable outside their supply chain if it is not possible to obtain full compensation from the other infringers. Parties are also granted protection as regards access to the files. As to the application of the Act, leniency concerns cartels only (generally in Polish law, leniency is also possible for vertical agreements).

Rationae temporis application of the Act

In accordance with the general principle of non-retroactivity of the law, the new substantial provisions of the Act, and in particular the above-mentioned presumptions, are only applicable to actions for damages as a result of infringements of competition rules (*i.e.* the facts causing liability) which took place after its entry into force *i.e.* from 27 June 2017 onwards.

However, Chapter 3 of the Act regarding the procedure and rules of the production of evidence apply to all proceedings initiated since 27 June 2017, regardless of when the breach of competition law occurred (Article 36 of the Act).

Provisions extending the limitation period apply in specific, intermediate cases, when the limitation period under new provisions introduced by the Act would have started or elapsed before the date of entry into force of the Act but would have not started under the previous wording of relevant provision (Article 442^1 § 1 of the Civil Code). In such a case, the period that has already elapsed is not taken into consideration, and the general three-years limitation period (Article 442^1 § 1 of the Civil Code) started on 27 June 2017.

3. What types of anti-competitive conduct are damages actions available for?

Violations of EU or national competition law are a requirement and include those relating to anti-competitive agreements and concerted practices or abuse of a market dominant position, pursuant to Articles 101 or 102 of the TFEU or Articles 6 and 9 of the Act on the Protection of Competition and Consumers.

4. What forms of relief may a private claimant seek?

The primary objective of damages actions under civil law provisions and the Act is to obtain full compensation for the harm caused by an infringement of competition law.

A private claimant can seek compensation for the damage suffered (*damnum emergens*), as well as for the benefits that it lost as a consequence of the unlawful conduct (*lucrum cessans*).

Causation between the fault and the damage must be direct, which means that the claimant must prove that the damage suffered and/or loss of profits results entirely from the anti-competitive behaviour.

In addition, private claimants are also entitled to claim interest. According to general rules, interests are due from the day of the court's decision awarding damages until the effective and full payment of the compensation. Depending on the specific circumstances of the case, private claimants might be also entitled to interests for the period before the court's decision. According to the Act, it might be the case if the basis for determining the compensation are prices from a date other than the date of determining the compensation (date of the court's decision), the injured party is entitled to statutory interest for the period from the date on which the prices were the basis for determining the compensation, to the date when the claim for damages is due. Under general rules, the injured party might be also entitled to claim interest for the time of delay in payment compensation from the day after the debtor has been called upon to pay until the payment.

5. Passing-on defence

As mentioned above, the Act provides for some presumptions which all aim to strengthen the situation of aggrieved persons and entities, one of them being the presumption that an overcharge is passed on to indirect purchasers. This presumption can be relied on solely by the indirect purchaser. Indirect purchasers can rely on the presumption that the overcharge was passed on to them by the direct purchasers in their claims against the infringer. This presumption is rebuttable, but the burden of proof in such respect lies entirely with the defendant (infringer).

The infringing party (defendant) cannot take advantage of this presumption as a part of the defence against the action brought by the direct purchaser – in such cases the infringer must prove that the overcharge was fully or partially passed on.

In both situations, in order to shift the burden of proof, the defendant (infringer) must prove that there was no passing-on from the direct purchaser to the indirect purchaser (when the indirect purchaser is the claimant) or that the overcharge was passed-on to the indirect purchaser (in the event the direct purchaser acts as the claimant). In such cases, the defendant must rely on standard evidentiary methods (documentary, economic analysis, expert opinions, witness statements, and so forth).

6. Pre-trial discovery and disclosure, treatment of confidential information

There is no typical pre-trial discovery under Polish law. However, the Act provides for a simplified procedure for obtaining evidence in support of damage claims under pending litigation. The claimant (the aggrieved party) can apply to the court to oblige the defendant, the OCCP or other third parties to disclose evidence being in their possession. The disclosure is granted based on a legally binding decision which constitutes an enforcement order.

The claimant can use the documents obtained only for the given court proceedings. The earliest moment when the disclosure procedure can start is at the filing of the lawsuit, as Polish law does not foresee any pre-trial disclosure.

The Act provides that the disclosure must be proportionate and must not relate to the leniency statements submitted under a leniency programme or settlement submissions. Misuse of disclosed evidence will result in the court handling the claim disregarding that evidence. A non-discretionary fine of up to PLN 20,000 (EUR 4,700) can be imposed on a party requesting the disclosure of evidence in bad faith.

As far as confidential information is concerned, if any such information occurs in the court files as a result of disclosure at the initiative of one of the parties, the court conducts the proceedings behind closed doors. Moreover, if such information is included in documents or other materials obtained because of the disclosure, the court limits the access to such evidence to the necessary degree or order on the specific rules of familiarization with such evidence.

7. Limitation periods

Polish civil law regarding torts provides for a general limitation period of three years from the day on which the injured party learned about the damage and about the person liable to redress it, or might have learned about it if he/she had exercised due diligence. However, such a time limit may not be longer than ten years from the day on which the event causing the damage occurred.

By way of exception, the three-years limitation period for damages claims arising out of competition law infringements has been extended to five years. This limitation period is suspended for the duration of proceedings conducted by the OCCP or other competent authorities (e.g. the European Commission or the competition authority of another Member State). This suspension will cease one year after the date of issuance of a legally binding decision or termination of the proceedings in a different way.

8. Appeal

First-instance court judgments in private antitrust litigation are subject to appeal at second instance courts (Courts of Appeal). Court of Appeal judgments are final and binding but can be subject to extraordinary appeal to the Supreme Court (limited to questions of breach of substantive law or severe procedural error which affected the outcome of the case). The appeal to the Supreme Court do not overturn the final and binding character of the Court of Appeal judgments.

9. Class actions and collective representation

In Poland, the mechanism of pursuing claims in group proceedings was introduced to the legal system by an Act of 17 December 2009. There have been very few group cases. However, in theory, it is possible for competitors of an entrepreneur who committed an act of unfair competition to make claims in group proceedings. Consumers seeking compensation for damages resulting from delicts can also make claims in group proceedings. There are only a few minor limitations of claims which cannot be subject to class actions.

Class actions are understood as proceedings where claims of the same type, based on the same or similar facts, are pursued by at least ten individuals. A representative of the group (a group member or certain authorized entity) conducts the proceedings on behalf of and for the benefit of all the group members. Although the practice has shown that it is difficult to prove that all claimants form a "class" (group), a significant number of class actions have been heard by Polish courts to date. According to publicly available data, in the period 2010-2021, there have been more than 320 class actions submitted to courts in civil and commercial cases and approximately 30% of them were rejected or refused.

10. Key issues

The entry into force of the presumptions facilitating private actions

Before the Act entered into force, it was extremely difficult, if not impossible, for claimants to initiate a procedure for damage claims for competition law infringements. The burden of proof was to a large extent borne by the aggrieved party, who at the same time had no actual access to evidence. The Act introduced a new type of tort, and provided several presumptions, strengthening the situation of the injured parties and facilitating the action for claims.

Starting point of the limitation period

Pursuant to Polish law regarding torts, the starting point for a limitation period is the day on which the injured party (i) learns about the damage and about the person liable to redress it, or (ii) the day on which he/she might have learned about the damage if he/she had exercised due diligence. The question may accrue depending on how this actual moment is understood. This is particularly vital with regard to follow-on actions. Some may argue whether the starting point in such cases is the moment of initiation of the proceeding by the OCCP, the issuance of the decision or the moment when the decision becomes final. It seems that the starting point for a limitation period would be the moment when the decision becomes final, as only then can the claimants obtain full clarity on the unlawfulness of the practice and the identification of the infringer.

Calculation of damages

One of the biggest practical problems in competition law infringement is calculating the damage suffered by an aggrieved party. In this respect, the Act introduces an important presumption that any breach of competition law causes damage. With regard to the methods of determining the amount of damage, the Act refers to the guidelines of the European Commission and indicates that the guidelines may be found helpful by Polish courts. As a rule, the calculation of damage is based on counterfactual analysis. It is necessary to make a comparison between the actual situation of the aggrieved party and the situation of the party if the infringement had not occurred. This can be done, for example, by means of comparative methods such as referring the actual situation to the period before or after the infringement or to the situation on other markets. Another way is to simulate market outcomes by use of economic models.

The Act enables courts to request assistance from the OCCP with the calculation of damages. Although not obligatory, the assistance of the OCCP, with the expertise of its employees and available tools, may prove invaluable for the aggrieved party.

11. Key cases in antitrust damages actions in Poland

As mentioned above, initiating a procedure for damage claims for competition law infringements proved difficult under the previous regime (before the Act entered into force). One private enforcement case under the previous regime that is worth mentioning concerns the cement cartel case (I ACa 1322/13). A private claimant submitted a statement of claims requesting damages against a leniency applicant before the infringement decision became final. The courts of all instances confirmed that it is the claimant who must prove the antitrust infringement if there is no final infringement decision. The lawsuit was dismissed, as the courts found that the private claimant did not prove all the aspects of the alleged collusions, in particular basing its case on the fact that the leniency applicant's admitted participation in a cartel is not enough.

Since the entry into force of the Act, only a few actions have been initiated and none of them have been finally decided to date.

As for Polish courts, private enforcement still seems to be a sort of *terra incognita*. A number of Polish entrepreneurs who were affected by international cartels have sought damages in countries with a much greater tradition and experience in that area *i.e.* in France, Germany or the United Kingdom.

The following paragraphs outline actions initiated after the entry into force of the Act and do not attempt to be exhaustive.

Interchange fees

In April 2018, a Polish entrepreneur filed a claim for damages against banks for higher interchange fees. The claim concerns damages for the overpayment of the interchange fee in the time period of 2008 to 2014.

The interchange fee is paid by each entrepreneur enabling card payment. The interchange fee is a fixed component of the fee from banks issuing payment cards or agents acting on their behalf. The interchange fee is charged on the gross value of a sales transaction, usually as a specified percentage of the transaction value and paid to issuing banks and card organizations such as Maestro, MasterCard, VISA and American Express. Ultimately, when a customer pays for a good with a card, the merchant receives the gross value less a commission (e.g., PLN 100 gross price of the goods – PLN 2 commission = PLN 98 receipt in the merchant's account). The entrepreneurs claimed that due to an anti-competitive agreement, the fee was higher than it ought to have been e.g., 0.3% instead of 0.2% of the gross value of each transaction.

The claimant derived the "right" fee from the entry into force of the amendment to the Act on Payment Services. The claimant claimed that the banks and card organizations agreed on jointly setting the interchange fees. In this respect, the claimants referred to the decision of the President of the OCCP of 29 December 2006, which, as of today is not legally binding (the OCCP decision was challenged by the allegedly infringing parties in the civil court, and the revision procedures are still pending). Moreover, the claimant also referred to the European Commission's decision in the VISA case (AT.39398 Visa MIF) and the CJEU's ruling in the MasterCard case (C-382/12). However, both the President of the OCCP's decision and the Commission's decisions have only evidential value, as the former concerns a different time period and the latter covers a different factual situation.

In the said case (XVI GC 457/18) the claim was dismissed by the court of first instance almost in its entirety as time-barred – the court established that the claimant learned about the infringer and the damage at the day of the entry into force of the amendment to the Act on Payment Services. The claims were granted only insofar as the infringement resulted in overcharge after the said day. The award was challenged but the Court of Appeal confirmed in November 2022 that the statutory limitation charges, granted by the court of first instance, were accurate (VII AGa 933/22).

Truck manufacturers cartel

Another lawsuit based on the Act as a part of a wider, European private enforcement action concerning a truck manufacturers cartel (European Commission's decision of 19 June 2016) is pending before the District Court in Wroclaw (X GC 790/17). However, since the Act fully applies only to infringements that occurred after 27 June 2017, some Polish entrepreneurs joined a private enforcement action which was initiated before German courts.

Cement cartel

In January 2019, a private enforcement action based on the Act was submitted to the Warsaw District Court by entities injured by cement producers. This case was resolved at the end of 2022 (XX GC 74/19) – the court dismissed the claim at the result of the statutory limitation of the claims. The court observed that the injured entity learned about the damage and the person obliged to repair it long before the decision of the OCCP was upheld by the Court of Appeal.

The cement cartel case is known as one of the biggest cases in the history of Polish competition law enforcement. In 2009 the President of the OCCP imposed the highest possible fine of PLN 411 million on the seven largest cement producers. The infringing parties had been dividing the market, exchanging confidential information and setting prices for more than eleven years. In 2018, after almost a decade of battling in court, the decision became final. However, the penalties were reduced by one third. This has given impetus to private enforcement actions initiated by aggrieved entrepreneurs, mostly those using cement as a semi-finished product, namely concrete producers.

Chemical products for the mining industry

In June 2020, two more private enforcement actions were submitted to the Katowice District Court (XIV GC 631/19) and Gliwice District Court (X GC 114/20) by two coal mines. The two lawsuits were based on the same non-final infringement decision of the President of the OCCP alleging price-fixing, market sharing and bid-rigging (the decision was repealed by the second instance court during the proceedings). Therefore, the Act's provisions are only applicable in part (*i.e.* evidence disclosure). Both claimants were obliged to prove their case and did not benefit from any presumption included in the Act.

Both cases are already resolved in the first instance and are now being heard by the Courts of Appeal. The District Courts dismissed the claims of coal mines finding that the claim was time-barred. The Courts observed in both cases that the claimants learned about the damage and the person obliged to repair it before the decision was issued by the OCCP, from the official correspondence received by the claimant from the OCCP in the course of the antimonopoly proceedings, in which claimants were asked to provide detailed information on contractual relations with the defendants, in the context of alleged infringements of competition law. This correspondence indicated the entities which were concerned by the antimonopoly proceedings, the charges which were brought against them as well as suggested that there was an overprice affecting the claimants.

In June 2023 the Court of Appeal dismissed the ruling of the Katowice District Court (XIV GC 631/19) and referred the case back. The Court of Appeal did not share the District Court's assessment on the statutory limitation of the claims – referring to the complexity of private enforcement cases and difficulties which might be faced by claimants in identifying the abuse of competition law and the damage, the Court held that the claimant learned about the damage and the person obliged to repair from the non-binding decision issued by the OCCP.

PORTUGAL

Eduardo Maia Cadete

Partner, Morais Leitão Advogados

With the support of Gonçalo Machado Borges, Partner, Morais Leitão Advogados,
and Miguel Mota Delgado, Junior Lawyer, Morais Leitão Advogados

Miguel Miranda

Partner, Raposo, Sá Miranda & Associados

With the support of Efigénia Marabuto Tavares,
Managing Associate & PRA, Raposo, Sá Miranda & Associados

Miguel Gorjão-Henriques

Partner, Sérvulo & Associados

Gonçalo Anastácio

Partner, SRS Advogados

Leyre Prieto

Partner, Telles Advogados

Nuno Cruz

Partner, JP CRUZ

Miguel Pena Machete

Partner, Cuatrecasas

In Portugal, private antitrust litigation, prior to the enactment of the Private Enforcement Directive, has been based on general rules of civil contractual and tort liability. On 5 June 2018 Law No. 23/2018 was approved, which entered into force on 4 August 2018, implementing EU Directive 2014/104, of 26 November 2014, on Antitrust Damages Actions ("Law 23/2018")

1. Jurisdiction

The primary authority in charge of enforcing competition law in Portugal is the Portuguese Competition Authority ("PCA"). The authority is only competent for public enforcement and not for private damages actions.

Victims of anti-competitive conducts can seek compensation before civil common courts if the cause of action is grounded non-exclusively on a competition law breach (for instance, abuse of dominance and cumulative breach of insurance sector rules) and before the specialised Competition Court, which has jurisdiction *ratione materiae* over the entire Portuguese territory, if the cause of action is exclusively based on a competition law breach. As such, the specialised Competition Court lacks competence to decide claims based on anti-competitive conducts combined with other grounds[1].

In private antitrust enforcement proceedings, claimants can bring actions based on a decision from the PCA, the European Commission, the competition authority of another EU member state or the court of another EU member state finding an infringement of competition law against the defendant(s) (follow-on actions) or, independently of a public enforcement procedure, on the basis of a stand-alone action.

Collective actions for indemnity, under the opt-out model in force in Portugal, can also be started to seek compensation for anti-competitive conducts.

2. Relevant legislation and legal grounds

The relevant legislation is enshrined in (i) Law No. 23/2018, of 5 June 2018, which entered into force on 4 August 2018, implementing EU Directive 2014/104 on Antitrust Damages Actions, (ii) Law No. 19/2012, 8 May 2012, as amended, which approves the national Competition Act, (iii) the Civil Code and the Civil Procedure Code, (iv) Law No. 83/95, 31 August 1995, as amended, on collective actions ("Law 83/95"), and (v) Law No. 62/2013, 26 August 2013, as amended, on the Organisation of the Judicial system ("Law 62/2013").

Pursuant to the framework introduced by Law 23/2018, a competition law infringement found by a final decision adopted by the PCA or judicially confirmed (*res judicata*) has binding evidentiary value in the form of a non-rebuttable presumption regarding the existence, nature, duration and material, personal and territorial scope of the antitrust

---

1 See Article 112(3-4) of Law 62/2013.

infringement. Further, the law confers a qualified evidentiary value on the basis of a rebuttable presumption to final decisions or rulings by competition authorities or courts of other EU member states[2].

3. What types of anti-competitive conduct are damages actions available for?

Damages actions are available for anti-competitive agreements, abuses of dominant position and abuses of economic dependency.[3] Among the classic illegal behaviours that can lead to a damage action, one can include price-fixing and/or allocation of customers among competitors or a refusal to supply or a non-justifiable discriminatory pricing policy set by an undertaking in a dominant position in a regulated or non-regulated sector of the economy. In parallel, the abuse of economic dependence consists of the abusive exploitation by one undertaking of the economic dependence of another undertaking due to the absence of the latter of an equivalent alternative for the supply of goods or the provision of services.

4. What forms of relief may a private claimant seek?

A private claimant under a private antitrust enforcement claim can seek compensation for the damage suffered (*damnum emergens*), as well as for the benefits (*lucrum cessans*) that it lost as a consequence of the unlawful conduct.[4]

Causation between the fault and the damage must be direct, which means that the claimant must prove that the damage suffered and /or loss of profits results exclusively from the anti-competitive behaviour.

In addition, private claimants are also entitled to delay interest (*juros de mora*), which is applied from the adoption date of the judicial decision that awards damages until effective and full payment of the compensation.[5]

If the anti-competitive conduct results from a joint behaviour of two or more undertakings, they are jointly and severally liable for the incurred damage[6], but the subsequent exceptions can apply to SMEs and leniency applicants. If the damage is caused by an SME, such undertaking is only liable before the respective direct or indirect customers or suppliers if (i) its market share in the market(s) affected by the infringement is below 5% during the infringement period and (ii) the application of joint and severally rules harms irreparably its economic viability and devaluates fully its assets[7]. The aforementioned exception for SMEs is not applicable if the SME is the ringleader or coerced other undertakings to participate in the infringement or has been condemned in another procedure for a competition law breach by a final decision. With regards to a leniency

---

2 See Article 7 of Law 23/2018.
3 See Article 1 and 2(I) of Law 23/2018.
4 See Article 3(1) and 4(1) of Law 23/2018.
5 See Article 4(2) of Law 23/2018.
6 See Article 5(1) of Law 23/2018.
7 See Article 5(2-3) of Law 23/2018.

applicant[8], the company is only liable to (i) the respective direct or indirect customers or suppliers, and (ii) any other victims, if these cannot obtain full reparation on the suffered damages from the other infringers.

5. Passing-on defence

The passing-on defence is expressly allowed under national rules: the defendant may invoke the fact that the claimant passed on (fully or in part) the overcharge resulting from the competition law infringement. The burden of proving that the overcharge was passed on rests with the defendant.[9] Conversely, indirect purchasers may seek compensation arguing that the overcharge was passed on them.

6. Pre-trial discovery and disclosure, treatment of confidential information

There is no pre-trial discovery procedure in Portugal similar to the one in force in the US legal system.

Still, any party to the proceedings, including the claimant, is entitled to request to the court the disclosure of documents that are considered as necessary to prove the alleged facts that are in the possession of the defendant or of any third party, including public authorities.[10]

In the case of documents from the file of the PCA, the European Commission or a national competition authority within the EU, the court may order the disclosure of the following categories of evidence only after the competition authority has closed its proceedings: (i) information that was prepared by a natural or legal person specifically for the proceedings of the competition authority, (ii) information that the competition authority has drawn up and sent to the parties in the course of its proceedings and (iii) settlement submissions that have been withdrawn.[11] Still, the court, per applicable rules, cannot request the following sets of documents from a competition authority: (i) leniency statements; and (ii) settlement proposals.[12]

There is also a specific procedure to protect business secrets from requested documents. Under this procedure the court can request the presentation by the parties of documents containing confidential information, albeit adopting adequate measures to protect the respective confidentiality, such as (i) deletion of excerpts from documents; (ii) hold hearings behind closed doors; (iii) restrict the number of persons authorised to have access to the evidence, namely, limit or access the legal representatives and defenders of the parties or individuals subject to the obligation of confidentiality; or (iv) request the preparation by a court-appointed expert of information in an aggregated or otherwise non-confidential manner.[13]

---

8 See Article 5(4) of Law 23/2018.

9 See Article 8 of Law 23/2018.

10 See Article 12, 13 and 14 of Law 23/2018.

11 See Article 14(4) of Law 23/2018.

12 See Article 14(5) of Law 23/2018.

13 See Article 12(7) of Law 23/2018.

In addition, before bringing an action for damages, the claimant, through a reasoned motion, can request the competent court to summon a party withholding information or means of proof and order it to present the said information or means of proof[14].

When there is serious evidence of a breach of competition law capable of causing damages, the injured party can ask the court for provisional measures to preserve the means of proof of that breach.[15]

Additionally, when there is a well-founded fear that the deposition of a certain party or the checking of certain facts by means of inspection will become impossible or very difficult, that deposition or inspection can take place before the action is brought.[16]

7. Limitation periods

Prior to the implementation of Directive 2014/104/EU by Law 23/2018 the relevant limitation period, for private antitrust claims based on tort liability, was three years from the date on which the injured party was aware of its right, even if unaware of the identity of the person liable and the full extent of the damage.[17] Yet, the Court of justice ruled in 2019 that this system of limitation period violated Article 102 TFEU and the principle of effectiveness: "a limitation period of three years, such as that at issue in the main proceedings, which, first, starts to run from the date on which the injured party was aware of its right to compensation, even if the infringer is not known and, secondly, may not be suspended or interrupted in the course of proceedings before the national competition authority, renders the exercise of the right to full compensation practically impossible or excessively difficult".[18]

Pursuant to Law 23/2018, the limitation period is now five years from the date the victim knows or can reasonably be expected to know of, cumulatively, the relevant conduct and the fact that it was anti-competitive, the identity of the wrongdoer; and the harm that it caused to the victim.[19]

In any case, the five-years limitation period does not start to run until the infringement has ceased. Further, said period is suspended when the PCA, other competition authority of other EU member state or the European Commission, starts a formal investigation regarding the infringement to which the indemnity claim is connected. Aforesaid suspension only ceases one year after the case is concluded by the relevant competition authority.[20]

---

14 See Article 13(1) of Law 23/2018. Articles 2 to 9 of Law 23/2018 are applicable, mutatis mutandis, to the request – see Article 13(2) of Law 23/2018. In accordance with the Civil Procedure Code, the summoned party can challenge this court order – see Article 1046(1) of the Civil Procedure Code.

15 See Article 17(1) of Law 23/2018.

16 See Article 17(2) of Law 23/2018.

17 See Article 498(1) of Law 23/2018.

18 CJEU, Case C-637/17, 28 March 2019, *Cogeco*, para. 53.

19 See Article 6 of Law 23/2018.

20 Please see preceding footnote.

8. Appeal

First instance civil court decisions and specialised Competition Court rulings can be subject to judicial review before the Court of Appeal and, if applicable procedural rules are met, by the Supreme Court of Justice.[21]

9. Class actions and collective representation

In the Portuguese jurisdiction, class actions are available for private antitrust enforcement under the opt-out model.[22]

The judicial claim must be introduced by (i) a natural person; (ii) a public prosecutor; (iii) an association or foundation whose aim is the protection of consumers; or (iv) an association of companies whose members were victims of anti-competitive conducts, even if the respective by-laws do not include in their scope the protection of competition.[23]

If the class action proceeds on the merits, the judicial decision determines the criteria to identify the victims of the anti-competitive conduct and the quantification of the damage suffered by each identifiable victim. If all victims are not individually identifiable, the court can award a global compensation amount. The judicial decision further identifies the entity responsible for the reception, management, and payment of the granted compensation to the victims which were not individually identifiable.[24]

10. Key issue

Popular Actions

Portugal is one of the few countries in Europe with opt-out regimes for antitrust infringements that are actually being put into practice.
It is rooted in a constitutional right of popular action and it is implemented by Article 19 of Law 23/2018 and, subsidiarily, by the general regime of popular actions Law 83/95.

It can be used to represent consumers and undertakings and active legitimacy is granted to individual consumers and associations. Third-party funding has been deemed irrelevant for the determination of active legitimacy in popular actions.

Courts have confirmed that popular actions may be used to seek (i) compensation for consumers injured by anticompetitive practices, (ii) pre-filing discovery and (iii) provisional measures.

Methodology for the selection of cases

The following database includes the most relevant publicly available cases in the Portuguese case law for both follow-on and stand-alone proceedings and it does not attempt to be exhaustive.

---

21 See Article 627 *et seq* of the Civil Procedure Code.

22 See Article 19 of Law 23/2018 and Articles 14 and 15 of Law 83/95.

23 See Article 19(2) of Law 23/2018 and Articles 2(1) and 15 of Law 83/95

24 See Article 19 of Law 23/2018.

List of Cases

All the case comments mentioned are available in the Concurrences e-Competitions Bulletin

Supreme Court

07/07/2022, Case 2/19.3YQSTR-G.L1.S1, e-Competitions Bulletin, Art. N° 116310
www.concurrences.com/116310
Miguel Miranda, Efigénia Marabuto Tavares

08/03/2022, Case 6/19.6YQSTR-C.L1.S1, e-Competitions Bulletin, Art. N° 116306
www.concurrences.com/116306
Miguel Miranda, Efigénia Marabuto Tavares

16/02/2016, Case 135/12.7TCFUN.L1.S1 *AA and BB vs CC*, e-Competitions Bulletin, Art. N° 111717
www.concurrences.com/111717
Eduardo Maia Cadete

20/06/2013, Case 178/07.2TVPRT.P1.S1 *AUTO-AA vs SC COMÉRCIO and SC-INDÚSTRIAS,* e-Competitions Bulletin, Art. N° 111718
www.concurrences.com/111718
Eduardo Maia Cadete, Miguel Mota Delgado, Morais Leitão Advogados

2010, Case 3130/08, *A. vs B*, judgment publicly available in physical format at Portuguese Colectânea de Jurisprudência, n.º 227, Tomo III/2010, e-Competitions Bulletin, Art. N° 111720
www.concurrences.com/111720
Eduardo Maia Cadete, Miguel Mota Delgado, Morais Leitão Advogados

Court of Appeal

22/03/2023, Case 18/21.0YQSTR.L1, e-Competitions Bulletin, Art. N° 116323
www.concurrences.com/116323
Miguel Miranda, Efigénia Marabuto Tavares

13/07/2022, Case 6/21.6YQSTR.L1-PICRS, e-Competitions Bulletin, Art. N° 116311
www.concurrences.com/116311
Miguel Miranda, Efigénia Marabuto Tavares

04/10/2011, Case 107/2001.L1-7, e-Competitions Bulletin, Art. N° 111719
www.concurrences.com/111719
Eduardo Maia Cadete, Miguel Mota Delgado, Morais Leitão Advogados

Competition Court

10/03/2023, Case 54/19.6YQSTR, e-Competitions Bulletin, Art. N° 116321
www.concurrences.com/116321
Miguel Miranda, Efigénia Marabuto Tavares

08/03/2023, Case 6/21.6YQSTR, e-Competitions Bulletin, Art. N° 116319
www.concurrences.com/116319
Miguel Miranda, Efigénia Marabuto Tavares

30/11/2022, Case 12/19.0YQSTR, e-Competitions Bulletin, Art. N° 116317
www.concurrences.com/116317
Miguel Miranda, Efigénia Marabuto Tavares

06/11/2022, Case 71/19.6YQSTR, e-Competitions Bulletin, Art. N° 116312
www.concurrences.com/116312
Miguel Miranda, Efigénia Marabuto Tavares

Court of First Instance

22/11/2016, Case 1774/11.9TVLSB, e-Competitions Bulletin, Art. N° 111722
www.concurrences.com/111722
Gonçalo Machado Borges

Cogeco Communications Inc v. Sport TV Portugal, case pending.
Daniela Cardoso

SPAIN

Juan Pablo Correa Delcasso
Partner, Laguard

Laura Pérez
Lawyer, Laguard

Rais Amils
Partner, Pérez-Llorca

Ana Parés
Lawyer, Pérez-Llorca

Belén Irissarry
Lawyer, Counsel, Clifford Chance

Fernando Giménez-Alvear
Counsel, Clifford Chance

Laura García-Valdecasas
Lawyer, Clifford Chance

In Spain, private damages actions have historically played a minimal role in enforcing Competition Law. As a result of enacting the current Spanish Competition Act 15/2007 of 3 July 2007 (the "SCA"), private enforcement of Competition Law was facilitated, increasing the number of antitrust damages actions brought before Spanish courts. However, there was still no specific regulation on the liability for such damages arising from antitrust infringements.

Private antitrust litigation has grown further as a result of the transposition of Directive 2014/104/EU of 26 November 2014 (the "Damages Directive") into Spanish Law through the Royal Decree-Law 9/2017 of 26 May 2017 (the "RDL 9/2017"), which approved certain specific rules, both substantive and procedural, in the field of private antitrust actions, by respectively amending the SCA and the Spanish Act 1/2000 of 7 January 2000 on Civil Procedure (the "SACP").

Both follow-on and stand-alone actions (*i.e.* based or not based on a previous final resolution issued by a Competition authority) are allowed under Spanish law.

1. Jurisdiction

Apart from the European Commission ("EC"), the main administrative bodies in charge of enforcing Competition law in Spain are the National Commission on Markets and Competition ("*Comisión Nacional de los Mercados y la Competencia*" or "*CNMC*") and several regional Competition authorities. However, they are only competent for public enforcement of Competition Law.

On the whole, judicial actions for damages resulting from infringements of Competition Law must be brought before the commercial courts, which are the competent courts for private enforcement of Competition Law, regardless of whether the victim is a public or a private entity.

In addition, certain anti-competitive conducts are qualified as a crime by the Spanish Criminal Code which may give rise to criminal liability. In such a case, criminal courts will have jurisdiction. However, the criminal catalogue does not correspond to the typology of competition infringements that are punishable by the EC or the CNMC. Criminal courts will deal with the civil liability *ex delicto* derived from such criminal offences under the Spanish Criminal Code, unless the injured party reserves its right to claim the damages in further civil proceedings.

The rules applicable to administrative and criminal proceedings are not covered in this overview which is focused only on private enforcement of Competition Law before the commercial courts.

2. Relevant legislation, legal grounds and burden of proof

Before the RDL 9/2017 came into force, and without prejudice to the specific antitrust legal provision breached, antitrust damages actions were generally founded on tort liability provisions contained in the Spanish Civil Code ("SCC"). SCC general provisions on contracts may also be invoked in certain cases. The applicable procedural rules were those generally provided by the SACP for any other civil ordinary proceedings.

In addition to these provisions, private antitrust actions are specifically governed in Title VI of the SCA, which regulates certain substantive aspects, and in Article 283 bis of the SACP, which sets out concrete rules on disclosure of evidence in proceedings regarding antitrust damages actions.

The SCA states that undertakings which have infringed Competition Law are liable for the damages caused by the infringement (Article 71.1 of the SCA). As a result, any natural or legal person who has suffered damages caused by a breach of Competition Law is entitled to claim full compensation from the infringer (Article 72.1 of the SCA).

The burden of proof of the damages rests with the claimant (Article 76.1 of the SCA). Moreover, the claimant must bring evidence of the infringement and the causal link between it and the damages. In June 2023, the Supreme Court issued 15 judgments on cassation appeals on claims for damages related to the 'truck cartel', and several of them acknowledged the claimant's difficulties in providing concrete proof of the amount of the damage, justifying the application of a judicial quantification mechanism to determine the precise extent of the damage, especially considering that the existence of the damage has already been verified[1].

RDL 9/2017 amended the SCA to make it easier to comply with these evidence requirements so that:

- If a Spanish Competition authority (the CNMC or a regional authority) or a Spanish court had found an infringement of Competition Law in a final decision, such an infringement is deemed to be irrefutably established for the purposes of an action for damages (Article 75.1 of the SCA). The same rule applies to infringements of Articles 101 or 102 of the Treaty on the Functioning of the European Union (the "TFEU") found in judgments and EC decisions. The latter have direct effect and are legally binding on national courts. Therefore, there is no need for them to be final. However, there will only be a rebuttable presumption of the existence of those infringements of Competition Law declared in final decisions issued by Competition authorities or courts of other EU Member States (Article 75.2 of the SCA).
- When, based on the evidence available, it is practically impossible or extremely difficult to precisely quantify the damages suffered by a claimant due to an infringement of Competition Law, Spanish courts will be entitled to estimate an amount (Article 76.2 of the SCA).
- Spanish courts may request any Spanish Competition authority (the CNMC or a regional authority) to report on the criteria that should be considered for quantifying the damages (Article 76.4 of the SCA).
- There is a rebuttable presumption that cartels cause damages (Article 76.3 of the SCA). Regarding the rules applicable prior to the Damages Directive, the Supreme Court, in the recent judgments on the trucks cartel of June 2023, has also confirmed, quoting the principle of effectiveness of EU law, that the presumption

[1] *Inter alia*, judgment 950/2023 of the Supreme Court, 14 June 2023, Appeal 5855/2020.

by the Courts of Appeals that the cartel caused damage to the purchasers of trucks was admissible. Specifically, the Supreme Court has held that there is a presumption *iuris tantum*[2], which is grounded in the specific characteristics of the trucks cartel.

3. What types of anti-competitive conduct are damages actions available for?

Although damages actions are available for conducts falling within the scope of the Spanish Act 3/1991 of 10 January 1991 on Unfair Competition, the provisions included in the SCA by the RDL 9/2017 are only applicable to actions for damages resulting from the breach of Articles 101 or 102 of the TFEU or their national equivalent provisions, *i.e.,* Articles 1 or 2 of the SCA (Article 71.2.a of the SCA).

4. What forms of relief may a private claimant seek?

Without prejudice to other remedies when an antitrust action has to do with a contract (in which case SCC general provisions on agreements, and the remedies set therein, will also apply), pursuant to Article 72.1 of the SCA, claimants are entitled to obtain full compensation for the damages caused by any breach of Competition Law.

Full compensation means that the person who has suffered the damage must be placed in the position in which it would have been if the infringement had not been committed. The compensation shall therefore cover actual loss (*damnum emergens*) and loss of profit (*lucrum cessans*), plus interest (Article 72.2 of the SCA). The Directive and the Spanish rules of transposition state that overcompensation by means of punitive damages, in whatever form, is not allowed under Spanish law (Article 72.3 of the SCA).

The undertakings and parties involved in an antitrust infringement are jointly and severally liable for the damages caused. Thus, the injured party has the right to claim compensation in full for the damages from any of the infringers (Article 73.1 of the SCA).

Infringing undertakings which had compensated the injured party may seek a contribution from the rest of the infringers, the amount of which shall be determined in accordance with their relative responsibility for the damages caused by the infringement (Article 73.5 of the SCA).

There are two exceptions to the general principle of several and joint liability of infringers set out by Article 73.1 of the SCA:

- Where the infringer is a small- or medium-sized enterprise ("SME"), as defined in European Commission Recommendation 2003/361/EC, it will be liable only to its own direct and indirect purchasers, provided that certain conditions expressed by the Damages Directive are fulfilled (Articles 73.2 and 73.3 of the SCA).
- Where the infringer has been granted immunity by a Competition authority, it will be jointly and severally liable only to its own direct and indirect purchasers or

---

2 *Inter alia,* judgment 926/2023 of the Supreme Court, 12 June 2023, Appeal 4937/2020.

providers. Immunity recipients shall also be liable to other injured parties if full compensation for the damages caused by the infringement of Competition Law cannot be obtained from the other infringers (Article 73.4 of the SCA).

RDL 9/2017 introduced that parent companies may be jointly and severally liable for the damages caused by the infringements of Competition Law committed by their subsidiaries (Article 71.2.b of the SCA). Although the Damages Directive did not directly require the parent companies' liability rule, the European Court of Justice ("ECJ") has already ruled that the concepts of undertaking and economic unit in EU Competition Law also apply in damage claims for the purposes of the application of economic succession.[3] Since Article 71.2 of the SCA only provided for "upwards" extension of liability, i.e. from the subsidiary to the parent company, and only when the parent company exercises control over the infringing company, by Judgment dated 24 October 2019 the Barcelona Court of Appeal put a referral to the ECJ in order to clarify whether the ECJ was in favour of holding similar liability the other way round, i.e. the subsidiary being liable for the acts of its parent company (liability "downwards"). In its Sumal judgment[4], the ECJ also opened the door to downward liability and thus to the possibility of directing claims for damages against the subsidiary of the parent company that has been penalised. This downward liability could apply when there are "*economic, organisational and legal links*" between the parent company and the subsidiary and a "*specific link*" between the economic activity of the subsidiary and the subject matter of the infringement for which the parent company has been held liable. Article 71.2.b of the SCA therefore needs to be read in conformity with the Sumal judgment.

Finally, a recent judgment of the ECJ has also highlighted that the right to full compensation for damages suffered as a result of anticompetitive conduct according to Articles 101 of the TFEU and 3 of the Damages Directive precludes a national rule of civil procedure such as Article 394(2) of the SACP, under which, if the claim is upheld in part, costs are to be borne by each party and each party bears half of the common costs, except in cases of wrongful conduct.[5]

5. Passing-on defence

Right to full compensation for the damages caused by a breach of Competition Law does not cover the overcharge that the claimant passed on to its customers (Article 78.1 of the SCA).

The defendant may argue that the claimant passed on the whole or part of the overcharge resulting from the infringement. The burden of proof shall be on the defendant (Article 78.3 of the SCA).

Case law has extended the passing-on defence to subsidizing Administrations. If the expense and the overcharge are covered by a public subsidy, the loss is passed on its

---

3 ECJ, Case C-724/17, 14 March 2019, Skanska, para. 28-32.

4 ECJ, Case C-882/19, 6 October 2022, Sumal, para. 51.

5 ECJ, Case C-312/21, 16 February 2023, Tráficos Manuel Ferrer SL, para. 34-49.

entirety to the subsidizing public body, which is therefore entitled to claim for the damages caused by the anti-competitive infringement,[6] as well as any other private entity that has been adversely affected.

6. Pre-trial disclosure and treatment of confidential information

Article 283 bis of the SACP provides specific rules on the disclosure of evidence in proceedings relating to antitrust damages actions, in line with the Damages Directive.

Accordingly, the claimant and the defendant may reasonably request each other or a third party (typically, a Competition authority) to disclose relevant evidence in their control. The court shall limit the disclosure of evidence to that which can be considered proportionate.

Request for the disclosure of evidence may be submitted prior to filing the claim (in that case, the claim must be brought within twenty days from the date on which this disclosure had taken place), at the time of filing or over the course of the judicial proceedings.

The disclosure of evidence included in the file of a Competition authority is regulated explicitly by the SACP in a more restrictive manner than the disclosure of other evidence:

- Spanish courts cannot order the disclosure of the following categories of evidence before the closure of the relevant Competition proceedings: (i) information that a natural or legal person has prepared explicitly for such proceedings, (ii) information that the relevant Competition authority has drawn up and sent to the parties during the proceedings, and (iii) *settlement submissions* that have been withdrawn.
- Spanish courts cannot order the disclosure of *leniency statements* and *settlement submissions*.
- Spanish courts cannot order the disclosure from a Competition authority of evidence included in its file unless no other party can reasonably provide that evidence.

Regarding evidence containing confidential information, Spanish courts shall be empowered to order its disclosure where they consider it relevant. However, they must take effective measures to protect such information (e.g. redacting sensitive passages in documents, conducting closed hearings or restricting access to them, limiting the number of persons allowed to examine the evidence, instructing experts to produce summaries of the information in an aggregated or otherwise non-confidential form, redacting a non-confidential version of court resolutions containing confidential data and limiting access to certain sources of evidence to the parties' legal representatives and advocates and to experts subject to confidentiality obligations). The legal professional privilege shall be protected by the courts when ordering the disclosure of evidence.

As for the request of production of documents *ex novo*, the Commercial Court No. 3 of Valencia of 14 June 2019 referred a preliminary judgment to the ECJ asking if Article 5.1 of the Damages Directive "*include the disclosure of documents that must be created ex novo by the party to whom the request for information is made by compiling or*

[6] Barcelona Court of Appeals, judgment 1267/2022, 27 July 2022, para. 28-32.

classifying information, knowledge or data held by it'.[7] The ECJ concluded in its judgment of 10 November 2022 that Article 5.1 of the Damages Directive "*must be interpreted as meaning that the reference therein to the disclosure of relevant evidence in the control of the defendant or a third party also covers those documents which the party to whom the request to disclose evidence is addressed must create ex novo by compiling or classifying information, knowledge or data in its possession, subject to strict compliance with Article 5(2) and (3) of that directive, which requires the national courts seised to restrict the disclosure of evidence to that which is relevant, proportionate and necessary, taking into account the legitimate interests and fundamental rights of that party*".[8]

7. Limitation periods

RDL 9/2017 also implemented a relevant change in the limitation period for bringing antitrust damages actions. Prior to its entry into force, such actions had to be brought within the general time limit of one year provided for damages resulting from tort liability (Article 1968.2 of the SCC). The *dies a quo* for this one-year limitation period has been interpreted by the Spanish Supreme Court as the day on which the party suffering the damage knew about it and was able to bring the corresponding damages action.

RDL 9/2017, substantially modified the Spanish legal framework of the limitation period as follows:

- The five-years limitation period shall begin to run on the date when, once the infringement has ceased, the claimant has or can reasonably be expected to have knowledge of all the following circumstances: (i) the behaviour and the fact that it infringes Competition law, (ii) the damages caused by the infringement, and (iii) the identity of the infringer (Article 74.2 of the SCA).
- The limitation period shall be interrupted if a Competition authority initiates an investigation or sanctioning proceedings in respect of an infringement related to the action for damages. The interruption shall end one year after the resolution issued by the relevant Competition authority has become final, or the proceedings are otherwise terminated (Article 74.3 of the SCA).
- Likewise, the limitation period shall be interrupted during any out-of-court settlement process concerning the claim for damages for a maximum term of two years. The interruption shall apply only to those parties involved or represented in such a process (Articles 74.4 and 81 of the SCA).

Article 74.1 of the SCA now lays down a time limit of five years (the minimum required by the Damages Directive).

In relation to this five-years limitation period, the ECJ made valuable considerations when assessing the Volvo case C-267/20[9]. The ECJ pointed out that the Damages Directive distinguishes between procedural and substantive provisions and that the limitation period

---

[7] ECJ, Case C-163/21, 10 November 2022, AD and others v. ACCAR Inc, DAF Trucks NV and DAF Trucks Deutschland GmbH, para. 26.

[8] ECJ, Case C-163/21, 10 November 2022, AD and others v. ACCAR Inc, DAF Trucks NV and DAF Trucks Deutschland GmbH, paras. 69 and 70.

[9] ECJ, Case C-267/20, 22 June 2022, AB Volvo and DAF Trucks NV v. RM.

is substantive in nature. Each Member State is competent to regulate the right to seek compensation, including the limitation period, without prejudice to the preponderance of the Damages Directive and the laws for its transposition. However, the time limit cannot start to run until the injured party is aware or could have been aware of the existence of the infringement, the damages and the causal link. In the case under analysis, the ECJ held that the moment at which the limitation period began to run was the publication of the decision on penalties in the Official Journal of the European Union. The ECJ finally concluded that the five-years limitation period provided for in the Damages Directive should apply and, therefore, the action in that case was not time-barred.

Given the questions as to the applicability of the Damages Directive, the ECJ judgment considers Article 10 of the Damages Directive and Article 74(1) SCA applicable to these disputes because they are substantive provisions within the meaning of Article 22(1) of the Damages Directive. Therefore, there may be cases in which the limitation period for the action was foreseen under the previous one-year regulation and at the same time the action was not exhausted before the expiry of the period for transposition of the Damages Directive. In these cases, the five years limitation period will apply.

Briefly, the ECJ considered in a completely novel way that the relevant time for determining the applicable rule is the date on which the action was brought if, at the end of the transposition deadline, the one-year period laid down in the previous national legislation had not elapsed. The time at which the injured party becomes aware of the four elements referred to above would be relevant for these purposes, and not the date of the infringement.

8. Appeal

Judgments issued by Commercial Courts and dealing with damages actions based on antitrust infringements may be challenged before the corresponding Court of Appeal.

Judgments issued by the Court of Appeal may, in turn, be appealed before the Spanish Supreme Court, provided that certain requirements set out by the SACP are met.

9. Class action and collective representation

The SACP provides for a sort of collective legal standing of consumers' and users' associations that would also be available for antitrust damages actions.

There are two different types of collective actions, depending on whether they are aimed at defending collective interests (*i.e.* those of victims that are perfectly determined or easily determinable) or diffuse interests (*i.e.* those of victims that are undetermined or difficult to determine). Consumers' and users' associations are entitled to bring any of these two actions, as well as the public prosecutor. Actions in defence of collective interests can also be brought by entities whose purpose is the defence or protection of the affected consumers and users or by the own groups of them (Article 11 of the SACP).

The admission for processing of the complaint will be published in the media so that any affected party can join the proceedings (Article 15 of the SACP). In practice, if the complaint is upheld, the judgment will determine the consumers that will benefit from the compensation. If the individual determination of the affected consumers is not possible, the judgment will establish the basis for the calculation of the compensation to which any injured party is entitled.

However, we expect that the current system will be modified once Directive (EU) 2019/216 of the European Parliament and of the Council of 27 November 2019, regarding the better enforcement and modernisation of Union consumer protection rules, and Directive (EU) 2020/1828 of the European Parliament and of the Council of 25 November 2020, on representative actions for the protection of the collective interests of consumers and joint efforts, are transposed into Spanish law.

10. Key issues

The non-retroactivity of the substantive provisions introduced by the RDL 9/2017

Following the judgment of ECJ Volvo case C-267/20, issued on 22 June 2022, the procedural provisions may apply from the entry into force of the RDL 9/2017 and the substantive provisions may only apply (i) to new situations and after the entry into force of the RDL 9/2017[10] or (ii) to situations prior to the entry into force of the RDL 9/2017, but whose effects continue to occur after its entry into force[11].

Subsidiaries' liability for their parent companies' antitrust infringements found in European Commission decisions

In Spain, a significant number of actions for damages relating to the European cartel of truck manufacturers have been brought not against the companies sanctioned by the EC in its decision of 19 July 2016, but against their Spanish subsidiaries, assuming that the commitment of the infringement by the latter was irrefutably established as a result of such a decision, without the need of further evidence.

Since Spanish courts took two different positions in relation to this issue, the 15th Section of the Barcelona Court of Appeals, in its judgment of 24 October 2019, referred this question to the ECJ for a preliminary judgment. The ECJ replied, in its judgment dated 6 October 2021, case C-882/19, in the direction that subsidiaries may be liable for their parent companies infringements (i.e. liability "downwards") when there are "*economic, organisational and legal links*" between the parent company and the subsidiary and a "*specific link*" between the economic activity of the subsidiary and the subject matter of the infringement for which the parent company has been held liable.

The Supreme Court referred a preliminary judgment to the ECJ on 10 October 2022, in the AB Volvo v Transsaqui SL case (C-632/22) where the ECJ will have to analyse the national rules regarding notifications to parent companies established in other member States in connection with Article 47 of the EU Charter of Fundamental Rights (the "Charter"). In particular, the Supreme Court asked the ECJ whether article 47 of the Charter allows to service notifications against a parent company that has committed an

---

10 *Inter alia,* Barcelona Court of Appeal, judgment 1282/2022, 27July 2022; and Barcelona Court of Appeal, judgment 1582/2022, 3 November 2022.

11 *Inter alia*, ECJ, Case C-198/22 and C-199/22, C-267/20, 6 March 2023, Deutsche Bank AG; and Judgment 925/2023 of the Supreme Court, 12 June 2023, Appeal 4536/2020.

infringement of EU competition rules in the place of business of a subsidiary company established in the State in which legal proceedings are brought, whilst the parent company has not appeared in the proceedings and has remained in default. Answering in the affirmative may have implications in the current case law of the Spanish Constitutional Court on the service of process on parent companies established in another member States.

Calculation of damages

The presumption of damage is recognised in the Damages Directive and Article 76.3 SCD, as long as it has not been rebutted by the defendants and their experts.

Courts dealing with antitrust damages actions encounter a major difficulty when quantifying the damages suffered. In practice, Spanish courts will usually follow the guidance provided in the Communication from the European Commission on quantifying damages in actions for damages based on breaches of Article 101 or 102 of the TFEU (2013/C 167/07). They will compare the counterfactual, i.e. the actual position of the claimants with the position in which they would have had if the infringement had not occurred. To do so, they will assess the expert opinions filed by the parties and will infer their own criteria on how to calculate the damages.

Regarding the calculation of damages, judicial estimation of damages is probably one of the most debated aspects in Spain today. From an EU approach, it remains undecided whether, in a dispute between private individuals, one of them can invoke the *contra legem* application of the Damages Directive against the other when the national regulations transposing it have considered the judicial power to assess the damages as a substantive provision with no retroactive application.
Notwithstanding the above, the judgment of the ECJ of 16 February 2023 in case C-312/21, *Tráficos Manuel Ferrer SL and D. Ignacio versus Daimler AG* has provided guidance regarding when the judicial estimation of damages can apply. In response to the first request for a preliminary judgment of the 3rd Commercial Court of Valencia, the ECJ stated on the basis that article 17(1) that the judicial estimation of damages is based on the establishment of damages and applies when it is impossible or very difficult to quantify it precisely. Hence, all the parameters of damages and proof leading to such a finding must be taken into consideration.

The power of the courts to estimate the damage was already recognised in Spain's legal system, before the entry into force of the Damages Directive, by the principle of compensation of the injured party in Article 1902 of the SCC and 101 of the TFEU. The principle guiding the court's decisions is the principle of effectiveness of EU competition law (i.e. national procedural rules cannot make the application of EU competition rules impossible in practice or excessively difficult to enforce).

The insufficiency of the claimant's expert report to prove the amount of the damage or the fact that the defendant and third parties have not requested the production of evidence does not necessarily mean that the lack of proof of the damage is attributable to the claimant's inactivity.

Thus, in the recent judgments of the Supreme Court on the truck cartel, the courts considered that the judge should set the estimate of the damage (overcharge) at the percentage of 5% of the purchase price of the truck as long as it was not proven that the amount of the damage was higher or lower than that estimate[12]. In view of the concurrent circumstances of the parties' expert reports, the Supreme Court considered that the judicial estimate of the overcharge should be at least 5% in the absence of any other convincing or higher approximation of a specific percentage.

Pending amendments with the transposition of Directive (EU) 2020/1828 on consumer class actions

Directive (EU) 2020/1828, which is yet to be transposed, aims to harmonise a procedural regime for collective actions to defend consumers' and users' interests in member states. In addition, it also aims to minimise distortion of free and fair competition between businesses and to enhance national and cross-border consumer protection through legal remedies such as injunctions and actions for damage. However, its material scope does not alter national rules governing the settlement of contractual or non-contractual disputes, nor does it not affect private international law concerning jurisdiction management and the recognition and enforcement of judgments in civil and commercial matters.

The possible collective actions against infringing companies governed by Directive (EU) 2020/1828 and affecting the content of the CNMC Report of September 15 and the CNMC Report of December 21 are of a cross-border and representative nature. Representative actions to protect consumers' collective interests can be national and cross-border. National representative actions will be those brought before a national court by an entity authorised in Spain, i.e., a consumer organisation, on behalf of domestic and foreign consumers. A qualified entity may bring cross-border actions in another Member State to protect the collective interests of different consumers in different Member States.

On 9 January 2023, the Ministry of Justice published the Draft Bill on representative actions for the protection of the collective interests of consumers (the "Draft Bill"). The purpose of the Preliminary Draft is to advance with the process of transposition in Spain of Directive (EU) 2020/1828 of the European Parliament and of the Council of 25 November 2020, on representative actions for the protection of the collective interests of consumers, whose deadline for transposition into the internal legislation of the different Member States of the European Union expired on December 25, 2022.

The new procedural system once adopted, will ensure that entities entitled to bring injunctions and remedies in favour of consumers and users whose rights have been affected by an infringement have standing to sue.

Methodology for the selection of cases

The selection focuses on the court decisions issued after the entry into force of the RDL 9/2017, which transposed the Damages Directive into Spanish law. Prior and more paradigmatic cases, such as those related to the damages caused by the cartel of sugar producers, have also been included. These cases raise issues of particular legal interest and are mostly connected to the European cartel of truck manufacturers.

---

12 *Inter alia,* judgment 627/2023 12 June 2023, Appeal 6019/2020.

List of Cases

All the case comments mentioned are available in the Concurrences e-Competitions Bulletin

Supreme Court

07/11/2023, Case 651/2013, e-Competitions Bulletin, Art. N° 111675
www.concurrences.com/111675
Juan Pablo Correa Delcasso, Laura Pérez Poza and Paula Belén Pérez Chávez

04/09/2023, Case 528/2013, e-Competitions Bulletin, Art. N° 111678
www.concurrences.com/111678
Jesús Almoguera, Juan Pablo Correa Delcasso, Laura Pérez Poza

14/06/2023, Case 949/2023, e-Competitions Bulletin, Art. N° 116233
www.concurrences.com/116233
Belén Irissarry, Fernando Giménez-Alvear and Laura García-Valdecasas

14/06/2023, Case 5855/2020, e-Competitions Bulletin, Art. N° 116273
www.concurrences.com/116273
Rais Amils & Ana Parés

14/06/2023, Case 5408/2020, e-Competitions Bulletin, Art. N° 116273
www.concurrences.com/116273
Rais Amils & Ana Parés

12/06/2023, Case 6019/2020, e-Competitions Bulletin, Art. N° 116254
www.concurrences.com/116254
Rais Amils & Ana Parés

12/06/2023, Case 586/2020, e-Competitions Bulletin, Art. N° 116253
www.concurrences.com/116253
Rais Amils & Ana Parés

07/10/2022, Case 45/2021, e-Competitions Bulletin, Art. N° 116201
www.concurrences.com/116201
Rais Amils & Ana Parés

08/03/2022, Case 4079/2018, e-Competitions Bulletin, Art. N° 116208
www.concurrences.com/116208
Rais Amils & Ana Parés

26/02/2019, Order, Case 262/2018, e-Competitions Bulletin, Art. N° 111694
www.concurrences.com/111694
Rais Amils, Belén Irissarry, Juan Pablo Correa Delcasso, Laura Pérez Poza

08/06/2012, Case 344/2012, e-Competitions Bulletin, Art. N° 111674
www.concurrences.com/111674
Jesús Almoguera, Juan Pablo Correa Delcasso, Laura Pérez Poza

Courts of Appeal

03/03/2023, Case 104/2023, e-Competitions Bulletin, Art. N° 116230
www.concurrences.com/116230
Belén Irissarry, Fernando Giménez-Alvear and Laura García-Valdecasas

14/02/2023, Case 44/2023, e-Competitions Bulletin, Art. N° 116229
www.concurrences.com/116229
Belén Irissarry, Fernando Giménez-Alvear and Laura García-Valdecasas

10/02/2023, Case 65/2022, e-Competitions Bulletin, Art. N° 116228
www.concurrences.com/116228
Belén Irissarry, Fernando Giménez-Alvear and Laura García-Valdecasas

03/02/2023, Case 99/2003, e-Competitions Bulletin, Art. N° 116226
www.concurrences.com/116226
Belén Irissarry, Fernando Giménez-Alvear and Laura García-Valdecasas

17/01/2023, Case 53/2023, e-Competitions Bulletin, Art. N° 116225
www.concurrences.com/116225
Belén Irissarry, Fernando Giménez-Alvear and Laura García-Valdecasas

23/12/2022, Case 375/2022, e-Competitions Bulletin, Art. N° 116224
www.concurrences.com/116224
Belén Irissarry, Fernando Giménez-Alvear and Laura García-Valdecasas

16/12/2022, Case 736/2022, e-Competitions Bulletin, Art. N° 116223
www.concurrences.com/116223
Belén Irissarry, Fernando Giménez-Alvear and Laura García-Valdecasas

02/12/2022, Case 1417/2022, e-Competitions Bulletin, Art. N° 116217
www.concurrences.com/116217
Belén Irissarry, Fernando Giménez-Alvear and Laura García-Valdecasas

11/11/2022, Case 745/2022, e-Competitions Bulletin, Art. N° 116205
www.concurrences.com/116205
Belén Irissarry, Fernando Giménez-Alvear and Laura García-Valdecasas

04/11/2022, Case 1596/2022, e-Competitions Bulletin, Art. N° 116199
www.concurrences.com/116199
Belén Irissarry, Fernando Giménez-Alvear and Laura García-Valdecasas

06/10/2022, Case 1791/2021, e-Competitions Bulletin, Art. N° 116200
www.concurrences.com/116200
Rais Amils & Ana Parés

19/09/2022, Case 84/2020, e-Competitions Bulletin, Art. N° 116198
www.concurrences.com/116198
Rais Amils & Ana Parés

07/09/2022, Case 986/2021, e-Competitions Bulletin, Art. N° 116195
www.concurrences.com/116195
Rais Amils & Ana Parés

18/07/2022, Case 1762/2021, e-Competitions Bulletin, Art. N° 116202
www.concurrences.com/116202
Rais Amils & Ana Parés

27/06/2022, Case 109/2021, e-Competitions Bulletin, Art. N° 116219
www.concurrences.com/116219
Rais Amils & Ana Parés

13/06/2022, Case 1785/2021, e-Competitions Bulletin, Art. N° 116218
www.concurrences.com/116218
Rais Amils & Ana Parés

19/05/2022, Case 292/2021, e-Competitions Bulletin, Art. N° 116213
www.concurrences.com/116213
Rais Amils & Ana Parés

16/03/2022, Case 735/2021, e-Competitions Bulletin, Art. N° 116209
www.concurrences.com/116209
Rais Amils & Ana Parés

15/02/2022, Case 1405/2021, e-Competitions Bulletin, Art. N° 116206
www.concurrences.com/116206
Rais Amils & Ana Parés

07/02/2022, Case 2112/2021, e-Competitions Bulletin, Art. N° 116204
www.concurrences.com/116204
Rais Amils & Ana Parés

31/01/2022, Case 43/2021, e-Competitions Bulletin, Art. N° 116203
www.concurrences.com/116203
Rais Amils & Ana Parés

10/12/2021, Case 736/2019, e-Competitions Bulletin, Art. N° 116337
www.concurrences.com/116337
Rais Amils & Ana Parés

19/11/2021, Case 180/2020, e-Competitions Bulletin, Art. N° 116335
www.concurrences.com/116335
Rais Amils & Ana Parés

01/07/2021, Case 693/2021, e-Competitions Bulletin, Art. N° 116333
www.concurrences.com/116333
Rais Amils & Ana Parés

26/02/2021, Case 2882/2019, e-Competitions Bulletin, Art. N° 116354
www.concurrences.com/116354
Rais Amils & Ana Parés

16/12/2019, Case 1126/2019, e-Competitions Bulletin, Art. N° 111712
www.concurrences.com/111712
Juan Pablo Correa Delcasso, Laura Pérez Poza and Paula Belén Pérez Chávez

16/12/2019, Case 1071/2019, e-Competitions Bulletin, Art. N° 116367
www.concurrences.com/116367
Juan Pablo Correa Delcasso, Laura Pérez Poza and Paula Belén Pérez Chávez

05/12/2019, Case 1169/2019, e-Competitions Bulletin, Art. N° 111709
www.concurrences.com/111709
Jesús Almoguera, Juan Pablo Correa Delcasso, Laura Pérez Poza

24/10/2019, Case 775/2019, e-Competitions Bulletin, Art. N° 111708
www.concurrences.com/111708
Jesús Almoguera, Juan Pablo Correa Delcasso, Laura Pérez Poza, Rais Amils

20/06/2019, Case 180/2019, e-Competitions Bulletin, Art. N° 111699
www.concurrences.com/111699
Rais Amils, Belén Irissarry, Juan Pablo Correa Delcasso, Laura Pérez Poza

03/07/2017, Case 475/2015, e-Competitions Bulletin, Art. N° 111677
www.concurrences.com/111677
Rais Amils, Belén Irissarry, Juan Pablo Correa Delcasso, Laura Pérez Poza

Commercial Courts

02/06/2023, Case 307/2023, e-Competitions Bulletin, Art. N° 116196
www.concurrences.com/116196
Juan Pablo Correa Delcasso, Laura Pérez Poza and Paula Belén Pérez Chávez

01/12/2022, Case 583/2022, e-Competitions Bulletin, Art. N° 116210
www.concurrences.com/116210
Belén Irissarry, Fernando Giménez-Alvear and Laura García-Valdecasas

21/10/2022, Case 148/2022, e-Competitions Bulletin, Art. N° 116212
www.concurrences.com/116212
Rais Amils & Ana Parés

07/09/2022, Case 135/2022, e-Competitions Bulletin, Art. N° 116339
www.concurrences.com/116339
Rais Amils & Ana Parés

08/06/2022, Case 221/2022, e-Competitions Bulletin, Art. N° 116216
www.concurrences.com/116216
Rais Amils & Ana Parés

03/06/2022, Case 969/2021, e-Competitions Bulletin, Art. N° 116214
www.concurrences.com/116214
Rais Amils & Ana Parés

22/03/2022, Case 2250/2019, e-Competitions Bulletin, Art. N° 116211
www.concurrences.com/116211
Rais Amils & Ana Parés

17/02/2022, Case 1639/2022 and 1764/2022, e-Competitions Bulletin, Art. N° 116207
www.concurrences.com/116207
Rais Amils & Ana Parés

30/06/2021, Case 1722/2015, e-Competitions Bulletin, Art. N° 116330
www.concurrences.com/116330
Rais Amils & Ana Parés

18/05/2021, Case 588/2018, e-Competitions Bulletin, Art. N° 116326
www.concurrences.com/116326
Rais Amils & Ana Parés

15/03/2020, Case 52/2019, e-Competitions Bulletin, Art. N° 111696
www.concurrences.com/111696
Jesús Almoguera, Rais Amils, Juan Pablo Correa Delcasso, Laura Pérez Poza

03/03/2020, Case 127/2019, e-Competitions Bulletin, Art. N° 111716
www.concurrences.com/111716
Jesús Almoguera, Juan Pablo Correa Delcasso, Laura Pérez Poza

30/12/2019, Case 317/2019, e-Competitions Bulletin, Art. N° 111714
www.concurrences.com/111714
Jesús Almoguera, Juan Pablo Correa Delcasso, Laura Pérez Poza

02/10/2019, Case 211/2019, e-Competitions Bulletin, Art. N° 111707
www.concurrences.com/111707
Jesús Almoguera, Juan Pablo Correa Delcasso, Laura Pérez Poza, Rais Amils

12/09/2019, Case 501/2018, e-Competitions Bulletin, Art. N° 111705
www.concurrences.com/111705
Rais Amils, Belén Irissarry, Juan Pablo Correa Delcasso, Laura Pérez Poza

27/09/2019, Case 1/2018, e-Competitions Bulletin, Art. N° 111706
www.concurrences.com/111706
Jesús Almoguera, Juan Pablo Correa Delcasso, Laura Pérez Poza

10/09/2019, Case 118/2019, e-Competitions Bulletin, Art. N° 111704
www.concurrences.com/111704
Jesús Almoguera, Juan Pablo Correa Delcasso, Laura Pérez Poza, Rais Amils

30/08/2019, Case 151/2019, e-Competitions Bulletin, Art. N° 111703
www.concurrences.com/111703
Jesús Almoguera, Juan Pablo Correa Delcasso, Laura Pérez Poza, Rais Amils

26/07/2019, Case 117/2019, e-Competitions Bulletin, Art. N° 111702
www.concurrences.com/111702
Jesús Almoguera, Juan Pablo Correa Delcasso, Laura Pérez Poza

03/07/2019, Case 584/2018, e-Competitions Bulletin, Art. N° 116241
www.concurrences.com/116241
Jesús Almoguera, Juan Pablo Correa Delcasso, Laura Pérez Poza

02/07/2019, Case 265/2019, e-Competitions Bulletin, Art. N° 111700
www.concurrences.com/111700
Jesús Almoguera, Juan Pablo Correa Delcasso, Laura Pérez Poza

14/06/2019, Case 338/2019, e-Competitions Bulletin, Art. N° 111698
www.concurrences.com/111698
Jesús Almoguera, Juan Pablo Correa Delcasso, Laura Pérez Poza

07/05/2019, Case 338/2018, e-Competitions Bulletin, Art. N° 111679
www.concurrences.com/111679
Jesús Almoguera

13/03/2019, Case 309/2018, e-Competitions Bulletin, Art. N° 111695
www.concurrences.com/111695
Jesús Almoguera, Juan Pablo Correa Delcasso, Laura Pérez Poza

20/02/2019, Case 287/2018, e-Competitions Bulletin, Art. N° 111693
www.concurrences.com/111693
Juan Pablo Correa Delcasso, Laura Pérez Poza and Paula Belén Pérez Chávez, Jesús Almoguera

23/01/2019, Case 899/2017, e-Competitions Bulletin, Art. N° 111692
www.concurrences.com/111692
Rais Amils, Belén Irissarry, Juan Pablo Correa Delcasso, Laura Pérez Poza

13/12/2018, Case 198/2018, e-Competitions Bulletin, Art. N° 111690
www.concurrences.com/111690
Jesús Almoguera, Juan Pablo Correa Delcasso, Laura Pérez Poza

07/12/2018, Case 644/2017, e-Competitions Bulletin, Art. N° 111689
www.concurrences.com/111689
Jesús Almoguera, Juan Pablo Correa Delcasso, Laura Pérez Poza

27/09/2018, Case 274/2018, e-Competitions Bulletin, Art. N° 111688
www.concurrences.com/111688
Juan Pablo Correa Delcasso, Laura Pérez Poza and Paula Belén Pérez Chávez

10/09/2018, Case 320/15, e-Competitions Bulletin, Art. N° 111687
www.concurrences.com/111687
Rais Amils, Belén Irissarry, Juan Pablo Correa Delcasso, Laura Pérez Poza

05/09/2018, Case 32/15, e-Competitions Bulletin, Art. N° 111686
www.concurrences.com/111686
Rais Amils, Belén Irissarry, Juan Pablo Correa Delcasso, Laura Pérez Poza

05/09/2018, Case 31/15, e-Competitions Bulletin, Art. N° 111685
www.concurrences.com/111685
Rais Amils, Belén Irissarry, Juan Pablo Correa Delcasso, Laura Pérez Poza

08/06/2018, Case 189/2015, e-Competitions Bulletin, Art. N° 111683
www.concurrences.com/111683
Rais Amils, Belén Irissarry, Juan Pablo Correa Delcasso, Laura Pérez Poza

06/06/2018, Case 30/2015, e-Competitions Bulletin, Art. N° 111684
www.concurrences.com/111684
Juan Pablo Correa Delcasso, Laura Pérez Poza and Paula Belén Pérez Chávez, Rais Amils, Belén Irissarry, Jesús Almoguera

06/06/2018, Case 15/1, e-Competitions Bulletin, Art. N° 111680
www.concurrences.com/111680
Rais Amils, Belén Irissarry, Juan Pablo Correa Delcasso, Laura Pérez Poza

07/05/2018, Case 241/2015, e-Competitions Bulletin, Art. N° 111679
www.concurrences.com/111679
Juan Pablo Correa Delcasso, Laura Pérez Poza and Paula Belén Pérez Chávez

Court of First Instance

06/02/2020, Case 342/2019, e-Competitions Bulletin, Art. N° 111715
www.concurrences.com/111715
Jesús Almoguera, Juan Pablo Correa Delcasso, Laura Pérez Poza

SWEDEN

Claes Langenius
Partner, Advokatfirman Hammarskiold & Co
Sofia Falkner
Partner, Advokatfirman Hammarskiold & Co

The applicable framework regulating private enforcement of competition law infringements in Sweden is the Competition Damages Act (2016:964) (the "Competition Damages Act"), which entered into force on 27 December 2016 and implements Directive 2014/104/EU on antitrust damages actions (the "Damages Directive"). The former rules continue to apply to damage claims relating to infringements that occurred before 27 December 2016.

It hascc have violated the competition rules since the entry into force of the Swedish Competition Act in 1993. Despite this possibility, private enforcement of competition law has been limited.

The low number of antitrust damages cases is most likely due to the long-standing judicial tradition in Swedish law, which is based on a general restrictive approach to tort law. It is likely that the frequency of follow-on damages claims in particular (and the likelihood of success of those claims) may increase over time following the enactment of the Competition Damages Act. Indeed, the Competition Damages Act introduces a number of clarifications and new provisions that will benefit future claimants.

1. Jurisdiction

The authority responsible for public enforcement of competition law in Sweden is the Swedish Competition Authority (the "SCA") or *Konkurrensverket.*

Private enforcement claims based on the Competition Damages Act can be brought by anyone that has suffered damage due to a competition law infringement. Such claims shall be made to the Swedish Patent and Market Court in Stockholm which, since September 2016 has jurisdiction over competition damages actions as well as competition cases brought by the SCA. The Patent and Market Court of Appeal is the court of second -and generally final- instance in such cases.

2. Relevant legislation and legal grounds

The Swedish Competition Act (2008:549) ("The Competition Act") governs in principle all aspects of Swedish competition law. The act contains two general prohibitions: the prohibition of anti-competitive agreements and the prohibition of abuse of a dominant position (Chapter 2 Sections 1 and 7). The Competition Act also includes regulations on control of concentrations as well as relevant procedural rules relating to (for example) dawn raids and other investigatory measures of the SCA.

The two general prohibitions against anti-competitive agreements and abuse of dominance correspond to Articles 101 and 102 of the Treaty on the Functioning of the European Union (the "TFEU") and are to be interpreted in line with EU law and the case-law of the courts of the European Union. Furthermore, Articles 101 and 102 TFEU are directly applicable to practices that may affect trade between EU Member States.

The Competition Act refers to the Competition Damages Act for provisions regarding damages due to competition law infringements. The Competition Damages Act provides that anyone who intentionally or negligently infringes competition law shall compensate the harm suffered. Consequently, in order for damages to be awarded under the Competition Damages Act, it must be established that (i) there has been an infringement of competition law, (ii) the infringement has been committed intentionally or negligently, and (iii) there is a causal link between the infringement and the damage subject to the claim. The burden of proof in relation to these conditions lies with the claimant seeking damages.

As regards the first criterion, the Competition Damages Act provides that a final infringement decision of the Swedish Competition Authority or a Swedish court shall constitute full proof before the civil courts that the infringement occurred. The finding of a breach of the provisions of the Competition Act in a final ruling may not be re-examined in a subsequent action for damages.

There is also a relaxation of the burden of proof with regard to the third criterion. Indeed, Chapter 3 Section 4 of the Competition Damages Act establishes a rebuttable presumption that cartels cause harm. This presumption of harm does not apply to other types of competition law infringements.

3. *Rationae temporis* application of the Competition Damages Act

In accordance with the principle of non-retroactivity of the law established in the Swedish Constitution (Instrument of Government), the new substantial provisions of the Competition Damages Act, including but not limited to rules on limitation periods and presumptions relating to e.g. harm of cartels and passing on of costs, are applicable only to actions for damages resulting from infringements of competition rules (*i.e.* the facts causing liability) arising after the entry into force of the Competition Damages Act on 27 December 2016.

The transitional provisions of the Competition Damages Act explicitly establish that the following procedural rules of the Competition Damages Act shall apply to all actions brought after 25 December 2014:

- **Stay of proceedings** under Chapter 5 § 3 of the Competition Damages Act, according to which the Court may declare a case suspended if two or more parties have initiated a dispute settlement in good faith in relation to a claim covered by the case. The case before the Court shall be resumed no later than two years from the decision to suspend the proceedings.
- The **limitations to the possibility of general disclosure injunction** in accordance with the Swedish Code of Judicial Procedure (1942:740) that are included in chapter 5 §§ 4 -7 of the Competition Damages Act (see also section 7 below).
- **Limitations to invoking certain written evidence** under Chapter 5 § 8 of the Competition Damages Act, according to which certain documents that have been provided to the SCA as part of leniency programmes or settlement proceedings cannot be used as evidence in a follow-on damages action.
- The principle of ***res judicata*** contained in Chapter 5 § 9 of the Competition Damages Act, establishing that if a violation of competition law has been established through a final decision under the Competition Act, the question of infringement may not be re-examined in a case for damages under the Competition Damages Act.

4. What types of anti-competitive conduct are damages actions available for?

The Competition Damages Act is applicable for damages claims arising from an "infringement of competition law" which are defined to include:

i. Article 101 and Article 102 TFEU;

i. Sections 1 and 7 in Chapter 2 of the Competition Act (the equivalent to Article 101 and 102 TFEU under Swedish law); and

i. Equivalent national competition law of an EU Member State in accordance with Article 3(1) of Regulation No 1/2003 on the implementation of the rules on competition laid down in Articles 101 and 102 TFEU.

5. What forms of relief may a private claimant seek?

According to Chapter 3 Section 1 of the Competition Damages Act, the forms of relief avaicf, or damage to, property) and loss of profit (including loss of interest).

The purpose is to restore the claimant's financial situation in which it would have been if the infringement never occurred *i.e.* the hypothetical financial situation absent the infringement. Punitive or exemplary damages are not available.

In addition, successful damages claimants are awarded interest. Interest accrues from the day the harm occurred to the day compensation payment is effectuated. The interest rate is 2% above the reference rate of the Swedish Central Bank from the time the damage was caused until legal proceedings to claim compensation were initiated. Thereafter, the interest rate is 8% above the reference rate.

6. Passing-on defence

Passing-on defence is available under Chapter 3 Section 2 of the Competition Damages Act. The right to compensation for actual loss can be reduced by an amount equivalent to any overcharge the injured party has passed on to its own buyers or any undercharge the injured party has passed on to its own suppliers. The same applies in the case of undercut prices passed on by the injured party to its suppliers. The burden of proof lies with the defendant.

Corresponding to Article 14 of the Damages Directive, the Competition Damages Act also provides for a rebuttable presumption that indirect customers have suffered some level of overcharge harm, to be estimated by the court. The Swedish legislator has also chosen to introduce a corresponding passing on presumption in relation to indirect suppliers.

7. Pre-Trial discovery and Disclosure, treatment of confidential information

Under the general principles of the Swedish Code of Judicial Procedure (1942:740), anyone in possession of written documents (interpreted widely) that can reasonably be expected to be of evidentiary value in a civil case can be obliged by the court to disclose such evidence to the court. Such disclosure may be ordered by injunction against an opposing party as well as a third party.

The possibility of making use of this general disclosure injunction for an antitrust damages claim is subject to two main exceptions provided for in the Competition Damages Act.

First, a party can only direct such injunctions for the disclosure of materials held by the SCA when a third party cannot provide the same information conveniently. Neither is such disclosure allowed when it is reasonable to assume that such disclosure would seriously hamper the SCA's ability to perform its duties.

Second, documents that have been provided to the SCA as part of leniency programmes or settlement proceedings, information produced by a natural or legal person specifically for the handling of a case by the SCA and information produced by the SCA and provided to the parties during the processing of a case are exempted from disclosure. There are also limitations imposed as to the use of such documents as evidence in damages proceedings. Furthermore, copies of other documents than those already mentioned and which someone has obtained *only* through access to the SCA's case file may be relied on as evidence only by that person or someone who has taken over his/her rights.

In addition, the general disclosure injunction can never be used for disclosure of information subject to legal privilege. There are also other exceptions governing personal integrity, trade secrets and public interests.

8. Limitation periods

Different limitation periods apply for damages that occurred prior to the entry into force of the New Competition Damages Act (27 December 2016) and damages that occurred post that date.

Damage that occurred prior to the entry into force of the new Competition Damages Act

According to the previous rules, the right to damages caused by an intentional or negligent infringement of any of the prohibitions contained in Chapter 2, Article 1 or 7 of the Swedish Competition Act, or in Article 101 and 102 TFEU shall lapse if no legal action is brought within ten years from the date on which the damage occurred.

For damage that has occurred before 1 August 2005, the earlier statute of limitation of the Competition Act applies, according to which the right to damages shall lapse if no legal action is brought within five years from the date on which the damage occurred.

Damages that have occurred after the entry into force of the Competition Damages Act

Under the Competition Damages Act, claimants can initiate damages claims within five years from the time the infringement has ceased and the claimant knows, or can reasonably be expected to know: (i) of the behaviour and the fact that it constitutes an infringement of competition law, (ii) of the fact that the infringement of competition law caused harm to it, and (iii) the identity of the infringer.

The limitation period is interrupted if a competition authority in the EU takes action in respect of the infringement to which the claim relates. A new deadline runs from the day when there is a final infringement decision or when the authority terminates its procedure in some other way. In line with the Damages Directive, there are important rules about breach of the statute of limitation, e.g. in relation to settlement proceedings.

9. Appeal

Actions under the Competition Damages Act must be brought before the Patent and Market Court. A Patent and Market Court judgment may be appealed before the Patent and Market Court of Appeal.

As a general rule, the judgments and decisions of the Patent and Market Court of Appeal relating to competition damages cannot be further appealed. However, the Patent and Market Court of Appeal can allow for a ruling to be appealed to the Supreme Court if it is important for the application of the law that the appeal is examined by the Supreme Court.

10. Class actions and collective representation

It is possible to bring class action claims for antitrust damages claims. Such actions are regulated by the Swedish Group Proceedings Act (2002:599). The Group Proceedings Act contains specific procedural rules on group/class actions and is applicable to civil claims in general.

There are three ways in which group actions can be instituted under Swedish law: (i) class actions brought by an individual member of a group who is a natural person or a legal entity (private class actions), (ii) by an association of consumers or wage-earners (organisation class actions), and (iii) by a designated public authority (public class actions). The Group Proceedings Act does not specify any minimum number of claimants required for a group action to be brought. However, the court may accept a class action only if:

- the claims of the members of the group are based on circumstances that are common or of a similar nature;
- the class action is not deemed unmanageable due to substantial differences in the legal basis of the claims of different members of the group;
- the majority of the claims to which the action relates cannot be equally well pursued by private actions brought by individual members of the group;
- the group, taking into consideration its size and ambit, is otherwise appropriately defined; and
- the claimant, bringing the action on behalf of the group, is deemed an appropriate representative, taking into consideration the claimant's interest in the substantive matter, the claimant's financial capacity to bring a class action and other relevant circumstances.

Class actions are initiated on an opt-in basis through personal notice given to the court by each group member. Each member of the group must give notice to the court in writing within the period of time determined by the court that he or she wishes to be included in the group action. In the absence of such notice, the member is deemed to have withdrawn from the group. New group members can be allowed also in later stage of the proceedings, provided that this does not cause any significant delay of the case or other substantial inconvenience for the defendant.

Class actions are rare in Sweden, and there has not been any class action in relation to competition damages claims. It should also be mentioned that the general rule under the Code of Conduct of the Swedish Bar Association is that contingency fees are not allowed. However, contingency fees can be allowed in class actions and other cases where access to justice may be denied if contingency fees are not allowed.

11. Key Issues

Although the provisions on damages for infringements of competition rules have been in force for more than twenty years, only a limited number of competition damages cases have been tried by Swedish courts. To date, no final judgment of the Swedish courts has been based on the Competition Damages Act that entered into force on 27 December 2016. Therefore, it is too early to identify key issues in the application of the Competition Damages Act.

In relation to existing judgments, a key issue identified is the challenge for the claimants to fulfil its burden of proof in relation to the existence of an infringement causing ground for damages. The new Competition Damages Act brings about important rules which will probably open up for further follow-on competition damage litigations in Sweden.

One interesting new case pending before the Swedish Patent- and Market Court is Pricerunners' SEK 22 billion in damages claim against Google following the EU Google-shopping saga. The claim was brought in February 2022 (case PMT 1860-22) and is ongoing before the court. We have no indication on when to expect a judgment in that case.

Methodology for the selection of cases

Although the provisions on damages for infringements of competition rules have been in force for more than twenty years, only a limited number of competition damages cases have been finally tried by Swedish courts.

Excluded from the report are all cases where none of the court instances that tried the case has found an infringement of the competition rules and thus no basis for review of damages claims.

Also excluded are cases where the parties have settled out of court and those subject to arbitration procedure. In relation to such cases, only limited information and no legal assessment of the circumstances is publicly available.

List of Cases

All the case comments mentioned are available in the Concurrences e-Competitions Bulletin

Court of Appeal

21/12/2017, *Tele2 v Telia* (T 5365-16), e-Competitions Bulletin, Art. N° 111671
www.concurrences.com/111671
Claes Langenius, Sofia Falkne

29/06/2017, *Yarps v Telia* (T 2673-16), e-Competitions Bulletin, Art. N° 111672
www.concurrences.com/111672
Claes Langenius, Sofia Falkner

19/01/2011, *Europe Investor Direct et. al. v Euroclear Sweden* (T 10012-08) , e-Competitions Bulletin, Art. N° 111673
www.concurrences.com/111673
Claes Langenius, Sofia Falkner

TURKEY

Sahin Ardıyok
Partner, Dentons

Private enforcement is yet to be developed for the Turkish competition regime. The jurisprudence of the judicial authorities has not been settled yet as there is a severe lack of finalised court rulings on action(s) for damages resulting from competition law infringements.

Accordingly, private enforcement of competition law is recognised in a form of antitrust litigation, which is governed by civil procedural rules in Turkey. Considering the extremely limited number of damages actions finalised by the High Court of Appeal in Turkey (due to the untested enforcement trends and difficulties in calculating the damage amounts), the elbowroom for this type of enforcement is rather restricted. However, the ongoing discussions on potential ways to improve private enforcement remain at the forefront among Turkish scholars, enforcers, and practitioners of competition law.

1. Jurisdiction

The Turkish Competition Authority ("Authority") together with its decisional arm the Turkish Competition Board ("Board") is the competent regulatory body responsible for the public implementation of Law No. 4054 on the Protection of Competition (the "Competition Law").

When it comes to private enforcement, Article 58 of the Competition Law provides that anyone who has suffered from a competition infringement that has an impact on the Turkish market for goods and services is entitled to seek damages. Actions for such damages can be brought before civil courts, commercial courts, or consumer courts based on the circumstances surrounding the case (such as the merchant status deemed for the parties or the amount of the damages). In other words, the Turkish judicial system does not provide for specialised courts to review cases related to competition law infringements. Considering the high number of cases coupled with the tremendous workload of the judicial system, specific local courts have been seen to gain meaningful experience or particular skills for such cases. However, on the administrative law side, the 13th Chamber of the Council of State has been driving the final review of the appeals concerning Board decisions. Therefore, it would be fair to say that the 13th Chamber, in comparison to the other judicial authorities, has earned more experience with competition law cases.

Under Turkish law, compensation claims arising from competition law violations are pursued in the form of unlawful acts. Hence, this procedure is governed by the Code of Civil Procedure ("CCP") which provides that the establishment of the unlawful act must fall under the jurisdiction of the court of the geographical district in which (i) the act has been committed, (ii) the damage has arisen, or (iii) the domicile of the claimant is located. The Law on the Protection of Consumers also grants power to adjudicate to the court of the geographic district where the consumer's domicile is located.

2. Relevant legislation and legal grounds

As mentioned above, private antitrust actions are governed under the Competition Law. As per Article 57, any person (legal or natural) responsible for the prevention, distortion, or restriction of competition through practices, decisions, contracts, agreements or abuse of dominance shall be obliged to compensate for any damages of the injured party. Additionally, the general provisions of the Code of Obligations on liability for unlawful acts, which are stipulated under Article 49, are also applicable in such instances.

Any party who has suffered from an unlawful act (e.g. a competition law infringement) has to cumulatively establish the following four conditions: (i) infringement of the Competition Law (which can automatically be fulfilled if there is a finalised Board decision on the infringement), (ii) fault, (iii) damage, and (iv) causation between the infringement and the damage suffered.

The burden of proof falls on the claimant for such claims. Although the Competition Law does not explicitly provide that indirect customers may raise claims, they can do so as long as there is a sufficient causal link between the infringement and the damages they have suffered. However, considering the difficulties in linking the damages to the infringement for indirect customers, the general opinion among practitioners and legal literature is that such claims are unlikely to prevail under Turkish law. As such, Turkish law does not provide special tools to help indirect victims in demonstrating their damages. However, there is no tangible example in case law on these issues.

As to stand-alone claims, according to the jurisprudence of the High Court of Appeal, a final Board decision (*i.e.* a decision that has gone through the administrative judicial review) is required to determine that there is an infringement of the Competition Law. In other words, civil, commercial and/or consumer courts do not rule on the violation of competition rules and the High Court of Appeals only recognises finalised Board decisions for the establishment of such violation. On this basis, even if an injured party intends to raise a stand-alone claim, such procedure will eventually evolve into a follow-on claim due to the jurisprudential requirement of a settled Board decision to establish the infringement. Hence, the theoretic ability to raise stand-alone claims is not thoroughly enforceable in practice.

3. What types of anti-competitive conduct are damages actions available for?

Anti-competitive agreements and abuse of dominant position are explicitly deemed by Article 57 of the Competition Law as infringements which allow their victims to seek compensation. With that said, the possibility to claim compensation for infringement of the Competition Law by way of creating or reinforcing a dominant position via mergers and acquisitions, failure to notify, or gun-jumping types of violations is also a topic of discussion within the Turkish doctrine. Considering that the concept of private enforcement of antitrust law violations is not very developed in Turkey, subsections such as damages by way of gun-jumping have not been fully discovered.

4. What forms of relief may a private claimant seek?

The Turkish Code of Obligations, as a general rule, does not provide for any punitive damages and limits the amount of compensation that the injured party is entitled to obtain to the actual amount of the damages incurred (material damages).

Accordingly, the Code of Obligations provides that the court will determine the amount of compensation by taking into consideration the level of fault on the defendant and the circumstances surrounding the case. The "level of fault" element is used for determining what portion of the damages the damaging parties will be responsible for. In other words, if the applicant or any other party also has a fault in the damages, then the court may distribute the level of fault among the parties at fault and determine a corresponding level of compensation. Therefore, the "level of fault" element does not lead to the application of punitive damages. Instead, it is used to allocate the responsibility within the amount of actual (non-punitive) damages.

In parallel with the foregoing principles, the Competition Law determines the amount of compensation for antitrust related damages as the difference between the price the victims have paid and the price they would have paid had the infringement not taken place. The Competition Law also sets forth that competitors suffering from the infringement can claim compensation for all damages incurred by them.

Furthermore, private enforcement of competition rules – with the application of treble damages – grants an exception to the non-punitive compensation principle. Accordingly, if the infringement under consideration results from an agreement or decision of the infringing parties or the gross negligence thereof, the court – upon request – can determine a compensation amount up to three times the loss suffered by the claimant or the profits gained (or may be gained) via the infringing acts. The wording of this provision (*i.e.* Article 58) may be interpreted broadly to argue that all competition law violations include gross negligence and therefore warrant treble damages. However, Article 58 designates separate provisions for requesting compensation and for requesting treble damages (*i.e.* Article 58(1) and Article 58(2), respectively). Considering that only the treble damages provision refers to gross negligence, we may argue that the law attributes a somewhat higher level of negligence for such cases. Additionally, the treble damages provision also refers to the concept of agreement/decision, which seems to exclude bilateral violations and violations where the multilateral decision aspect is not present. Due to the lack of case law examples and jurisprudential guidance on the issue, we cannot fully anticipate the potential enforcement trends. On another note, fines imposed by the Board at the end of the investigation are not contingent on private enforcement processes and are not considered by the courts.

Claimants are also entitled to seek interim measures if there is an immediate risk arising from a delayed decision, and to seek specific performance where the court orders the defendant to perform certain actions (e.g. supply certain goods to the claimant). The "interim measure" or the "specific performance" options are used in cases where, for example, the damaging party continues its harmful conduct. In such cases, if the court is convinced of the fact that the applicant will suffer severe damage until the final verdict, it may order the defendant to act in a certain way or not to take certain actions until the trial is over. This is a general protective option granted to the courts. Therefore, if the infringement damaging the applicant is still going on (despite the Board decision, as the case may be) the court reviewing the damages action will be entitled to put the damaging actions on hold over the course of the trial. As explained above, there are no legal obstacles against issuing a stand-alone claim. By extension, there are no legal obstacles against requesting interim measures in a stand-alone claim. However, the High Court of Appeals has consistently ruled that there should be a finalised Board decision for a damages action to proceed. Accordingly, if the damaged party asks for an interim measure from the court in a damages action (without a finalised Board decision), the court would be expected to treat the issue as a prejudicial question and wait for the Board's decision before rendering a judgment on the matter.

In case of a collective infringement, the participants in the infringement can be held jointly and severally liable. In other words, the claimant is entitled to request and collect the total amount of compensation from any of the defendants. In such a case, if the defendant – from whom the compensation is collected – is of the view that it has overpaid, it can initiate a recourse proceeding before the court to recover such extra amount from the other defendants, based on the unjust enrichment principles. During the recourse process, the court will distribute the compensation liability proportionally based on the level of fault concerning the damages for each of the infringing parties.

Lastly, infringing parties who were leniency applicants during the investigation of the Authority are not protected from the follow-on litigations and neither the Code of Obligations nor the Competition Law provides for any beneficial treatment for such parties.

5. Passing-on defence

Under the CCP, the burden of proof is on the claimant in actions for private antitrust litigations. Subject to the general evidence rules of civil law applicable to unlawful acts, the claimant has to establish the infringement of the Competition Law (via the finalised decision of the Board, which also fulfils the element of fault), the damages, and a causal link between the damage and infringement.

The decisional practice of the High Court of Appeal has not yet recognised the concept of passing-on defence. Therefore, if invoked during the court proceedings, the passing-on defence would be subject to the general provisions of the Code of Obligations and the defendant rising the passing-on defence would have to bear the burden of proof pursuant to Article 50.

6. Pre-trial discovery and disclosure, treatment of confidential information

The Turkish system does not contain any pre-trial discovery instruments as US civil law does. However, some of the discovery proceedings under the Turkish system are of similar nature with the common law jurisdictions' pre-trial discoveries.

At any rate, the pre-trial discovery process is deemed irrelevant for private antitrust litigations in Turkey because there is a jurisprudential requirement to obtain a Board decision prior to initiating an action for competition law related damages.

In general, testimonials, documentaries or any other kind of tangible documents are accepted as means of evidence in the court proceedings. On that basis, such evidence of tangible nature shall be relevant and shall be deemed sufficient to prove or disprove a fact in connection with the merits of the case. Confession, oath, documents, and definitive judgment are classified as direct means of evidence while witness reports, expert opinions and viewing are referred to, by the CCP, as circumstantial means of evidence. Both direct and circumstantial means of evidence are admissible during private antitrust litigation. As court judgments constitute direct evidence, decisions of the Board in which an infringement of the Competition Law has been established will have the same effect. The parties are also entitled to request submission of evidence at the third parties' disposal to the court. The court, should it deem necessary, may also request evidence from third parties or governmental institutions.

If the court requests documents in the investigation file from the parties or the Authority during the litigation process, the requested party and/or the Authority are under the obligation to fully comply with this request and submit all documents without having the opportunity to omit any trade secrets or confidential information. As the leniency applicants are not protected from follow-on actions, the disclosure requirement shall also be applicable for the leniency applicants.

7. Statute of Limitation

The Competition Law does not regulate the statute of limitation for private antitrust litigation. Therefore, such claims are subject to the statute of limitation that applies to unlawful acts. Under CCP, the statute of limitation to request compensation is two years. This term starts from the date the claimant became aware of the damages and the responsible party. The general lack of case law guidance also continues here, however, and considering that the Board decisions are published in the public domain, it may be taken into account in determining the statute of limitation.

At any rate, the statute of limitation shall not exceed a total term of ten years, from the date of the act subject to compensation. In other words, the ten-years limitation – as of the date of the act – serves as a longstop date to bring the relevant claims.

8. Appeal

In civil law, decisions of the court of first instance are subject to a dual legal remedy mechanism. After the court of first instance renders its final decision, the parties might appeal the ruling before the Regional Court of Appeal. The Regional Court of Appeal is authorised to examine the procedural grounds of the ruling and its merits. Such review will include procedural and factual errors as well as any errors of law.

Once the Regional Court of Appeal passes its judgment, the parties may appeal this decision at the High Court of Appeal. High Court of Appeal is the third instance within the judicial review and is the last authority to render a judgment in civil procedure. The High Court will only review the procedural issues. Lastly, if the subject of the case (e.g. the amount of damages subject to compensation claim) is less than a certain monetary value, parties are not entitled to appeal the judgment. The appeal threshold is renewed periodically. Cases with a monetary value under approximately USD 650 do not qualify for the first stage of the appeal process (*i.e.* the Regional Court of Appeals), while cases with a monetary value under approximately USD 10,000 do not qualify for the second stage of the appeal process (*i.e.* the High Court of Appeals).

9. Class actions and collective representation

The CCP provides that associations and other legal entities of similar content are entitled to initiate an action for determination concerning the rights of its sole members. Associations may also file to cure a breach of law or to prevent the breach of future rights. The context of the lawsuit and the content of the dispute must be connected with the objectives of the relevant association and there must be sufficient grounds to demonstrate the interest of the association members. The question of whether the Articles of Association grant the ability to launch a lawsuit is also a topic of discussion while assessing the standing of associations in such lawsuits.

However, a class action that would include any potential claimant is not available under Turkish law.

10. Key issues

The key issue preventing the private enforcement of antitrust in Turkey may be singled out as the lack of tangible jurisprudential guidance. This issue not only decreases the associated degree of certainty among the ranks of antitrust practitioners but also presents a discouraging impact on the potential applicants that have suffered from a competition law violation.

In most cases, parties suffering from a competition law violation are reluctant to even initiate a damages action despite the existence of a Board decision establishing the unlawful act. The primary reasons for such reluctance emerge as the length of lawsuit before reaching a finalised ruling (three to five years on average), as well as the uncertainty of the case law and final outcome. Due to the general lack of case law examples, we cannot anticipate the practicality of settlements in antitrust related damages actions. Similarly, another important factor is the lack of guidance for the calculation of the damages and, in certain cases, the fear of commercial retaliation from the infringing party.

On the other hand, the above issue also indicates that Turkish practice for antitrust damages is open to developments. Accordingly, as the number of cases increases and the courts are, in one way or another, finalising their rulings; an increase in the number of new applications is believed to be seen in an array of applicants ranging from ordinary customers to large conglomerates in competition with the accused infringer.

Another key issue in Turkey is the interplay between the Authority's decision and private enforcement options. As explained, Turkish courts do not accept stand-alone cases and requires a finalized decision by the Authority. That said, the Authority may take different types of decisions in each competition investigation.

If the Authority decides that there are no violations, the prospects of a damages action will be significantly lowered. By parity of reasoning, if the Authority decides that Competition Law was violated, this will give a clear legal basis for the following damages action.

On the other hand, there are three other types of decisions, which are introduced by the recent amendments on the Competition Law on 24 June 2020 (namely, (i) commitment, (ii) settlement and (iii) *de minimis* procedures). These procedures aim to better allocate the Authority's resources and provide procedural efficiency. That said, they include different levels of determinations with respect to the infringement. Accordingly, it will be beneficial to assess the legal basis for damages actions in investigations that resulted in a commitment, settlement or *de minimis*.

The commitment mechanism

The commitment mechanism is regulated under Article 43 of the Competition Law and the Communiqué No: 2021/2[1]. As per Article 43 of the Competition Law, undertakings (or associations of undertakings) may offer commitments to eliminate the competition concerns during an ongoing investigation process. If the Board decides that the proposed commitments can resolve the competition concerns, it may render these commitments binding for the relevant undertakings. Therefore, in cases where the Board accepts commitments offered by the investigated undertakings during a preliminary investigation or a full-fledged investigation, the question of whether there is an infringement of competition law will remain unanswered since the Board will finalize its decision by accepting commitments and will not render a decision based on the finding of violation.

Due to the absence of the determination of infringement by the Authority, there is legal uncertainty as to whether and how it will be possible to bring damages actions before civil courts since the party suffering from an unlawful act is required to prove an infringement of competition law to seek compensation. Furthermore, it is not clear how and to what extent the investigated undertaking offering commitments will be obliged to compensate for any damage without a Board's decision on the existence or non-existence of a competition law infringement.

As stated above, in practice, damages claims are brought in the form of follow-on actions due to jurisprudential requirements and are based on the finding of competition law infringement. For this reason, even if there is the possibility of filing a compensation lawsuit without the Board's explicit decision on infringement, civil courts usually require the Board's decision on the violation of competition law before rendering their judgment on the merits of the case. The issue in question is not regulated under the Competition Law and as the commitment mechanism is a new procedure in Turkish competition law, there is yet to be an example in practice regarding the enforcement and assessment of commitment decisions in relation to damages actions. That said, the commitment mechanism merely intends to address competition law concerns without having to complete the entire investigation process. If the courts will not allow damages actions in cases closed with commitments, this may raise an unintended level of restriction against the right to seek damages.

On the other hand, it may be argued that if the case is closed with commitments, the Authority has already raised valid competitive concerns based on findings and evidence.

---

1 Communiqué on the Commitments to be Offered in Preliminary Inquiries and Investigations Concerning Agreements, Concerted Practices and Decisions Restricting Competition and Abuse of Dominant Position.

Accordingly, even if the Board's decision does not determine whether there is a violation or not, the findings in the case file may serve as *prima facie* evidence. In such a case, the courts should review all the findings in the case file and decide whether there was a violation or not. There are pending damages actions in cases closed with commitments and the courts' position remains to be seen.

10.1 *The settlement mechanism*

The settlement procedure regulated under Article 43 of the Competition Law and the Settlement Regulation[2] allows the undertakings to request a settlement from the Board until the notification of the investigation report or the Board to initiate a settlement procedure *ex officio*. Unlike the commitment mechanism, the Board may also render a settlement decision as regards hardcore violations.

Depending on the Board's decision to initiate the settlement procedure and conclude the ongoing investigation with a settlement decision, certain disadvantages arise for the settling undertaking concerning the effect of the settlement decision in relation to damages actions. Although the investigated parties that settle with the Board will benefit from a reduction of the administrative fines at a rate between 10% and 25%, they will also admit and accept the existence of competition law infringement, therefore, the settlement decision will make clear the acceptance of violation of competition law by the settling undertakings.

Therefore, as regards its effect on the private litigation process, the settlement decision could be used as acceptance and determination of the violation, which will put the settling undertaking at a disadvantage regarding the assessment of the scope of the alleged violation by the courts in antitrust damages actions.

10.2 *The De Minimis principle*

With the adoption of the *De Minimis* principle under Article 41 of the Competition Law and the Communiqué No: 2021/3[3], it is at the discretion of the Board to initiate an investigation where competition is not significantly restricted by taking into account the market share and turnover thresholds, excluding naked and hardcore infringements. This aims to allow the Authority focus on cases with more impact on the market and not engage in infringements that remain below a certain threshold.

Therefore, in cases where the Board does not initiate an investigation for violations falling under the *de minimis* principle, a legal uncertainty arises as regards the injured party's application to the courts for private damages actions since the condition of proving the violation of competition law through a Board investigation or decision would not be possible.

---

2 Regulation on the Settlement Procedure Applicable in Investigations on Agreements, Concerted Practices, and Decisions Restricting Competition and Abuses of Dominant Position.

3 Communiqué on Agreements, Concerted Practices and Decisions and Practices of Associations of Undertakings that Do Not Significantly Restrict Competition.

Given the uncertainty arising from the application of the De Minimis mechanism, the question of whether and how the courts will determine the existence of a breach of competition law in the absence of a Board investigation or decision remains unclear. That said, similar to the commitment mechanism, *de minimis* mechanism does not intent to restrict third parties' right to seek damages. Accordingly, if the Authority did not engage in a potential violation due to de minimis rules, the courts should still be able to accept the damages actions and assess whether there has been a violation.

Methodology for the selection of cases

The selection criteria predominantly focus on cases where the judicial review has been initiated and the ruling has been finalised. Among such finalised rulings, only the cases where the courts have ruled in favour of the applicant and granted quantifiable compensation for the antitrust related damages are referenced. Considering that the decisional practice of the Turkish courts provides only a limited number of examples, the selection criteria do not narrow the scope by applying a further materiality threshold based on the amount of the award or the damage.

List of Cases

All the case comments mentioned are available in the Concurrences e-Competitions Bulletin

Regional Court of Appeals

22/03/2019, 2015/1008 E., 2017/1325 K. – (Based on the infringement decision of the Turkish Competition Board numbered 8 March 2013 and numbered 13-13/198-100), e-Competitions Bulletin, Art. N° 111670
www.concurrences.com/111670
Şahin Ardıyok

Commercial Court of First Instance

22/06/2022, Ongoing case (Based on the infringement decision of the Turkish Competition Board dated 6 June 2011 and numbered 11-34/742-230), e-Competitions Bulletin, Art. N° 116257
www.concurrences.com/116257
Şahin Ardıyok

UKRAINE

Olexander Martinenko
Partner, Kinstellar

Daryna Ushchapivska
Associate, Kinstellar

The number of private antitrust damages actions in Ukraine is quite limited. This is due mostly to the lack of a specific regulation in this area. While Ukraine's Antimonopoly Committee (the "AMC") has been successful in promoting fair competition in Ukraine since 2015, national competition legislation is still under reconstruction. Particularly, further harmonisation of the Ukrainian competition regulation with that of the European Union is anticipated as stipulated by the Ukraine-EU Association Agreement.

1. Jurisdiction

Although it has exclusive jurisdiction to enforce competition law in Ukraine, the AMC is not competent to resolve private antitrust damages actions.

Victims of anti-competitive practices may however seek compensation before commercial courts. In particular, the *Protection of Economic Competition Law* (the "Competition Law") entitles a person who suffered damages as a result of concerted practices, abuse of dominance, merger control violations or any other violations provided by this law to file a claim for the compensation for such damages with a commercial court.

Also, some violations, for instance, illegal use of business entity's reputation, illegal collection and disclosure of business secrets, inducing to boycott, and so forth, qualify as anti-competitive practices under the *Protection from Unfair Competition Law* (the "Unfair Competition Law"). Victims of such violations are also entitled to seek compensation for damages before the Ukrainian court. While the Unfair Competition Law does not provide that commercial courts have exclusive jurisdiction over damages actions resulting from a breach of this law, such claims are heard by commercial courts as well.

Ukrainian law does not expressly establish that the AMC findings of antitrust violations serve as a pre-requisite to pursuing antitrust damages action (follow-on actions). However, the existence of relevant AMC decision is implied. This is due to the exclusive authority of the Ukrainian antitrust authority in establishing antitrust violations. In other words, the Ukrainian court lacks jurisdiction to establish a fact of the antitrust violation.

For instance, in case *Nibulon v. Ukrzaliznytsya* No 910/4425/16 dated 3 July 2018, the Supreme Court rendered a landmark decision (the "Nibulon Case") setting further principles, including in relation to potential inadmissibility of stand-alone actions under Ukrainian law.

In the *Nibulon Case*, the Supreme Court concluded that the AMC has exclusive authority to decide whether an undertaking violated the Competition Law. Therefore, a victim that allegedly suffered damage is entitled to seek compensation for antitrust damages before the Ukrainian court, provided that a relevant AMC decision has been rendered. The court has no jurisdiction to decide whether certain actions shall qualify as a violation of the Competition Law. Although the Supreme Court did not consider the issue of stand-alone actions specifically, considering the reasoning of the court in terms of the exclusive competence of the AMC, stand-alone claims may be regarded by Ukrainian courts inadmissible.

Therefore, in Ukraine, only follow-on actions are available to victims of antitrust violations.

2. Relevant legislation and legal grounds

To be valid, a claim for damages must be based on both:

i. civil liability legislation:
   - the Civil Code of Ukraine (Articles 22, 1166, 1167 and 1190 of the Civil Code of Ukraine); and / or
   - the Commercial Code of Ukraine (Articles 224-227, 255 of the Commercial Code of Ukraine);

(ii) and the relevant antitrust legislation: the Competition Law (Article 55) or the Unfair Competition Law (Article 24) which, from a procedural point of view, is subject to the same enforcement regime.

As stated above, private antitrust damages actions are considered by commercial courts. Therefore, the proceedings are regulated by the Commercial Procedure Code of Ukraine.

There are four component elements of any tort claim (including antitrust damages actions), in particular:

(i) unlawful behaviour, *i.e.* the anti-competitive behaviour by an undertaking held liable for competition law infringement (the relevant decision of the AMC, which has a preclusive effect);

(ii) the damage (actual (direct) damages, loss of profit[1], moral damages[2]);

(iii) causation between the unlawful behaviour and damages such claimant has suffered. Damages shall serve as a direct and objective consequence of relevant violation; and

(iv) fault. Under Ukrainian law fault is presumed. Fault in this context means an intention to cause harm or negligence.

The above criteria are cumulative. The burden of proving damages, unlawful behaviour and causal link between the same rests on the claimant, while the defendant has to prove the absence of its fault.

As stated above, any person who suffered damage as a result of a violation of either the Competition Law or Unfair Competition Law is entitled to bring a claim for recovery of damages. Therefore, indirect purchasers and ultimate customers potentially may also bring actions for damages.

3. What types of anti-competitive conduct are damages actions available for?

Damages actions are not limited to certain types of Competition Law or Unfair Competition Law violations.

---

1 Ukrainian law provides that claims for compensation for damages in the form of loss of profit shall be duly substantiated with specific calculations and evidence confirming real opportunity of obtaining such income. Presence of theoretical opportunity of receipt of the income does not constitute a ground for its recovery.

2 Compensation for moral damages is available under the Commercial Code of Ukraine.

In turn, the Competition Law provides that double damages are available for the following types of violations:

(i) concerted practices;
(ii) abuse of dominance;
(iii) implementation of a notifiable transaction failing to obtain merger clearance;
(iv) implementation of a conditionally approved merger or concerted practices failing to comply with conditions imposed by the AMC; and
(v) imposition of restrictions on business activity of an undertaking following its application to the AMC with a complaint regarding an alleged antitrust violation.

Double damages are not available in actions resulting from so-called informational violations,[3] illegal use of business entity's reputation, illegal collection and disclosure of business secrets, inducing to boycott, and so forth.

4. What forms of relief may a private claimant seek?

Neither the Competition Law nor the Unfair Competition limits forms of relief available to potential claimants in addition to compensation for damage suffered. There exist different forms of relief that are potentially available to victims of antitrust violations:

(i) Compensation for damage suffered

The effective law does not establish any mechanism for calculation of antitrust damages.

As stated under Section 3, the Competition Law provides that double damages are available for certain types of Competition Law violations. However, punitive damages are not available under Ukrainian law.

Damages, which resemble a monetary value of harm, may, pursuant to Article 22(2) of the Civil Code of Ukraine, consist of:

(1) actual (direct) damages (*i.e.*, losses incurred by a person as well as expenses, which a person has incurred or should incur in order to restore its violated rights;
(2) loss of profit.

Ukrainian law provides that claims for compensation for damages in the form of loss of profit shall be duly substantiated with specific calculations and evidence confirming real opportunity of obtaining such income. Presence of theoretical opportunity of receipt of the income does not constitute a ground for its recovery. Moral damages are also available and may be awarded both to individuals and legal entities.[4]

The fine imposed by the AMC does not influence the amount of damages that may be awarded to a successful claimant.

The highest amount of antitrust damages that have ever been awarded in Ukraine is *circa* USD 4,500,000 in the *Nibulon Case.*

---

3 For instance, untimely provision of information in response to the AMC request, provision of untrue, incomplete data or failure to provide information.

4 Compensation for moral damages is available under the Commercial Code of Ukraine.

Updates in legislation:

As mentioned previously, according to the current Ukrainian legislation[5], for certain types of Competition Law violations damages are to be compensated in the double amount of the damage caused.

In 2021, the Parliament of Ukraine proposed to amend antitrust legislation by reducing the sum of compensation to single amount of the damage caused.[6] As of today the draft law has not been adopted.

Also, the Parliament proposed to introduce the grounds and procedure for exemption from liability of participants in anticompetitive concerted actions. Such grounds for exemption from liability include:

a. disclosure of such anticompetitive concerted actions to the AMC;
b. cease to participation in anticompetitive concerted actions immediately after filing an application for exemption from liability;
c. cooperation with the bodies of the AMC, etc.[7]

Furthermore, if the entity is exempt from liability it shall reimburse damages exclusively to its direct buyers or suppliers or other persons who have suffered damage, only if compensation for damage cannot be obtained from other business entities that were defendants in the same case of violation of the legislation on protection of economic competition.

(ii) Other forms of relief

A claimant may also ask the court to invalidate an agreement (certain provision of an agreement). Such relief is available if such an agreement was made in violation of the Competition Law or the Unfair Competition Law and, as a result, affected the rights of a claimant.

Further, suppose an antitrust violation involves the publication of false and/or inaccurate, or incomplete information regarding a business entity. In that case, such entity may claim for a public refutation of such information. So far, we have not identified any such case.

In addition to the above mentioned forms of relief, a claimant may also apply for interim relief. For instance, a court may issue a freezing injunction over the defendant's assets or prohibit the defendant or third parties to take certain actions.

The court may grant interim relief on an *ex parte* basis. Before granting interim relief, the court will weigh up the interests of parties and consider:

(a) the potential harm for either of parties resulting from the granting or non-granting of such interim relief, and

---

5 Article 55(2) of Law of Ukraine "On the protection of economic competition" No. 2210-III dated 11 January 2001.

6 Draft Law "On Amendment to Certain Legislative Acts of Ukraine on Improving the Activities of the Antimonopoly Committee of Ukraine" No. 5431 dated 27 April 2021.

7 Draft Law "On Amendment to Certain Legislative Acts of Ukraine on Improving the Activities of the Antimonopoly Committee of Ukraine" No. 5431 dated 27 April 2021.

(b) whether the rights and interests of third parties will be (are likely to be) infringed by such interim relief.

Accordingly, a party seeking interim relief should convince the court that it would suffer irreparable harm if interim relief is not granted.

Importantly, the court may order a party applying for interim relief to provide a cross-undertaking (security) in the form of a deposit lodged on the account of the court, a bank guarantee, security, etc.

5. Passing-on defence

The passing-on defence is not yet regulated under Ukrainian law. While there is no court practice involving passing-on defence, such defence (if appropriate) may be raised. Considering that there is no specific rule regulating the issue either prohibiting or allowing the passing-on defence, there is no statutory limitation with respect to its availability. Under Ukrainian law, there is no presumption that a direct or indirect purchaser is deemed to have passed on the surcharge to its own customers.

Considering the requirements of the Commercial Procedure Code that each party should prove those circumstances to which it refers to support its claim or defence, it is for the defendant to prove that the claimant in fact passed on the surcharge to its own customers.

6. Pre-trial discovery and disclosure, treatment of confidential information

Ukrainian law does not provide for a discovery procedure. However, a claimant is entitled to request the disclosure of documents (or any other evidence) by the defendant if:

(i) the claimant cannot obtain such documents; and

(ii) such documents are considered as necessary to prove the alleged facts relevant to the case.

The judge may also order the production of documents from third parties, including from the AMC. As a matter of practice, the AMC is reluctant to disclose its case files even when its own decisions are being challenged. In addition, the AMC usually applies for closed court proceedings relying on confidentiality of materials submitted by parties to the AMC investigation. Confidentiality does not apply automatically to materials submitted by parties to relevant AMC investigation. First, such documents shall be marked as confidential. Second, parties shall provide justification when applying for confidentiality.

Furthermore, a leniency applicant is entitled to apply for non-disclosure of its identity. Such application may be allowed by the AMC if the applicant provided justification that such non-disclosure will be beneficial for the AMC investigation. Notably, the effective Competition Law envisages that only first leniency applicant may enjoy benefits of the leniency programme.

7. Limitation periods

A general limitation period of three years is applicable. The limitation period starts when the claimant learned or could have learned of the violation upon its rights or when the claimant learned who violated its rights.

In the *Nibulon Case*, the Supreme Court confirmed that the limitation period starts from the day on which the AMC's decision is issued.

8. Appeal

A decision of the court of first instance may be appealed to the court of appeal on the grounds of:

(i) failure to fully identify the circumstances relevant to the case;
(ii) lack of evidence with respect to circumstances relevant to the case;
(iii) inconsistency of the conclusions set forth in the first instance court's decision with the established circumstances of the case;
(iv) breach of material law or procedural law (if the latter resulted in an improper court decision).

A cassation appeal against the decision of the Court of Appeal (on limited grounds) may be filed with the Supreme Court (Commercial Cassation Court of the Supreme Court). In exceptional circumstances, the Supreme Court may transfer a case to the Grand Chamber of the Supreme Court, if it considers that it is necessary to deviate from the finding on an issue of law made in similar circumstances, or if the case concerns an exceptional legal problem and such transfer is required to ensure formation of the consistent court practice. A case shall be transferred to the Grand Chamber if parties to such proceedings challenge jurisdiction: either the subject matter jurisdiction rules or subjective jurisdiction rules.

9. Class actions and collective representation

Ukrainian law does not provide for class actions. However, several claimants may file a joint action against the same defendant(s) if:

(i) the subject matter of the dispute is related to the claimants' / defendants' common rights or obligations;
(ii) the rights or obligations of several claimants or defendants arose from the same reasons;
(iii) the subject matter of the dispute is the similar rights and obligations.

The criteria mentioned above are cumulative.

Each of the claimants or defendants shall however act independently in the court proceedings.

Methodology for the selection of cases

In Ukraine all court decisions are public and should be published in the Unified State Register of Court Judgments.[8] The cases related to damages actions have been selected for this chapter.

8 According to Article 2 of the Law of Ukraine "On access to court decisions", all court decisions are public and should be published in the electronic form not later than on the next day after their issuance and signature subject to certain exceptions. If the trial was closed, the court decision shall be published with the exception of the information which under the court decision is protected from disclosure. According to paragraph 3 of Final and Transitional provisions of the Law of Ukraine "On access to court decisions", the regular disclosure of electronic copies of court decisions of the Supreme Court of Ukraine, higher specialized courts, appeal and local administrative courts, appeal and local commercial courts, appeal courts of general jurisdiction in the Unified State Register of Court Judgments should be ensured by no later than 1 June 2006. In turn, the disclosure of court decisions of local courts of general jurisdiction should be ensured by no later than 1 January 2007.

List of Cases

All the case comments mentioned are available in the Concurrences e-Competitions Bulletin

Supreme Court

16/02/2023, Case No 910/14588/21, e-Competitions Bulletin, Art. N° 116262
www.concurrences.com/116262
Danylo Volkovetskyi

03/10/2022, Case No 910/17197/21, e-Competitions Bulletin, Art. N° 116260
www.concurrences.com/116260
Danylo Volkovetskyi

08/02/2022, Case No 916/3563/20, e-Competitions Bulletin, Art. N° 116269
www.concurrences.com/116269
Danylo Volkovetskyi

03/07/2018, Case No 910/4425/16, e-Competitions Bulletin, Art. N° 111636
www.concurrences.com/111636
Daryna Ushchapivsk

26/04/2018, Case No 927/81/16, e-Competitions Bulletin, Art. N° 111631
www.concurrences.com/111631
Daryna Ushchapivska

Commercial Court of Appeal

11/04/2023, Case No 910/1925/21, e-Competitions Bulletin, Art. N° 116267
www.concurrences.com/116267
Danylo Volkovetskyi

28/03/2023, Case No 910/18575/21, e-Competitions Bulletin, Art. N° 116265
www.concurrences.com/116265
Danylo Volkovetskyi

23/11/2022, Case No 910/17196/21, e-Competitions Bulletin, Art. N° 116261
www.concurrences.com/116261
Danylo Volkovetskyi

16/11/2022, Case No 910/147/22, e-Competitions Bulletin, Art. N° 116259
www.concurrences.com/116259
Danylo Volkovetskyi

09/12/2021, Case No 922/3779/19, e-Competitions Bulletin, Art. N° 116268
www.concurrences.com/116268
Danylo Volkovetskyi

16/04/2019, Case No 910/12634/18, e-Competitions Bulletin, Art. N° 111637
www.concurrences.com/111637
Daryna Ushchapivska

UNITED KINGDOM

Andrew Bartlett
Partner, Osborne Clarke LLP

Penny Coombs
Associate Director, Osborne Clarke LLP

The contents of this note relate to the law of England and Wales, which is formally a separate jurisdiction within the United Kingdom. Where reference is made to law deriving from European law this is the same throughout the United Kingdom, and the principles set out will apply broadly in Scotland and Northern Ireland. However, this note does not specifically address the position in those jurisdictions.

In the United Kingdom there is a long-established regime for individual and corporate claimants to bring claims against others for losses caused by anti-competitive behaviour, that is breaches of Article 101 or Article 102 on the Treaty on the Functioning of the European Union ("TFEU") and/or Chapter 1 (anti-competitive agreements) and Chapter 2 (abuse of a dominant position) of the Competition Act 1998, as amended ("CA 1998"). The CA 1998 was expanded in 2015 by the Consumer Rights Act 2015 ("CRA 2015") and further updated from 9 March 2017 to implement the EU Damages Directive to the extent that the Directive's provisions were not already part of United Kingdom law.

As discussed in Section 10, Brexit has not materially changed the current regime, since it is based on United Kingdom statute (some of which implements EU Directives, and which is otherwise closely aligned with EU law) and common law. It is not expected that the UK will diverge significantly from the EU on the key aspects of private damages claims described below in future.

1. Jurisdiction

The United Kingdom has a specialist competition claims court, the Competition Appeal Tribunal ("CAT"), but claims, other than collective actions, may also be brought in the High Court of England and Wales. The established regime in the United Kingdom makes it an attractive jurisdiction for such claims because of the experience of judges in such cases, and the availability of specialist economic experts in the CAT (who form part of the tribunal).

In addition, a specialist CAT regime, introduced in October 2015, allows collective actions to be brought efficiently on behalf of groups of claimants (both on an "opt-in" and an "opt-out" basis). These can only be brought in the CAT. Other than the collective actions the CAT and the High Court have a broadly similar function in respective of competition claims. The CAT also offers a "fast track" procedure for less complex claims which it aims to decide quickly (as soon as practicable and in any event within six months) with limited risk as to costs.

2. Relevant legislation and legal grounds

A civil claim for damages arising from anti-competitive behaviour is generally brought as a claim in tort for breach of statutory duty, namely breach of CA 1998 and/or the TFEU (where the finding was made prior to the end of the Brexit transition period). A claimant may bring a private action based on an infringement decision of the United Kingdom competition authorities (principally, the Competition and Markets Authority

("CMA") but also certain sector regulators with competition law powers) (often known as a "follow-on" claim) or, in cases where no decision has been reached, a so-called "stand-alone claim". These claims may now be brought in either the High Court or the CAT. Prior to the implementation of the CRA 2015 the CAT could not hear stand-alone claims.

Follow-on claims (where the decision binds the court) can still be brought in respect of decisions of the European Commission where the relevant decision was published prior to the end of the Brexit transition period.

If the English court has jurisdiction, claims can be brought under foreign laws as well as English law.

Where there has been such a regulatory decision, this is binding evidence of the defendant's anti-competitive conduct under English common law and section 58A of the CA 1998. Claimants will still need to prove causation (that is, that the particular behaviour caused them loss) and the quantum of the loss. The defendant may seek to argue "pass-on" in the context of proof of loss, to reduce any liability.

Claimants may also bring claims based on the torts of "interference with business by unlawful means" and "conspiracy to injure by the use of unlawful means". These are not specific competition-related claims, but may apply in situations where there has been a breach of competition law. In practice, these causes of action tend only to be relied on where it may be difficult to establish a breach of statutory duty because of the territorial scope of the infringement. One key challenge for claimants in bringing these actions is that they must demonstrate an intention to injure the claimant, which is often hard to establish.

Following the implementation of the Damages Directive[1] and other changes to the relevant law, slightly different rules apply to certain aspects of claims depending on when the infringing behaviour occurred or was established. These variations affect limitation periods and the collective actions regime in particular, and are dealt with in the relevant sections below. The Damages Directive provisions relating to limitation only apply in the United Kingdom where claims relate to infringements occurring after 9 March 2017.

3. What types of anti-competitive conduct are damages actions available for?

Claims may be brought in respect of any conduct which is a breach of competition law. United Kingdom competition law expressly permits claims in the CAT for damages arising from:

(a) agreements between undertakings that have as their object or effect the prevention, restriction or distortion of competition within the UK; and

(b) any conduct on the part of one or more undertakings which amounts to the abuse of a dominant position in a market is prohibited if it may affect trade within the United Kingdom.

---

[1] Directive 2014/104/EU of the European Parliament and of the Council of 26 November 2014 on certain rules governing actions for damages under national law for infringements of the competition law provisions of the Member States and of the European Union. See section 10 in relation to the status of this following Brexit.

As noted above, claims may also be brought in the High Court, and claims for "breach of statutory duty" may be based on other statutes regulating the behaviour of companies in certain sectors, such as the utilities; for example, there are some specific statutory provisions relating to fair access to networks. Such claims may therefore have the same objective as claims for breaches of the dedicated competition legislation.

4. What forms of relief may a private claimant seek?

The damages available in relation to competition claims are the same as those available for any tort under English law, and are subject to the same "tests" of liability, causation and proof of financial loss.

Claims are typically brought for financial loss arising from an overcharge in price, if the overcharge is not passed on by the claimant, loss of sales/profit arising from higher prices where the overcharge is passed on, and interest on the damages in either case. In cases of abuse of dominant position, the claimant typically seeks loss of profits and/or loss of opportunity.

In addition, where the claimant has a contract with the defendant that it believes is void for illegality because some or all of the provisions are contrary to competition law it may seek a declaration that the contract or certain clauses are unenforceable.

English courts, including the CAT, also have the power to grant injunctions based on a breach of competition law, requiring certain behaviour to cease, or compelling the defendant to take certain steps.

5. Passing-on defence

English law has recognised the principle of "pass-on" for some time, that is, that a defendant can challenge the amount of a claim by demonstrating that all or part of the loss caused by the anti-competitive behaviour was passed on to a customer of the claimant. Over the past ten years the courts have considered it more detail as more competition litigation claims have progressed all the way to trial. The *Sainsbury's v MasterCard* decision by the CAT,[2] which was confirmed by the Court of Appeal[3] was the first substantive decision on this point, and this has now been confirmed and further elaborated, most recently in *Royal Mail v DAF Trucks*[4].

Following the *Sainsbury's* judgment, defendants wishing to plead pass-on must establish a clear causal link between the overcharge arising from the anti-competitive behaviour and an increase in prices charged by the claimant. In cases where the claimant's prices are impacted by a large number of different elements and the cartelised product does not reflect a large proportion of the final product, a defendant is likely to find this difficult. In *Royal Mail* (which, like *Sainsbury's*, was also not subject to the provisions of the

---

2 *Sainsbury's v MasterCard* [2016] CAT 11

3 *Sainsbury's v MasterCard* [2018] EWCA 1536 (Civ)

4 *Royal Mail/BT v DAF ([2023]* CAT 6)

Damages Directive) the CAT summarised the four factors considered in *Sainsbury's* to be relevant to assessing whether this "causal link" could be established, namely:

(1) Knowledge of the overcharge or the specific increase in the cost in question (though this will generally be of limited application);
(2) The relative size of the overcharge against the claimant's overall costs and revenue;
(3) The relationship or association between the product subject to the overcharge and the "downstream" product sold by the claimant whose prices have been increased; and/or
(4) Whether there are realistic or known claims by identifiable "downstream" purchasers in respect of losses caused by the overcharge (which arises from considering the principle of the effectiveness of EU law).

Aspects of the pass-on principle have now also been codified by the Damages Directive. There is now a rebuttable presumption that there is 'upstream' pass-on of an overcharge to an indirect purchaser claimant. Furthermore, it is confirmed that the burden of proof in proving "downstream" pass-on (reducing the value of a claimant's claim) falls on the defendant. However, these new rules will only apply to claims arising (and brought) after the implementation of the Damages Directive.

6. Disclosure

The English rules regarding the disclosure by all parties to litigation of documents both supporting and adverse to their case remain a very important factor in competition litigation. Document disclosure is particularly important because it is often the case that the defendants will have control of many of the documents necessary to determine the overcharge and the precise nature of the infringing conduct. The disclosure regime in England is being adjusted in an attempt to reduce, where appropriate, the burden and cost to the parties, but these changes do not yet apply to competition claims.

The English Civil Procedure Rules contain a specific Practice Direction relating to the disclosure of documents in competition claims (Practice Direction 31C), although this does not expressly apply to claims in the CAT. This relates, in particular, to applications seeking evidence in the file of the competition authority, and implements (together with amendments to CA 1998) the provisions of the Damages Directive.

Documents that may be considered as simply "commercially confidential" are not afforded any protection under the English rules. They should be disclosed as long as they are relevant to the case of either party.

In general, the court will not expect a claimant to be able to present its evidential case in detail prior to disclosure where the evidence required by the claimant will only become available during the disclosure process.

7. Limitation periods

For claims not falling under the Damages Directive regime, the general limitation period for an English law tortious claim under the Limitation Act 1980 is six years from the date "*on which the cause of action accrued*". However, there is an important exception in section 32 of this act where there has been concealment of the facts giving rise to the action. In such a case the period of limitation does not begin to run until the claimant "*has discovered the fraud, concealment or mistake (as the case may be) or could with reasonable diligence have discovered it*".

The date on which this "discovery" occurs will depend on the facts of each individual case, where information may become available over a lengthy period in multiple jurisdictions but regulators may reveal few details. Importantly, recent case law (in a claim pre-dating the Damages Directive regime) has clarified that time may well **start** to run prior to the date of any regulatory decision and, where a claimant had awareness of the issuance of a Statement of Objections by a regulatory authority and the identity of the defendant(s), this may well start the limitation period running[5]. In practice the date of publication of a decision is likely to be the latest date on which time start to run, but what a claimant could reasonably be expected to have known is likely to depend on the characteristics of the claimant[6].

Prior to CRA 2015, a claim in the CAT could only be brought within two years of a final decision (subject to no further appeals). However the CAT limitation period (other than for collective claims, discussed below) has now been brought in line with the non-specialist courts for causes of action accruing after 1 October 2015 (when the CRA 2015 came into force). However, given the period that may elapse before a cartel is uncovered, this provision will continue to have force for some time to come.

Since the implementation of the Damages Directive, the date on which the limitation period starts to run has been codified across the EU for causes of action accruing after that date. Limitation for such causes of action now runs from the later of (i) the date when the infringing behaviour ceases or (ii) the "date of knowledge" of certain facts.

Where the CMA or other regulator is still investigating, however, or a decision has been appealed, the limitation period will be suspended until the investigation concludes, and any appeals are then determined. This is likely to mean that the date of any decision becomes the *de facto* start of the limitation period, since it will generally be hard to argue that any knowledge of the behaviour existed before the announcement of an investigation. It must be remembered, however, that this applies only to claims relating to infringements beginning on or after 9 March 2017, in accordance with the United Kingdom legislation implementing the Damages Directive.

8. Quantification of damages

For claims not caught by the Damages Directive there is no presumption of harm, but the courts have generally found that there are good *a priori* reasons for expecting a cartel to have adverse effects on competition and prices. It is nevertheless a matter for the claimant to prove that it has suffered **some** damage, and awards may be very low if it cannot do so. The assessment of loss is generally determined on the basis of a

---

5 *Gemalto Holding BV and others v Infineon Technologies AG and other companies* [2022] EWCA Civ 782 (Court of Appeal)

6 *Granville Technology Group Limited and ors v Infineon Technologies AG and ors [*2020] EWHC 415 (Comm)

combination of factual and economic evidence from each party, where estimates often vary widely. There have been very few judgments (since most cases settle) but the approach taken by the courts has been to focus on the specifics of each case rather than make assumptions as to what might be a "typical" overcharge. Most recently, the CAT awarded damages based on an overcharge of 5% in the *Royal Mail* trucks case, taking the particular characteristics of the Royal Mail contracts into account.

9. Appeal

Appeals against final judgments of the Competition Appeal Tribunal (which, despite its name, is a first instance court for civil competition claims) or the High Court, must be made to the Court of Appeal. Permission is required for all appeals, which may be granted by the lower court or, if not, sought from the Court of Appeal. The same rules apply to competition damages claims as to other civil claims in relation to the grounds on which appeals are permitted.

10. Collective claims (including "class actions")

The courts of England and Wales have long-established processes for coordinating and consolidating similar claims into group or multi-party claims of multiple (though not "mass") claimants, including a facility for "representative" claims although this is not widely used. Since 1 October 2015, the United Kingdom CAT regime also offers "opt-in" and "opt-out" collective actions, in which a single representative may be certified by the CAT to lead a claim on behalf of a wider, defined, group of claimants facing "common issues". The certified group may consist either of all claimants fulfilling defined criteria unless they actively choose not to participate (an "opt-out" action) or of all claimants fulfilling approved criteria who choose to participate ("opt-in"). The classes may encompass many thousands of claimants and the regime is at least partly aimed at litigating claims that may be too small to bring on an individual basis, such as those of consumers.

The process for bringing a collective action is as follows:

(a) A proposed "class representative" issues a claim form together with a detailed document setting out:

   (i) Whether the claim is to be certified as "opt-in" or "opt-out";
   (ii) How the class is to be defined;
   (iii) What the "common issues" faced by the members of the class are;
   (iv) Why the class representative is suitable to be certified; and
   (v) How the claim will be managed (communications with the class members, funding, how defendants' costs will be met in the event of an adverse costs order, distribution of any award, etc.).

(b) A hearing is held at which the CAT considers whether to certify (i) the class, and on what basis; and (ii) the class representative. (These decisions are taken independently.) The CAT may certify the class on a different basis to that in the representative's application. The defendants may oppose the certifications if they have reasonable grounds to do so.

(c) If the claim is certified it then proceeds in the usual way, except that it must be "advertised" to potential class members (for opt-in) or to class members who may wish to pursue a separate claim (for opt-out).
(d) If there is an award in favour of an opt-out class, the representative must make efforts to distribute it to all qualifying members. If the award is not fully distributed the default position is that the balance is payable to a nominated statutory charity. However, the CAT has the power to allow the release of funds to others, including for payment of the expenses of the claim including amounts due to a third party funder, or even return of a portion to the defendants.
(e) If a full or partial settlement is reached, the CAT must approve the terms.

The regime has proved very popular, with applications being made for both opt-in and opt-out actions, and relating to both follow-on actions (such as those arising from the EU Trucks cartel) and standalone claims. To date no collective claim has reached trial, and the regime is still evolving but important principles have been established by the CAT and the Court of Appeal in relation to what a suitable representative might look like, which of "competing" class representatives should be certified, how the "common issues" might be determined, how a certifiable class should be defined and what economic evidence might be required at the certification stage.

In an important judgment in 2017 the CAT confirmed that collective claims could benefit from third party litigation funding and that a portion of any damages awarded could be used to pay the funder's return as a legitimate expense of the claim.[7] In 2022, in a claim relating to the Trucks cartel, the CAT was asked to certify alternative claims, one on an opt-out and one an opt-in basis[8]. The CAT stressed that there was no presumption in favour of either approach, but, on the facts of the two proposed claims representatives and defined classes, it elected to certify only the opt-in claim brought on behalf of circa 10,000 truck purchasers. In its judgment in claims relating to 'forex' manipulation it refused to certify either of two opt-out claims[9].

Under the transitional provisions of the CRA 2015, if the facts giving rise to the claim arose **before** 1 October 2015, the collective claims procedure is only available to claimants where the claim is a follow-on claim and is based on a decision after that date (since the CAT did not have jurisdiction over stand-alone claims before 1 October 2015).

The two-years limitation period (from the date of the decision becoming final) for bringing a CAT claim still applies to the collective action regime where the facts giving rise to the claim arise before 1 October 2015, although this seems increasingly unlikely to arise. Where claims arise after 1 October 2015, the six-years limitation period set out in Section 7 above will apply.

---

7 [2017] CAT 16

8 *UK Trucks Claim Limited v Stellantis N.V. and Others/Road Haulage Association Limited v Man SE and Others* [2022] CAT 25

9 *Michael O'Higgins FX Class Representative Limited v Barclays Bank PLC and Others/Mr Phillip Evans v Barclays Bank PLC and Others* [2022] CAT 16

11. Key issues

As noted above, the regime for competition damages claims is well-established in the United Kingdom and many issues are settled law. Areas where the law continues to evolve include:

(i) **Limitation** – which, as described above, will begin to be affected by the provisions implementing the Damages Directive, but where there is still a long "tail" of cases that fall within the pre-Directive regime; and

(ii) **Collective actions** – where questions have yet to be finally answered on questions such as how detailed the methodology for calculating damages must be for very large classes, and how damages ultimately awarded should best be distributed in the case of mass claims; and

(iii) **Pass-on** – where the courts are seeking to balance the burden of proof on a defendant to show that a claimant has passed on any overcharge (further strengthened by the implementation of the Damages Directive), with the principle that a claimant should be permitted to recover only the loss it has actually suffered. This can be a difficult area, and very dependent on the facts relating to the particular business in question.

Brexit

The departure of the United Kingdom from the EU has to date had little effect on the current regime, much of which existed independent of EU law. Following withdrawal from the EU, the regulations implementing the Damages Directive remained in force, except that Commission infringement decisions published after Brexit (i.e. after 31 December 2020) ceased to be binding on UK courts. (They are nevertheless likely to continue to be very persuasive in UK courts and the CAT.)

At time of writing the UK Parliament is considering draft legislation which has the power to revoke or "sunset" certain statutes derived from EU law, and which could potentially include the regulations implementing the Damages Directive, although the outcome is uncertain and the process far from complete. In any event, as noted above, many of the core principles of the Directive existed in UK law prior to its implementation, and major change to the regime therefore seems unlikely.

United Kingdom claimants currently retain the right to bring follow-on claims in England and Wales for breaches of EU law arising from EU decisions pre-dating the date of the United Kingdom's withdrawal. Standalone claims in such circumstances (where the claim does not directly arise out of a decision) have always been, and remain, possible. Although EU infringement decisions made **after** the Brexit transition period are no longer **binding** on the English courts as regards follow-on claims, it is clear that the English courts will continue to view such Decisions as at least *prima facie* evidence of anti-competitive behaviour.

Whether or not a claimant (UK or foreign domiciled) can bring a claim in the UK courts will depend on the application of the jurisdictional rules. In very general terms, claims can often be brought where either a defendant is domiciled in the UK and/or loss was suffered in the UK. However, the jurisdictional rules are not quite the same as the EU jurisdictional rules under the Recast Brussels Regulation.

Methodology for the selection of cases

The United Kingdom has a substantial history of competition-related claims being brought in the High Court and the specialist Competition Appeal Tribunal. Most cases do not proceed to a full trial; it is assumed that they are settled. For this reason there is little information on the level of damages obtained by claimants, and any sums awarded in cases proceeding all the way to trial are likely to be misleading because they represent a substantially incomplete picture.

The cases selected by the authors represent those in which points of particular legal interest have been raised, primarily by way of interim applications. A number raise novel issues not yet decided and continue to be monitored. These relate in particular to the limitation and collective action issues discussed in the memo, and to the question of the jurisdiction of the English courts. The list is not exhaustive.

List of Cases

All the case comments mentioned are available in the Concurrences e-Competitions Bulletin

Supreme Court

17/06/2020, *Sainsbury's Supermarkets Limited v Visa Europe Services LLC and others*, Supreme Court judgment, e-Competitions Bulletin, Art. N° 111656
www.concurrences.com/111656
Penny Coombs

31/10/2019, *26 January 2015 – Appeal Judgment*, BritNed Development Ltd v ABB AB and ABB Ltd, e-Competitions Bulletin, Art. N° 111652
www.concurrences.com/111652
Penny Coombs

Apple Retail UK Limited and others v Qualcomm UK Limited and Qualcomm Incorporated, Jurisdiction judgments in May and October 2018. Case settled, e-Competitions Bulletin, Art. N° 111644
www.concurrences.com/111644
Penny Coombs

16/02/2018, *iiyama and Mouse Computer v Schott AG and others*, Issued 19 December 2014 – Court of Appeal judgment, e-Competitions Bulletin, Art. N° 111654
www.concurrences.com/111654
Penny Coombs

12/02/2016, *Streetmap.eu Limited v Google Inc, Google Ireland Limited and Google UK Limited*, Issued 15 March 2013 – Judgment, e-Competitions Bulletin, Art. N° 111655
www.concurrences.com/111655
Penny Coombs

25/09/2015, *Microsoft Mobile OY (Ltd) v Sony Europe Ltd and others*, e-Competitions Bulletin, Art. N° 111651
www.concurrences.com/111651
Penny Coombs

05/08/2015, *Arcadia Group Brands Ltd and others v Visa Inc and others*, e-Competitions Bulletin, Art. N° 111658
www.concurrences.com/111658
Penny Coombs

19/12/2014, *Vodafone Group Services Limited v Infineon Technologies AG and others*, Issued, e-Competitions Bulletin, Art. N° 111653
www.concurrences.com/111653
Penny Coombs

21/12/2010, *Safeway Stores Limited and others v Twigger and others*, e-Competitions Bulletin, Art. N° 111667
www.concurrences.com/111667
Penny Coombs

18/11/2010, *Emerald Supplies Ltd and others v British Airways Plc*, Claim issued 18 September 2008; Strike-out judgment, e-Competitions Bulletin, Art. N° 111664
www.concurrences.com/111664
Penny Coombs

23/07/2010, *Cooper Tire & Rubber Company and others v Shell Chemicals UK Limited and others [2009] EWHC 2609 (Comm)*, Issued 22 February 2008 – Judgment, e-Competitions Bulletin, Art. N° 111666
www.concurrences.com/111666
Penny Coombs

15/10/2008, *Devenish Nutrition Ltd and others v Sanofi-Aventis SA (France) and others*, Issued 14 May 2008 – Judgment, e-Competitions Bulletin, Art. N° 111665
www.concurrences.com/111665
Penny Coombs

29/09/2008, *Karen Murphy v Media Protection Services Ltd*, e-Competitions Bulletin, Art. N° 111663
www.concurrences.com/111663
Penny Coombs

02/02/2007, *Attheraces Ltd & Anor v The British Horseracing Board Ltd & Anor Rev 2 [2007] EWCA Civ 38, Court of Appeal Judgment*, e-Competitions Bulletin, Art. N° 111668
www.concurrences.com/111668
Penny Coombs

19/07/2006, *Bernard Crehan v Inntrepreneur Pub Company Limited and Brewman Group Limited ([2006] UKHL 38)*, House of Lords judgment, e-Competitions Bulletin, Art. N° 111669
www.concurrences.com/111669
Penny Coombs

Unlockd Ltd and Unlockd Media Technology Ltd v Google Ireland Ltd, Google Commerce Ltd and Google LLC, Claim withdrawn, e-Competitions Bulletin, Art. N° 111643
www.concurrences.com/111643
Penny Coombs

Competition Appeal Tribunal

31/03/2023, *Mr Phillip Evans [as class representative] v Barclays Bank PLC and others/ Michael O'Higgins FX Class Representative Limited v Barclays Bank PLC and others*, Issued (class certification), e-Competitions Bulletin, Art. N° 111638
www.concurrences.com/111638
Penny Coombs

07/02/2023, *Royal Mail Group Limited v DAF Trucks Limited and others/BT Group PLC v DAF Trucks Limited and others*, e-Competitions Bulletin, Art. N° 116318
www.concurrences.com/116318
Penny Coombs

08/06/2022, *Road Haulage Association Limited -v- Man SE and others*, Issued (class certification), e-Competitions Bulletin, Art. N° 1116642
www.concurrences.com/111642
Penny Coombs

08/06/2022, *UK Trucks Claim Limited v Iveco Magirus AG and Daimler AG*, (class certification), e-Competitions Bulletin, Art. N° 111641
www.concurrences.com/111641
Penny Coombs

18/01/2022, *Justin Gutmann v First MTR South Western Trains Limited and Another & Justin Gutmann v London & South Eastern Railway Limited*, Issued (class certification), e-Competitions Bulletin, Art. N° 111640
www.concurrences.com/111640
Penny Coombs

26/05/2017, *Socrates Training Limited v The Law Society of England and Wales*, Issued 04 April 2016 – Judgment, e-Competitions Bulletin, Art. N° 111649
www.concurrences.com/111649
Penny Coombs

31/03/2017, *Dorothy Gibson -v- Pride Mobility Products Limited*, Issued 25/05/2016, CAT judgment issued, e-Competitions Bulletin, Art. N° 111646
www.concurrences.com/111646
Penny Coombs

08/09/2016, *Walter Hugh Merricks CBE -v- MasterCard Inc and others*, Issued – Supreme Court judgment on preliminary issue awaited, e-Competitions Bulletin, Art. N° 111645
www.concurrences.com/111645
Penny Coombs

27/07/2016, *Peugeot Citroen Automobiles UK Ltd and others v Pilkington Group Limited and others (1244/5/7/15)*, Issued 22 December 2015 – Limitation judgment, e-Competitions Bulletin, Art. N° 111650
www.concurrences.com/111650
Penny Coombs

05/02/2016, *Shadhid Latif & Mohammed Abdul Waheed -v- Tesco Stores Limited*, Issued – Discontinued, e-Competitions Bulletin, Art. N° 111648
www.concurrences.com/111648
Penny Coombs

28/03/2013, *Albion Water v Dwr Cymru, Issued 18 June 2010* – Judgment, e-Competitions Bulletin, Art. N° 111662
www.concurrences.com/111662
Penny Coombs

18/12/2012, *Case 1241/5/7/15 (T) Sainsbury's Supermarkets Ltd -v- Mastercard Incorporated (2) Mastercard International Incorporated (3) Mastercard Europe SA*, Issued, e-Competitions Bulletin, Art. N° 111657
www.concurrences.com/111657
Penny Coombs

05/07/2012, *2 Travel Group PLC (in liquidation) v Cardiff City Transport Services Limited, Claim issued 14 January 2011* – Judgment, e-Competitions Bulletin, Art. N° 111659
www.concurrences.com/111659
Penny Coombs

Commercial Court (now Competition Appeal Tribunal)

25/02/2020, *Granville Technology Group Limited, OT Computers Limited and another v Infineon Technologies AG, Micron Europe Limited (and others)*, Issued: 18 May 2016, Judgment on part of the claim, e-Competitions Bulletin, Art. N° 111647
www.concurrences.com/111647
Penny Coombs

UNITED STATES OF AMERICA

Benjamin Holt
Partner, Hogan Lovells,
With the support of Holden Steinhauer, Senior Associate, Hogan Lovells,
and Jill Ottenberg, Knowledge Lawyer, Hogan Lovells

Private antitrust litigation is well-established in the United States where federal law has included a private right of action to enforce the antitrust laws for over one hundred years. Case law explicitly recognizes the role of private lawsuits in effective antitrust enforcement. Today, hundreds of cases are filed each year seeking damages or other relief as a result of alleged antitrust violations. While many of these cases follow government enforcement actions, substantial numbers are based on alleged conduct that has not been the subject of a government inquiry. The sections below provide more detail on the procedures and key issues related to private antitrust claims in the United States.

1. Jurisdiction

At the federal level, the Antitrust Division of the United States Department of Justice ("Antitrust Division") and the Federal Trade Commission ("FTC") share responsibility for enforcing the antitrust laws. In addition, state attorneys general enforce state antitrust laws within their respective states. This memorandum focuses largely on federal antitrust law and notes differences with state law where applicable.

Private antitrust claims may be brought in state or federal courts. Generally speaking, a claimant has the choice of filing a claim in any forum that has jurisdiction over the antitrust claim and the defendant. Antitrust claims that allege a violation of any federal antitrust law may be filed in any federal district court where either (i) the defendant resides, (ii) substantial parts of the events arose, or (iii) the defendant can be served (if there is no other appropriate forum). A defendant must live in or have sufficient minimum contact with the state in which the federal district court sits for that court to have jurisdiction over the defendant.

Most state courts have jurisdiction to adjudicate the federal antitrust claims if the federal court in that state would also have jurisdiction. Through a process called "removal", a defendant can transfer a case initially filed in state court to a federal court if the case otherwise meets the federal jurisdiction requirements.[1]

Both follow-on and stand-alone claims are available: private antitrust claims can (and often do) proceed in parallel to criminal investigations or adjudicatory proceedings. Additionally, a private claimant need not wait for a civil or criminal government enforcement action to sue for damages. Although there is no general rule staying civil proceedings while a criminal case is pending, courts will sometimes stay or defer discovery in civil proceedings based on requests from the Antitrust Division related to ongoing criminal investigations or proceedings.

1 A federal court has jurisdiction when (i) the case arises under the US Constitution or a federal statute, or (ii) the plaintiff(s) and defendant(s) are citizens of different states and/or countries and the amount in controversy is at least USD 75,000. 28 U.S.C. §§ 1331-1332.

2. Relevant legislation and legal grounds

Section 4 of the Clayton Act (15 U.S.C. § 15(a)) provides a private cause of action for suits brought pursuant to "the antitrust laws", which are set out in more detail below.

A claimant has standing to seek damages if (i) there is an actual case or controversy, the resolution of which directly impacts the claimant, (ii) the claimant is not too removed from the violation, and (iii) the claimant can demonstrate that it suffered an "antitrust injury" to have standing in federal court. Antitrust injury is "injury of the type the antitrust laws were intended to prevent." Atl. Richfield Co. v. USA Petroleum Co., 495 U.S. 328, 334 (1990). Claimants who purchased products or services indirectly from the defendant(s) are not permitted to bring antitrust damages claims under federal law but can do so under many state laws.

The Clayton Act provides that final judgments entered against a defendant in a civil or criminal antitrust proceeding brought by the government may be used in a later private suit arising out of the same facts as *prima facie* evidence against the defendant. 15 U.S.C. § 16(a).

3. What types of anti-competitive conduct are damages actions available for?

The "antitrust laws" include sections 1 and 2 of the Sherman Act (15 U.S.C. §§ 1, 2), section 7 of the Clayton Act (15 U.S.C. § 18), and section 2 of the Robinson Patman Act (15 U.S.C. § 13). Broadly speaking:

- Section 1 of the Sherman Act prohibits agreements in restraint of trade, including price-fixing agreements, group boycotts, market allocation, bid-rigging, and tying.
- Section 2 of the Sherman Act prohibits unlawful monopolisation.
- Section 7 of the Clayton Act prohibits mergers and acquisitions that substantially lessen competition or tend to create a monopoly.
- The Robinson Patman Act prohibits price discrimination in the sale of products to similarly situated buyers.

Many states' antitrust laws also provide for private rights of action.

4. What forms of relief may a private claimant seek?

Under section 4 of the Clayton Act (15 U.S.C. § 15(a)), claimants can obtain treble damages, *i.e.* three times the amount of damages sustained due to the claimant's antitrust violation, plus costs of suit, reasonable attorney's fees, and post-judgment interest.

Under section 16 of the Clayton Act (15 U.S.C. § 26), private claimants may obtain injunctive relief to prevent or terminate unlawful conduct or, in rare cases, divestiture. A claimant must establish that irreparable harm is likely unless injunctive relief is granted.

5. Passing-on defence

The passing-on defence, or the avoidance of antitrust liability through proof that a claimant passed on any antitrust injury to a third party, is not available in the US at the federal level, although some states do recognize it.[2] For example, the pass-on defence is available in California when "multiple levels of purchasers have sued, or where a risk remains they may sue."[3]

Further, under Illinois Brick Co. v. Illinois, indirect purchasers do not have standing to sue for damages under the federal antitrust laws; only direct purchasers may bring such claims[4]. However, 34 US states – including California and New York – as well as the District of Columbia permit indirect purchasers to sue under state antitrust laws.

6. Pre-trial discovery and disclosure, treatment of confidential information

Discovery in US antitrust cases is extensive and may include the production of documents, depositions, interrogatories, and requests for admissions. Discovery must be of non-privileged matters that are relevant to any party's claim or defense and proportional to the needs of the case, and is usually limited to a period of time before the earliest date of alleged wrongdoing through a date after the alleged wrongdoing ended. The number of depositions, interrogatories, and admissions is limited by the Federal Rules of Civil Procedure and state procedures (although such limitations are sometimes altered by agreement or court order).

Discovery of non-parties is also allowed; however, courts regularly narrow the scope of discovery when it is sought from non-parties.

Confidential information, if not otherwise subject to a legal privilege preventing disclosure, must be produced in response to appropriate discovery requests. Parties may protect such information from public disclosure through the use of protective orders that are either stipulated to by the parties or ordered by the court when the need for confidentiality of the information is shown "for good cause." Evidence introduced at trial is generally subject to the public's right of access to the courtroom and will not be blocked absent a compelling need.

If a criminal investigation is pending, investigators can seek a discovery stay in any pending damages actions sharing common questions of fact or law (e.g. follow-on actions). The judge presiding over the damages action has discretion as to whether to grant the stay. The files of a competition authority are often deemed protected by various exceptions to the discovery rules and as a result, are typically not accessible in private lawsuits. Additionally, documents submitted to the Antitrust Division in response to a Grand Jury subpoena are protected from disclosure by federal law.

---

2 Hanover Shoe, Inc. v. United Shoe Machinery Corp., 392 U.S. 481 (1968).

3 Clayworth v. Pfizer, Inc., 233 P.3d 1066, 1086 (Cal. 2010).

4 Illinois Brick Co. v. Illinois, 431 U.S. 720 (1977).

7. Limitation periods

The statute of limitations for federal private antitrust claims is four years from the date the cause of action accrued, which is defined as the date the claimant suffered injury. How to define the date the cause of action accrued and whether the injury is ongoing or not is regularly the subject of dispute within antitrust litigation matters. Individual US states may have statutes of limitations that differ from the federal rule; these statutes apply to any claims brought under the law of the particular state.

The statute of limitations period is considered procedural law. If the statute of limitations expires before a claimant files a case and no basis for suspension of the period exists, the claim will be dismissed with prejudice.

A statute of limitations may be suspended in the event of any one or more of the following situations: a pending government investigation or class action derived from the same facts as the claimant's case; fraudulent concealment; duress; or estoppel. A statute of limitations period may also be modified by contract between the parties, in what is often referred to as a "tolling" agreement.

8. Appeal

Unsuccessful claimants and defendants in private federal antitrust suits have the right to appeal a final decision of a federal district court.

In a private action, either side may appeal a final, unfavourable decision on the grounds of legal error that prejudiced the losing party. Appellate courts do not re-weigh the evidence; rather, they examine whether the trier of fact correctly applied the law to the facts as it (the trier of fact) found them.

For most competition cases, appeals from a federal district court are heard by the court of appeals in the circuit in which the district court is located. Further appeal to the United States Supreme Court – the country's highest court – is allowed, but the Supreme Court has discretion as to whether it will hear such an appeal.

State cases are appealed to the state appellate court in the state where the case was heard. Many states have two layers of appellate courts like the federal system. Under certain circumstances, a decision by the highest court in a state can be appealed to the United States Supreme Court.

9. Class actions and collective representation

Most U.S. antitrust class actions are filed in federal courts whether the claims arise under federal or state law. Rule 23 of the Federal Rules of Civil Procedure sets out the requirements for class actions, including antitrust class actions.

Rule 23(a) of the Federal Rules of Civil Procedure requires the class representative to establish (i) numerosity, (ii) commonality, (iii) typicality, and (iv) adequacy.

- Numerosity ensures that the size of the putative class is such that joining all members is impractical making class action a useful way to bring claims.

- Commonality requires that the class members have at least one question of law or fact in common.
- Typicality means that the claims or defenses of the class representative are typical of those of the other class members.
- Finally, the adequacy requirement ensures that the class representative is capable of fairly and adequately protecting the interests of the class.

A class representative also must satisfy one of three criteria set forth in Rule 23(b) of the Federal Rules of Civil Procedure:

- Trying individual actions would expose the defendant to the risk of inconsistent and incompatible judgments or would dispose of or harm the interests of non-parties;
- The defendant's conduct is such that injunctive or declaratory relief on behalf of the whole class is appropriate; or
- For damages actions, questions of law or fact common to the class predominate over questions affecting individual members.

10. Key issues

Standing of Direct and Indirect Purchasers

In 2019, the US Supreme Court ruled that iPhone users who purchased apps through Apple's App Store are considered direct purchasers of Apple's products, and therefore had standing to bring claims against Apple for alleged monopolisation of the market for iPhone apps. In *Apple v. Pepper* (2019), the Court rejected Apple's argument that longstanding Supreme Court precedent established in the *Illinois Brick* case – holding that indirect purchasers do not have standing to sue under federal antitrust law – should apply because iPhone users purchase apps from third-party developers, not from Apple. In rejecting this argument, the Court found that iPhone users should be considered direct purchasers with standing to bring claims for private damages under the antitrust laws because "the iPhone owners bought the apps directly from Apple and therefore are direct purchasers under Illinois Brick." The Court's decision in this case may expose other companies offering platform services for third-party vendors to antitrust claims brought by consumers of goods and services purchased from third parties through those platforms.

Evolving Class Action Certification Standards

US courts have been providing evolving standards with respect to certification of antitrust class actions. There is currently a split among the federal circuit courts of appeal as to whether a class containing uninjured members may be certified. Some circuits have held that Rule 23(b)(3)'s predominance requirement forbids certification where the proposed class contains uninjured members that cannot be identified and removed without individualised inquiries. Others have allowed certification as long as the class does not contain "a great many" uninjured members. More recently, one circuit court of appeals held that "courts must apply Rule 23(b)(3) on a case-by-case basis, rather than rely on a per se rule that a class cannot be certified if it includes more than a *de minimis* of uninjured class members."

To date, the Supreme Court has declined to address under what circumstances the presence of uninjured class members precludes the certification of a class, and this issue is likely to continue to be raised in antitrust class action cases. Nevertheless, in June 2021, the Supreme Court held that only plaintiffs "concretely harmed" by a defendant's statutory violation have standing under Article III of the US Constitution to seek damages against that private defendant in federal court. The Court clarified that, for the purpose of establishing Article III standing, the "mere risk of future harm, without more, cannot qualify as a concrete harm in a suit for damages." Although the decision specifically declined to address how this holding would impact class certification standards under Rule 23, the lower courts are likely to consider the Supreme Court's decision in future cases dealing with class certification issues.

Wage Fixing and No-Poach Litigation

A series of class actions cases have followed the increased interest from the Department of Justice and state attorneys general in reviewing "no-poach" agreements – agreements between competitors not to compete for employees – for antitrust violations. A key issue in these private actions is whether the alleged "no-poach" agreement should be analysed under the *per se* or rule of reason standard. The *per se* standard would allow claimants to argue that a "no-poach" agreement is *per se* illegal under the antitrust laws, while applying the rule of reason would require a court to evaluate the pro-competitive features of the "no-poach" agreement against its anti-competitive effects. The Department of Justice has filed Statements of Interest in a number of these private actions, citing its strong interest in ensuring that the federal antitrust laws are "fully and correctly applied to all markets – including labor markets." The Department has taken the position that no-poach and no-hire agreements are not deserving of "anything less than *per se* treatment" because there is no "cognizable ancillary-restraints argument" to justify the use of such agreements. DOJ has also filed a statement of interest in private litigation arguing that non-compete provisions may be considered horizontal restraints on competition and therefore *per se* unlawful, leaving the door open to potential criminal scrutiny of these common employment contract provisions.

Information Exchanges

There has been increased scrutiny from the claimants' bar in recent years on the exchange of information between competitors. While some exchange of information between competitors is a practical necessity of legally-sufficient conspiracy allegations, under federal antitrust law an agreement to exchange information is itself a standalone violation of the Sherman Act, evaluated under the rule of reason.

The use of information exchanges in various industries has been a focus of recent antitrust litigation. A number of antitrust class actions have been filed in the food industry, including cases against major producers of broiler chickens, pork, and turkey alleging a conspiracy to fix prices and/or limit production with the intent to increase prices. A central component of these cases is allegations that competitors exchanged commercially-sensitive production information. In addition, in October 2022 a series of lawsuits were filed by renters against some of the largest residential real estate managers and landlords in the United States, alleging that the landlords illegally shared price information through the use of data analytics software with the aim of suppressing price competition for multifamily residential real estate leases. Shortly thereafter – following public pressure from Congress – it was reported that DOJ had opened an investigation into whether the rent-setting software facilitated collusion among landlords.

Against this backdrop of private antitrust litigation focused on information exchanges, in February 2023, DOJ announced that it is breaking from years of antitrust enforcement precedent by withdrawing certain policy statements with the FTC related to antitrust enforcement in health care. Specifically, DOJ is withdrawing "safe harbors" for mergers, joint ventures, and joint purchasing agreements between or of health care providers, as well as guidance regarding health care information exchanges and accountable care organizations. With respect to DOJ's guidance on information exchanges, while the policy statement at issue is focused on the health care industry, the decision to withdraw from this policy has impacts beyond health care, since US antitrust practitioners have relied upon the guidance in other industries as well. While the effect that DOJ's abandonment of decades-old enforcement policy will have on private antitrust litigation remains to be seen, the private antitrust bar may take the agency's more rigid assessment of the potential competitive effects of information exchanges as license to pursue more cases focused on this issue.

Multi-Sided Platforms

In a 2018 Supreme Court case, *Ohio v. American Express*, the Court held that the anti-steering provisions in American Express's merchant contracts do not violate federal antitrust law. The anti-steering provisions prohibit merchants who accept American Express credit card payments from offering customers an incentive to use another credit card – such as Visa or MasterCard – at the point of sale to avoid American Express's comparatively higher merchant fees. In its decision, the Court found that the credit-card market should be considered a single market – rather than two separate markets for merchants and cardholders – because "credit-card networks are best understood as supplying only one product – the transaction – that is jointly consumed by a cardholder and a merchant." The court found that in this single market context, the claimants had not adequately met their burden of proving that the anti-steering provisions had anticompetitive effects because they focused their argument on just one side of the market. The court found that "evidence of a price increase on one side of a two-sided transaction platform cannot, by itself, demonstrate an anti-competitive exercise of market power." In order for their claim to be successful, claimants would have had to prove that the anti-steering provisions increased the cost of credit-card transactions above a competitive level, reduced the number of transactions, or otherwise stifled competition in the two-sided credit card market.

Methodology for the selection of cases

The cases included in the compilation below consist of both follow-on and stand-alone actions and represent some of the most important and recent decisions shaping antitrust litigation in the United States. The compilation is not exhaustive. Instead, the focus was on decisions from the US Supreme Court or federal courts of appeal addressing important issues that regularly arise in US antitrust litigation.

List of Cases

All the case comments mentioned are available in the Concurrences e-Competitions Bulletin

Supreme Court

25/06/2018, *Ohio v. American Express Co., 138 S.Ct. 2274 (2018)*, e-Competitions Bulletin, Art. N° 111620
www.concurrences.com/111620
Benjamin Holt

14/06/2018, *Animal Science Products, Inc. v. Hebei Welcome Pharmaceutical Co. Ltd., 138 S.Ct. 1865 (2018)*, e-Competitions Bulletin, Art. N° 111629
www.concurrences.com/111629
Benjamin Holt

Courts of Appeal

08/04/2022, *Olean Wholesale Grocery Cooperative Inc. v. Bumble Bee Foods*, e-Competitions Bulletin, Art. N° 16352
www.concurrences.com/16352
Benjamin Holt

07/03/2022, *Indirect Purchaser Plaintiffs v. Samsung Elecs. Co. (In re Dynamic Random Access Memory (DRAM) Indirect Purchaser Antitrust Litigation)*, e-Competitions Bulletin, Art. N° 116351
www.concurrences.com/116351
Benjamin Holt

22/01/2018, *In re Processed Egg Products Antitrust Litigation, 881 F.3d 262 (3d Cir. 2018)*, e-Competitions Bulletin, Art. N° 111625
www.concurrences.com/111625
Benjamin Holt

02/10/2017, *Valspar Corp. v. E.I. Du Pont, 873 F.3d 185 (3d Cir. 2017)*, e-Competitions Bulletin, Art. N° 111617 www.concurrences.com/111617
Benjamin Holt

12/01/2017, *In re Apple iPhone Antitrust Litigation, 846 F.3d 313 (9th Cir. 2017)*, e-Competitions Bulletin, Art. N° 111622
www.concurrences.com/111622
Benjamin Holt

23/05/2016, *Gelboim v. Bank of America Corp., 823 F.3d 759 (2d Cir. 2016)*, e-Competitions Bulletin, Art. N° 111628
www.concurrences.com/111628
Benjamin Holt

Table of Cases

THE EUROPEAN UNION

Court of Justice of the European Union

20/04/2023, CJEU, Case C-25/21, Repsol Comercial de Productos Petrolíferos, ECLI:EU:C:2023:298, e-Competitions Bulletin, Art. N° 116294
www.concurrences.com/112694
François Brunet, Pierre Chellet

16/02/2023, CJEU, Case C-312/21, Tráficos Manuel Ferrer, ECLI:EU:C:2023:99, e-Competitions Bulletin, Art. N° 116292
www.concurrences.com/116292
François Brunet, Pierre Chellet

12/01/23, CJEU, Case C-57/21, RegioJet, ECLI:EU:C:2023:6, e-Competitions Bulletin, Art. N° 116290
www.concurrences.com/112690
François Brunet, Pierre Chellet

22/06/2022, CJEU, Case C-267/20, Volvo and DAF Trucks, ECLI:EU:C:2022:494, e-Competitions Bulletin, Art. N° 116288
www.concurrences.com/112688
François Brunet, Pierre Chellet

06/11/2021, CJEU, Case C-882/19, Sumal, ECLI:EU:C:2021:800, e-Competitions Bulletin, Art. N° 116193
www.concurrences.com/116193
François Brunet, Pierre Chellet

12/12/2019, CJEU, Case C-435/18, Otis GmbH, ECLI:EU:C:2019:1069, e-Competitions Bulletin, Art. N° 111913
www.concurrences.com/111913
François Brunet, Pierre Chellet

29/07/2019, CJEU, Case C-451/18, Tibor-Trans Fuvarozó és Kereskedelmi Kft, ECLI:EU:C:2019:635, e-Competitions Bulletin, Art. N° 111878
www.concurrences.com/111878
François Brunet, Pierre Chellet

28/03/2019, CJEU, Case C-637/17, Cogeco Communications Inc., ECLI:EU:C:2019:263, e-Competitions Bulletin, Art. N° 111882
www.concurrences.com/111882
François Brunet, Pierre Chellet

14/03/2019, CJEU, Case C-724/17, Skanska Industrial Solutions Oy, ECLI:EU:C:2019:204, e-Competitions Bulletin, Art. N° 111884
www.concurrences.com/111884
François Brunet, Pierre Chellet

24/11/2018, CJEU, Case C-595/17, Apple Sales International, ECLI:EU:C:2018:854, e-Competitions Bulletin, Art. N° 111876
www.concurrences.com/111876
François Brunet, Pierre Chellet

05/07/2018, CJEU, Case C-27/17, AB "flyLAL-Lithuanian Airlines", ECLI:EU:C:2018:533, e-Competitions Bulletin, Art. N° 111877
www.concurrences.com/111877
François Brunet, Pierre Chellet

23/11/2017, CJEU, Case C-547/16, Gasorba SL, ECLI:EU:C:2017:891, e-Competitions Bulletin, Art. N° 111883
www.concurrences.com/111883
François Brunet, Pierre Chellet

21/05/2015, CJEU, Case C-352/13, Cartel Damage Claims (CDC) Hydrogen Peroxide SA, ECLI:EU:C:2015:335, e-Competitions Bulletin, Art. N° 111875
www.concurrences.com/111875
François Brunet, Pierre Chellet

05/06/2014, CJEU, Case C-557/12, Kone AG, ECLI:EU:C:2014:1317, e-Competitions Bulletin, Art. N° 111912
www.concurrences.com/111912
François Brunet, Pierre Chellet

27/02/2014, CJEU, Case C-365/012 P, EnBW Energie Baden-Württemberg AG, ECLI:EU:C:2014:112, e-Competitions Bulletin, Art. N° 111874
www.concurrences.com/111874
François Brunet, Pierre Chellet

06/06/2013, CJEU, Case C-536/11, Donau Chemie AG, ECLI:EU:C:2013:366, e-Competitions Bulletin, Art. N° 111873
www.concurrences.com/111873
François Brunet, Pierre Chellet

14/06/2011, CJEU, Case C-360/09, Pfleiderer AG, ECLI:EU:C:2011:389, e-Competitions Bulletin, Art. N° 111872
www.concurrences.com/111872
François Brunet, Pierre Chellet

Court of Justice of the European Communities

20/09/2001, CJEC, Case C-453/99, Courage and Crehan, ECLI:EU:C:2001:465, e-Competitions Bulletin, Art. N° 111879
www.concurrences.com/111879
François Brunet, Pierre Chellet

13/07/2006, CJEC, Cases C-295/04 to C-298/04, Manfredi, ECLI:EU:C:2006:461, e-Competitions Bulletin, Art. N° 111880
www.concurrences.com/111880
François Brunet, Pierre Chellet

AUSTRIA

Supreme Court

21/12/2022, Case 5 Ob 193/22a; LKW Kartell, e-Competitions Bulletin, Art. N° 116297
www.concurrences.com/116297
Andreas Traugott

22/05/2022, Case 16 Ok 1/22s; Austrian Construction Cartel, e-Competitions Bulletin, Art. N° 116296
www.concurrences.com/116296
Andreas Traugott

27/09/2016, Case 1 Ob 104/16z; LIBOR, e-Competitions Bulletin, Art. N° 111954
www.concurrences.com/111954
Stefanie Stegbauer

30/08/2016, Case 4 Ob 131/16t; LIBOR, e-Competitions Bulletin, Art. N° 111953
www.concurrences.com/111953
Stefanie Stegbauer

30/08/2016, Case 4 Ob 120/16z; LIBOR, e-Competitions Bulletin, Art. N° 111952
www.concurrences.com/111952
Stefanie Stegbauer

16/06/2015, Case 4 Ob 95/15x; Aufzugskartell, e-Competitions Bulletin, Art. N° 111951
www.concurrences.com/111951
Stefanie Stegbauer

29/10/2014, Case Eg: Case 7 Ob 121/14s; Aufzugskartell, e-Competitions Bulletin, Art. N° 111950
www.concurrences.com/111950
Stefanie Stegbauer

25/05/2014, Case 8 Ob 81/13i; Aufzugskartell, e-Competitions Bulletin, Art. N° 111949
www.concurrences.com/111949
Stefanie Stegbauer

15/05/2014, Case 6 Ob 47/14a; Aufzugskartell, e-Competitions Bulletin, Art. N° 111948
www.concurrences.com/111948
Stefanie Stegbauer

16/12/2013, Case 6 Ob 186/12i; Aufzugskartell, e-Competitions Bulletin, Art. N° 111947
www.concurrences.com/111947
Stefanie Stegbauer

12/02/2013, Case 4 Ob 168/12b; Aufzugskartell, e-Competitions Bulletin, Art. N° 111947
www.concurrences.com/111947
Stefanie Stegbauer

17/10/2012, Case 7 Ob 48/12b; Aufzugskartell, e-Competitions Bulletin, Art. N° 111945
www.concurrences.com/111945
Stefanie Stegbauer

14/08/2012, Case 5 Ob 39/11p; Aufzugskartell, e-Competitions Bulletin, Art. N° 111944
www.concurrences.com/111944
Stefanie Stegbauer

02/08/2012, Case 4 Ob 46/12m; Bankomatvertrag, e-Competitions Bulletin, Art. N° 111943
www.concurrences.com/111943
Stefanie Stegbauer

15/05/2012, Case 3 Ob 1/12m; Aufzugskartell, e-Competitions Bulletin, Art. N°111942
www.concurrences.com/111942
Stefanie Stegbauer

14/07/2010, Case 7 Ob 127/10t; Aufzugskartell, e-Competitions Bulletin, Art. N° 111941
www.concurrences.com/111941
Stefanie Stegbauer

BELGIUM

Court of Appeal

15/02/2008, Review Toepassingen van Communicatie BVBA / De Schepper J. and Raad voor de Mededinging, e-Competitions Bulletin, Art. N° 111937
www.concurrences.com/111937
Gerrit Oosterhuis

Commercial Courts

29/04/2022, A.J. Veurinck BV / DAF Trucks NV en Paccar Financial Holdings Europe BV (A/18/02226), e-Competitions Bulletin, Art. N° 116300
www.concurrences.com/116300
Vincent Mussche

23/03/2017, Herman Verboven e.a. / Honda Motor Europe Logistics, e-Competitions Bulletin, Art. N° 111940
www.concurrences.com/111940
Gerrit Oosterhuis

24/04/2015, Belgische Staat/liftenproducenten, e-Competitions Bulletin, Art. N° 111939
www.concurrences.com/111939
Gerrit Oosterhuis

24/11/2014, Europese Commissie/Otis e.a. (A.R. A/08/06816), e-Competitions Bulletin, Art. N° 111938
www.concurrences.com/111938
Gerrit Oosterhuis

BRAZIL

Federal Supreme Court

02/10/1997, "Process No. 964.306 (Extraordinary Appeal), e-Competitions Bulletin, Art. N° 111932
www.concurrences.com/111932
Joyce Honda, Thales Lemos

Superior Court of Justice

Process No. 7099345-90.2009.8.13.0024 (civil lawsuit); Interlocutory Appeal in Special Appeal nº 332865-MG, e-Competitions Bulletin, Art. N° 111936
www.concurrences.com/111936
Joyce Honda, Thales Lemos

Federal District Appellate court

07/08/2013, Process No. 0036211-12.2013.8.07.0001 (Civil Appeal), e-Competitions Bulletin, Art. N° 111929
www.concurrences.com/111929
José Gabriel Assis de Almeida, Mickael Viglino

Regional Federal Appellate Courts

26/08/2017, Process No. 1050035-45.2017.8.26.0100 (Civil Appeal); Process No. 1076834-28.2017.8.26.0100 (Civil Appeal); Process No. 1076386-55.2017.8.26.0100 (Civil Lawsuit); Process No. 1076640-28.2017.8.26.0100 (Civil Lawsuit); Process No. 1076741-65.2017.8.26.0100 (Civil Lawsuit); and others, e-Competitions Bulletin, Art. N° 111930
www.concurrences.com/111930
Joyce Honda, Thales Lemos

16/12/2013, Process No. 0004954-43.2013.8.21.0012 (civil lawsuit), e-Competitions Bulletin, Art. N° 111935
www.concurrences.com/111935
Joyce Honda, Thales Lemos

03/10/2006, Process No. 70068906171 (Civil Appeal), e-Competitions Bulletin, Art. N° 111933
www.concurrences.com/111933
Joyce Honda, Thales Lemos

26/08/2005, Process No. 3002976-90.2005.8.26.0506 (Civil Appeal), e-Competitions Bulletin, Art. N° 111928
www.concurrences.com/111928
José Gabriel Assis de Almeida, Mickael Viglino

05/04/1999, Process No. 0012334-56.1999.4.05.8300 (Civil Appeal), e-Competitions Bulletin, Art. N° 111934
www.concurrences.com/111934
Joyce Honda, Thales Lemos

03/04/1995, Process No. 0051034-04.1995.4.03.6100 (Civil Appeal), e-Competitions Bulletin, Art. N° 111931
www.concurrences.com/111931
Joyce Honda, Thales Lemos

CHILE

Competition Court

21/04/2020 (Date of admission), Demanda de Papelera Cerrillos S.A. contra CMPC Tissue S.A. y otra, CIP-3-2020, e-Competitions Bulletin, Art. N° 111927
www.concurrences.com/111927
Benjamín Grebe, Daniella Ibaceta

25/06/2019 (Date of admission), CIP- 3- 2019, e-Competitions Bulletin, Art. N° 111926
www.concurrences.com/111926
Benjamín Grebe, Daniella Ibaceta

14/12/2017 (Date of admission), Demanda de Sandra Fuentes Salazar y otros contra Empresa de Transportes Rurales Limitada y otros, CIP-1-2017, e-Competitions Bulletin, Art. N° 111925
www.concurrences.com/111925
Benjamín Grebe, Manuela Barros

FRANCE

Supreme Courts

01/03/2023, French Supreme Judiciary Court, n° 20-18.356, e-Competitions Bulletin, Art. N° 116314
www.concurrences.com/116314
Marie Louvet, Agathe Esch

19/10/2022, French Supreme Judiciary Court, n° 21-19197, e-Competitions Bulletin, Art. N° 116325
www.concurrences.com/116325
Marie Louvet, Agathe Esch

28/09/2022, French Supreme Judiciary Court, n° 21-20.731, e-Competitions Bulletin, Art. N° 116327
www.concurrences.com/116327
Marie Louvet, Agathe Esch

17/06/2022, French Supreme Judiciary Court, n° 454189, e-Competitions Bulletin, Art. N° 116331
www.concurrences.com/116331
Marie Louvet, Agathe Esch

Courts of Appeal

17/02/2023, Paris Administrative Court of Appeal, n° 14PA02419, e-Competitions Bulletin, Art. N° 116315
www.concurrences.com/116315
Marie Louvet, Agathe Esch

14/09/2022, Paris Court of Appeal, sections 5-4, n° 20/17560, e-Competitions Bulletin, Art. N° 116329
www.concurrences.com/116329
Marie Louvet, Agathe Esch

23/02/2022, Paris Court of Appeal, sections 5-4, n° 19-19239, e-Competitions Bulletin, Art. N° 116334
www.concurrences.com/116334
Marie Louvet, Agathe Esch

09/02/2022, Paris Court of Appeal, n° 19/19969, e-Competitions Bulletin, Art. N° 116336
www.concurrences.com/116336
Marie Louvet, Agathe Esch

05/01/2022, Paris Court of Appeal, sections 5-4, n° 19/22293, e-Competitions Bulletin, Art. N° 116340
www.concurrences.com/116340
Marie Louvet, Agathe Esch

24/11/2021, Paris Court of Appeal, sections 5-4, n° 20/04265, e-Competitions Bulletin, Art. N° 116341
www.concurrences.com/116341
Marie Louvet, Agathe Esch

24/09/2021, Paris Court of Appeal, sections 5-11, n° 20/14416, e-Competitions Bulletin, Art. N° 116342
www.concurrences.com/116342
Marie Louvet, Agathe Esch

23/06/2021, Paris Court of Appeal, sections 5-4, n° 17/04101, e-Competitions Bulletin, Art. N° 116344
www.concurrences.com/116344
Marie Louvet, Agathe Esch

06/03/2019, Paris Court of Appeal, Pôle 5 Ch. 4, n° 17/21261, e-Competitions Bulletin, Art. N° 111849
www.concurrences.com/111849
Marie Louvet

12/09/2018, Paris Court of Appeal, pôle 5, ch.4, n° 18/04914, e-Competitions Bulletin, Art. N° 111850
www.concurrences.com/111850
Marie Louvet

27/05/2015, Paris Court of Appeal, ch.5-4, n° 14/14758, e-Competitions Bulletin, Art. N° 111852
www.concurrences.com/111852
Marie Louvet

20/12/2017, Paris Court of Appeal, pôle 5, ch.4, n° 15/07266, e-Competitions Bulletin, Art. N° 111853
www.concurrences.com/111853
Marie Louvet

20/09/2017, Paris Court of Appeal, n° 12/04441, e-Competitions Bulletin, Art. N° 111854
www.concurrences.com/111854
Marie Louvet

05/07/2017, Paris Court of Appeal, n° 15/12365, e-Competitions Bulletin, Art. N° 111855
www.concurrences.com/111855
Marie Louvet

10/05/2017, Paris Court of Appeal, pôle 5, ch.4, n° 15/05918, e-Competitions Bulletin, Art. N° 111858
www.concurrences.com/111858
Marie Louvet

14/12/2016, Paris Court of Appeal, Pôle 5, ch.4, n° 13/08975, e-Competitions Bulletin, Art. N° 111859
www.concurrences.com/111859
Marie Louvet

07/12/2016, Paris Court of Appeal, ch.5-4, RG 14/01036, e-Competitions Bulletin, Art. N° 111860
www.concurrences.com/111860
Marie Louvet

13/04/2016, Paris Court of Appeal, Pôle 5, ch.4, n° 13/24840, e-Competitions Bulletin, Art. N° 111861
www.concurrences.com/111861
Marie Louvet

25/11/2015, Paris Court of Appeal, Pôle 5, ch.4, n° 12/02931, e-Competitions Bulletin, Art. N° 111862
ww.concurrences.com/111862
Marie Louvet

22/10/2015, Paris Court of Appeal, ch.5-4, RG 14/03665, e-Competitions Bulletin, Art. N° 111863
www.concurrences.com/111863
Marie Louvet

02/10/2015, Paris Court of Appeal, pôle 5, ch.11, n° 14/15779, e-Competitions Bulletin, Art. N° 111864
www.concurrences.com/111864
Marie Louvet

02/07/2015, Paris Court of Appeal, Pôle 5, ch.5, n° 13/22609, e-Competitions Bulletin, Art. N° 111865
www.concurrences.com/111865
Marie Louvet

27/06/2012, Paris Court of Appeal, Pôle 5, ch. 4, n° 10/04245, e-Competitions Bulletin, Art. N° 111869
www.concurrences.com/111869
Marie Louvet

24/06/2004, Versailles Court of Appeal, 12e ch.2, n° 2002-07434, e-Competitions Bulletin, Art. N° 111871
www.concurrences.com/111871
Marie Louvet

Commercial Courts

27/10/2022, Lyon Commercial Court, n° 2018J191, e-Competitions Bulletin, Art. N° 116324
www.concurrences.com/116324
Marie Louvet, Agathe Esch

09/03/2023, Paris Commercial Court, n° 2019063474, e-Competitions Bulletin, Art. N° 116313
www.concurrences.com/116313
Marie Louvet, Agathe Esch

23/01/2023, Paris Commercial Court, n° 2021037634, e-Competitions Bulletin, Art. N° 116316
www.concurrences.com/116316
Marie Louvet, Agathe Esch

10/02/2021, Paris Commercial Court, 10 February 2021, n° 2020035242, e-Competitions Bulletin, Art. N° 116345
www.concurrences.com/116345
Marie Louvet, Agathe Esch

20/02/2020, Paris Commercial Court, 3e ch., n° 2017021571, e-Competitions Bulletin, Art. N° 111847
www.concurrences.com/111847
Marie Louvet

30/03/2011, Paris Commercial Court, 6e ch., n° 2009-073089, e-Competitions Bulletin, Art. N° 111870
www.concurrences.com/111870
Marie Louvet

Tribunal of First Instance

06/06/2017, Lille Tribunal of First Instance, n° 15/10938, e-Competitions Bulletin, Art. N° 111856
www.concurrences.com/111856
Marie Louvet

GERMANY

Federal Court of Justice

08/08/2022, VBL-Gegenwert III, KZR 111/18, e-Competitions Bulletin, Art. N° 116264
www.concurrences.com/116264
Christian Ritz, Carolin Marx, Dr. Judith Solzbach, Hanna Weber

28/06/2022, Stahl-Strahlmittel, KZR 46/20, e-Competitions Bulletin, Art. N° 116263
www.concurrences.com/116263
Christian Ritz, Carolin Marx, Dr. Judith Solzbach, Hanna Weber

13/06/2022, Financialright Vla, ZR 418/21, e-Competitions Bulletin, Art. N° 116246
www.concurrences.com/116246
Christian Ritz, Carolin Marx, Dr. Judith Solzbach, Hanna Weber

13/07/2022, Air Deal II, ZR 84/20, e-Competitions Bulletin, Art. N° 116364
www.concurrences.com/116364
Christian Ritz, Carolin Marx, Dr. Judith Solzbach, Hanna Weber

13/04/2021, Truck Cartel, KZR 19/20, e-Competitions Bulletin, Art. N° 116363
www.concurrences.com/116363
Christian Ritz, Carolin Marx, Dr. Judith Solzbach, Hanna Weber

10/02/2021, Schienenkartell VI, KZR 63/18, e-Competitions Bulletin, Art. N° 116362
www.concurrences.com/116362
Christian Ritz, Carolin Marx, Dr. Judith Solzbach, Hanna Weber

23/09/2020, Schienenkartell V, KZR 4/19, e-Competitions Bulletin, Art. N° 116360
www.concurrences.com/116360
Christian Ritz, Carolin Marx, Dr. Judith Solzbach, Hanna Weber

23/09/2020, Truck Cartel, KZR 35/19, e-Competitions Bulletin, Art. N° 116359
www.concurrences.com/116359
Christian Ritz, Carolin Marx, Dr. Judith Solzbach, Hanna Weber

19/05/2020, Schienenkartell III, KZR 70/17, e-Competitions Bulletin, Art. N° 116357
www.concurrences.com/116357
Christian Ritz, Carolin Marx, Dr. Judith Solzbach, Hanna Weber

19/05/2020, Schienenkartell IV, KZR 8/18, e-Competitions Bulletin, Art. N° 116358
www.concurrences.com/116358
Christian Ritz, Carolin Marx, Dr. Judith Solzbach, Hanna Weber

28/01/2020, Schienenkartell II, KZR 24/17, e-Competitions Bulletin, Art. N° 111839
www.concurrences.com/111839
Christian Ritz, Carolin Marx, Dr. Judith Solzbach, Hanna Weber

29/10/2019, Berufungszuständigkeit II, KZR 60/18, e-Competitions Bulletin, Art. N° 111835
www.concurrences.com/111835
Christian Ritz, Carolin Marx, Dr. Judith Solzbach, Hanna Weber

11/12/2018, Schienenkartell I, KZR 26/17, e-Competitions Bulletin, Art. N° 111825
www.concurrences.com/111825
Christian Ritz, Carolin Marx, Dr. Judith Solzbach, Hanna Weber

27/11/2018, Zuckerkartell X, ARZ 321/18, e-Competitions Bulletin, Art. N° 111824
www.concurrences.com/111824
Christian Ritz, Carolin Marx, Dr. Judith Solzbach, Hanna Weber

12/06/2018, Grauzementkartell II, KZR 56/16, e-Competitions Bulletin, Art. N° 111817
www.concurrences.com/111817
Christian Ritz, Carolin Marx, Dr. Judith Solzbach, Hanna Weber

12/07/2016, Lottoblock II, KZR 25/14, e-Competitions Bulletin, Art. N° 111813
www.concurrences.com/111813
Christian Ritz, Carolin Marx, Dr. Judith Solzbach, Hanna Weber

14/07/2015, Trinkwasserpreise, KVR 55/14, e-Competitions Bulletin, Art. N° 111812
www.concurrences.com/111812
Christian Ritz, Carolin Marx, Dr. Judith Solzbach, Hanna Weber

18/11/2014, Calciumcarbid-Kartell II, KZR 15/12, e-Competitions Bulletin, Art. N° 111810
www.concurrences.com/111810
Christian Ritz, Carolin Marx, Dr. Judith Solzbach, Hanna Weber

28/06/2011, ORWI, KZR 75/10, e-Competitions Bulletin, Art. N° 111809
www.concurrences.com/111809
Christian Ritz, Carolin Marx, Dr. Judith Solzbach, Hanna Weber

Higher Regional Courts

24/02/2022, Truck Cartel 2 U 64/20, e-Competitions Bulletin, Art. N° 116227
www.concurrences.com/116227
Christian Ritz, Carolin Marx, Dr. Judith Solzbach, Hanna Weber

16/12/2021, Truck Cartel 2 U 4/20, e-Competitions Bulletin, Art. N° 116215
www.concurrences.com/116215
Christian Ritz, Carolin Marx, Dr. Judith Solzbach, Hanna Weber

17/11/2021, Sugar Cartel 6 U 56/20 Kart, e-Competitions Bulletin, Art. N° 116366
www.concurrences.com/116366
Christian Ritz, Carolin Marx, Dr. Judith Solzbach, Hanna Weber

10/02/2021, HDF-Platten U (Kart) 8/19, e-Competitions Bulletin, Art. N° 116361
www.concurrences.com/116361
Christian Ritz, Carolin Marx, Dr. Judith Solzbach, Hanna Weber

12/05/2020, Drogeriekartell 11 U 98/18, e-Competitions Bulletin, Art. N° 111844
www.concurrences.com/111844
Christian Ritz, Carolin Marx, Dr. Judith Solzbach, Hanna Weber

09/01/2020, Truck Kartell 29 W 1380/19 Kart, e-Competitions Bulletin, Art. N° 111837
www.concurrences.com/111837
Christian Ritz, Carolin Marx, Dr. Judith Solzbach, Hanna Weber

14/10/2019, HEMA-Vertriebskreis II 3 U 1876/18, e-Competitions Bulletin, Art. N° 111834
www.concurrences.com/111834
Christian Ritz, Carolin Marx, Dr. Judith Solzbach, Hanna Weber

08/05/2019, Schienenkartell III VI-U (Kart) 11/18, e-Competitions Bulletin, Art. N° 111830
www.concurrences.com/111830
Christian Ritz, Carolin Marx, Dr. Judith Solzbach, Hanna Weber

23/01/2019, Schienenkartell I VI-U (Kart) 18/17, e-Competitions Bulletin, Art. N° 111826
www.concurrences.com/111826
Christian Ritz, Carolin Marx, Dr. Judith Solzbach, Hanna Weber

28/06/2018, Schienenkartell; 2 U 13/14 Kart , e-Competitions Bulletin, Art. N° 111820
www.concurrences.com/111820
Christian Ritz, Carolin Marx, Dr. Judith Solzbach, Hanna Weber

28/06/2018, Weichenkartell; 29 U 2644/17 Kart, e-Competitions Bulletin, Art. N° 111822
www.concurrences.com/111822
Christian Ritz, Carolin Marx, Dr. Judith Solzbach, Hanna Weber

26/09/2018, Verkürzter Versorgungsweg VI-U (Kart) 24/17, e-Competitions Bulletin, Art. N° 111823
www.concurrences.com/111823
Christian Ritz, Carolin Marx, Dr. Judith Solzbach, Hanna Weber

03/04/2018, Herausgabe von Beweismitteln II; VI-W (Kart) 2/18, e-Competitions Bulletin, Art. N° 111816
www.concurrences.com/111816
Christian Ritz, Carolin Marx, Dr. Judith Solzbach, Hanna Weber

06/07/2017, Zuckerkartell; 18 AR 7/17, e-Competitions Bulletin, Art. N° 111814
www.concurrences.com/111814
Christian Ritz, Carolin Marx, Dr. Judith Solzbach, Hanna Weber

18/02/2015, CDC; VI-U (Kart) 3/14, e-Competitions Bulletin, Art. N° 111811
www.concurrences.com/111811
Christian Ritz, Carolin Marx, Dr. Judith Solzbach, Hanna Weber

28/01/2004, Vitamin Kartell; 6 U 183/03, e-Competitions Bulletin, Art. N° 111808
www.concurrences.com/111808
Christian Ritz, Carolin Marx, Dr. Judith Solzbach, Hanna Weber

Regional Courts

04/05/2020, Zuckerkartell 18 O 50/16, e-Competitions Bulletin, Art. N° 111842
www.concurrences.com/111842
Christian Ritz, Carolin Marx, Dr. Judith Solzbach, Hanna Weber

05/03/2020, Truck Kartell – Nigeria-Exportfahrzeuge 30 O 261/17, e-Competitions Bulletin, Art. N° 111841
www.concurrences.com/111841
Christian Ritz, Carolin Marx, Dr. Judith Solzbach, Hanna Weber

07/02/2020, Truck Kartell 37 O 18934/17, e-Competitions Bulletin, Art. N° 111840
www.concurrences.com/111840
Christian Ritz, Carolin Marx, Dr. Judith Solzbach, Hanna Weber

19/12/2019, Truck Kartell 30 O 8/18, e-Competitions Bulletin, Art. N° 111836
www.concurrences.com/111836
Christian Ritz, Carolin Marx, Dr. Judith Solzbach, Hanna Weber

25/09/2019, Schienenkartell 2-06 O 649/12, e-Competitions Bulletin, Art. N° 111833
www.concurrences.com/111833
Christian Ritz, Carolin Marx, Dr. Judith Solzbach, Hanna Weber

07/06/2019, Löschfahrzeug-Kartell 37 O 6039/18, e-Competitions Bulletin, Art. N° 111832
www.concurrences.com/111832
Christian Ritz, Carolin Marx, Dr. Judith Solzbach, Hanna Weber

24/04/2019, Truck Kartell 14 O 117/18 Kart, e-Competitions Bulletin, Art. N° 111829
www.concurrences.com/111829
Christian Ritz, Carolin Marx, Dr. Judith Solzbach, Hanna Weber

14/03/2019, Truck Kartell 30 O 234/17, e-Competitions Bulletin, Art. N° 111828
www.concurrences.com/111828
Christian Ritz, Carolin Marx, Dr. Judith Solzbach, Hanna Weber

23/01/2019, Zuckerkartell 14 O 110/18 Kart, e-Competitions Bulletin, Art. N° 111827
www.concurrences.com/111827
Christian Ritz, Carolin Marx, Dr. Judith Solzbach, Hanna Weber

03/08/2018, Truck Cartel; 9 O 49/18, e-Competitions Bulletin, Art. N° 111821
www.concurrences.com/111821
Christian Ritz, Carolin Marx, Dr. Judith Solzbach, Hanna Weber

27/06/2018, Truck Kartell; 8 O 13/17 [Kart], e-Competitions Bulletin, Art. N° 111819
www.concurrences.com/111819
Christian Ritz, Carolin Marx, Dr. Judith Solzbach, Hanna Weber

18/06/2018, HEMA-Vertriebskreis; 19 O 9571/14, e-Competitions Bulletin, Art. N° 111818
www.concurrences.com/111818
Christian Ritz, Carolin Marx, Dr. Judith Solzbach, Hanna Weber

13/09/2017, Schienenkartell; 8 O 30/16 [Kart], e-Competitions Bulletin, Art. N° 111815
www.concurrences.com/111815
Christian Ritz, Carolin Marx, Dr. Judith Solzbach, Hanna Weber

ITALY

Supreme Court of Cassation

16/12/2015, S.F. / Alleanza Toro Assicurazioni S.p.A., No. 25323, e-Competitions Bulletin, Art. N° 111791
www.concurrences.com/111791
Jacques Moscianese, Irene de Angelis

25/11/2015, S.F. / Milano Assicurazioni S.p.A., No. 24114, e-Competitions Bulletin, Art. N° 111792
www.concurrences.com/111792
Jacques Moscianese, Irene de Angelis

11/09/2015, S.D. /. Reale Mutua Assicurazioni S.p.A., No. 17996, e-Competitions Bulletin, Art. N° 111793
www.concurrences.com/111793
Jacques Moscianese, Irene de Angelis

06/07/2015, L.L. / Fondiaria – Sai S.p.A., No. 13890, e-Competitions Bulletin, Art. N° 111795
www.concurrences.com/111795
Jacques Moscianese, Irene de Angelis

04/06/2015, Comi S.r.l. et al. / Cargest S.r.l., No. 11564, e-Competitions Bulletin, Art. N° 111796
www.concurrences.com/111796
Pietro Merlino, Tommaso Olivieri, Giulia Scrivanti

Courts of Appeal

15/10/2021, Agroservizi srl in liquidazione, cerved group spa, italservice sipca srl, italservice cgc srl, its novum Srl in liquidazione c. agenzia dell'entrate. Number General Registry. 2194/2020, e-Competitions Bulletin, Art. N° 116276
www.concurrences.com/116276
Guido Carducci

21/09/2021, Digital World Television S.R.L., c. Sky Italia – S.r.l., Number General Registry 3949/2019, e-Competitions Bulletin, Art. N° 116277
www.concurrences.com/116277
Guido Carducci

18/06/2021, Eutelia S.p.A. / Vodafone Omnitel N.V. S.p.A., No. 1919, e-Competitions Bulletin, Art. N° 116278
www.concurrences.com/116278
Veronica Pinotti, Patrizia Pedretti, Michela Francavilla

06/04/2021, Alicargo and others / SEA Società esercizi aeroportuali S.p.A., No. 1097, e-Competitions Bulletin, Art. N° 116281
www.concurrences.com/116281
Veronica Pinotti, Patrizia Pedretti, Michela Francavilla

21/05/2020, Società Esercizi Aeroportuali S.E.A. S.p.A. / Qatar Airways – Linee Aeree Del Qatar No. 1242/2020 (General Registry: 3798/2018), e-Competitions Bulletin, Art. N° 116282
www.concurrences.com/116282
Pietro Merlino, Tommaso Olivieri, Giulia Scrivanti

21/01/2020, Iveco S.p.A./Cave Marmi Vallestrona S.r.l., No. 188/2020 (General Registry: 4525/2018), e-Competitions Bulletin, Art. N° 116372
www.concurrences.com/116372
Pietro Merlino, Tommaso Olivieri, Giulia Scrivanti

Commercial Courts

25/10/2022, Coprem – Costruzione prefabbricati modulari S.r.l. / Bonna Sabla S.A., No. 8365, e-Competitions Bulletin, Art. N° 116266
www.concurrences.com/116266
Jacques Moscianese, Irene de Angelis

21/10/2022, Nippon Cargo Airlines Co., Ltd. / SEA S.p.A., No. 8292, e-Competitions Bulletin, Art. N° 116270
www.concurrences.com/116270
Jacques Moscianese, Irene de Angelis

20/10/2022, G.V. / Intesa Sanpaolo S.p.A., No. 8267, e-Competitions Bulletin, Art. N° 116272
www.concurrences.com/116272
Jacques Moscianese, Irene de Angelis

27/09/2022, Codacons / Rolex Italia S.p.A., No. 7389, e-Competitions Bulletin, Art. N° 116274
www.concurrences.com/116274
Jacques Moscianese, Irene de Angelis

20/04/2022, Fallimento RS Italia S.r.l. / Gruppo Inox S.r.l., No. 3458, e-Competitions Bulletin, Art. N° 116275
www.concurrences.com/116275
Jacques Moscianese, Irene de Angelis

30/05/2019, D.F. S.r.l. / I.C.E. S.p.A. and P.C.A. S.p.A., General Registry No. 56090, e-Competitions Bulletin, Art. N° 111781
www.concurrences.com/111781
Guido Carducci

15/03/2018, Brussels Airlines SA/NV, American Airlines Inc. and Aegean Airlines SA / SEA S.p.A., No. 3011, e-Competitions Bulletin, Art. N° 111783
www.concurrences.com/111783
Pietro Merlino, Tommaso Olivieri, Giulia Scrivanti

24/07/2017, Ministry of Health and Ministry of Economy and Finance / Pfizer Italia S.r.l., No. 15020, e-Competitions Bulletin, Art. N° 111784
www.concurrences.com/111784
Pietro Merlino, Tommaso Olivieri, Giulia Scrivanti

24/06/2016, Alpina Società Immobiliare S.r.l., Arno S.r.l., Enrico Belloti / Banco di Brescia Sanpaolo Cab S.p.A., Banca Popolare Commercio e Industria S.p.A., No. 7884, e-Competitions Bulletin, Art. N° 111787
www.concurrences.com/111787
Jacques Moscianese, Irene de Angelis

23/06/2016, Franco Bartolomei / Banco Popolare soc. coop., No. 7796, e-Competitions Bulletin, Art. N° 111789
www.concurrences.com/111789
Jacques Moscianese, Irene de Angelis

28/07/2015, BT Italia S.p.A. / Vodafone Omnitel N.V., No. 9109, e-Competitions Bulletin, Art. N° 111794
www.concurrences.com/111794
Pietro Merlino, Tommaso Olivieri, Giulia Scrivanti

15/07/2015, Best Office S.p.A. / Intesa Sanpaolo S.p.A., No. 8720, e-Competitions Bulletin, Art. N° 111797
www.concurrences.com/111797
Jacques Moscianese, Irene de Angelis

14/04/2014, Airline Logistic S.r.l., Globe Air Cargo S.r.l., Swissport Cargo Services Italia S.r.l., Worldair S.r.l., Sasco S.r.l. / SEA S.p.A., No. 3324, e-Competitions Bulletin, Art. N° 111799
www.concurrences.com/111799
Pietro Merlino, Tommaso Olivieri, Giulia Scrivanti

Court of Milan

24/05/2021, A.B.E. S.N.C and others/Iveco S.p.A and others, No. 4491, e-Competitions Bulletin, Art. N° 116280
www.concurrences.com/116280
Veronica Pinotti, Patrizia Pedretti, Michela Francavilla

04/10/2018, Cave Marmi Vallestrona/Iveco, No. 9759, e-Competitions Bulletin, Art. N° 111782
www.concurrences.com/111782
Veronica Pinotti, Patrizia Pedretti

27/06/2016, Swiss International Airline S.p.A. / SEA Società esercizi aeroportuali S.p.A., No. 7970, e-Competitions Bulletin, Art. N° 111785
www.concurrences.com/111785
Veronica Pinotti, Patrizia Pedretti

21/06/2016, Teleunit S.p.A. / Telecom Italia S.p.A. No. 8008, General Registry 76561/2008, e-Competitions Bulletin, Art. N° 111786
www.concurrences.com/111786
Guido Carducci

05/04/2016, Eutelia S.p.A. / Vodafone Omnitel N.V. S.p.A., No. 4255, e-Competitions Bulletin, Art. N° 111788
www.concurrences.com/111788
Jacques Moscianese, Irene de Angelis

24/12/2015, Arslogica Sistemi S.r.l./ IBM Italia S.p.A., No. 4620, e-Competitions Bulletin, Art. N° 111790
www.concurrences.com/111790
Veronica Pinotti, Patrizia Pedretti

14/05/2014, Intermatica S.p.A. / Telecom Italia S.p.A. No. 6621, General Registry 8025/2009, e-Competitions Bulletin, Art. N° 111798
www.concurrences.com/111798
Guido Carducci

27/12/2013, Brennercom S.p.A /Telecom Italia S.p.A., No. 16319, General Registry 22423/2010, e-Competitions Bulletin, Art. N° 111804
www.concurrences.com/111804
Guido Carducci

04/06/2013, Viaggiare s.r.l. / Ryanair Ltd., No. 7825, e-Competitions Bulletin, Art. N° 111805
www.concurrences.com/111805
Guido Carducci

13/02/2013, OKCom S.p.A / Telecom Italia S.p.A, No. 2159, General Registry 76568/2008, e-Competitions Bulletin, Art. N° 111806
www.concurrences.com/111806
Guido Carducci

KOREA

Supreme Court

29/08/2019, Case No. 2017Da276679, Republic of Korea v. SK Engineering & Construction co., Ltd. and et al, e-Competitions Bulletin, Art. N° 116299
www.concurrences.com/116299
Cecil Chung

12/10/2018, Case No. 2016Da243115, Korea Electric Power Corporation v. Daehan Cable & Solution Co., Ltd. et al, e-Competitions Bulletin, Art. N° 116301
www.concurrences.com/116301
Cecil Chung

NETHERLANDS

Supreme Court

08/07/2016, Case ECLI:NL:HR:2016:1483, e-Competitions Bulletin, Art. N° 111732
www.concurrences.com/111732
Gerjanne te Winkel, Niels van Loon

Courts of Appeal

10/03/2020, Cases ECLI:NL:GHAMS:2020:714 and ECLI:NL:GHAMS:2020:713, e-Competitions Bulletin, Art. N° 111730
www.concurrences.com/111730
Gerjanne te Winkel, Niels van Loon

26/11/2019, Case ECLI:NL: GHARL:2019:10165, e-Competitions Bulletin, Art. N° 111738
www.concurrences.com/111738
Gerjanne te Winkel, Niels van Loon

05/02/2019, Case ECLI:NL:RBMNE:2016:4284, e-Competitions Bulletin, Art. N° 111737
www.concurrences.com/111737
Gerjanne te Winkel, Niels van Loon

02/09/2014, Case ECLI:NL: GHARL:2014:6766, e-Competitions Bulletin, Art. N° 111730
www.concurrences.com/111730
Gerjanne te Winkel, Niels van Loon

District Courts

26/09/2018, Case ECLI:NL:RBROT:2018:8001, e-Competitions Bulletin, Art. N° 111736
www.concurrences.com/111736
Gerjanne te Winkel, Niels van Loon

20/07/2017, Case ECLI:NL:RBMNE:2016:4284, e-Competitions Bulletin, Art. N° 111735
www.concurrences.com/111735
Gerjanne te Winkel, Niels van Loon

29/03/2017, Case ECLI:NL:RBGEL:2017:1724, e-Competitions Bulletin, Art. N° 111734
www.concurrences.com/111734
Gerjanne te Winkel, Niels van Loon

16/11/2016, Case ECLI:NL:RBLIM:2016:9897 and ECLI:NL:RBLIM:2015:1791, e-Competitions Bulletin, Art. N° 111733
www.concurrences.com/111733
Gerjanne te Winkel, Niels van Loon

10/06/2015, Case ECLI:NL:RBGEL:2015:3713, e-Competitions Bulletin, Art. N° 111731
www.concurrences.com/111731
Gerjanne te Winkel, Niels van Loon

16/01/2013, Case ECLI:NL: RBONE:2013:BZ0403, e-Competitions Bulletin, Art. N° 111729
www.concurrences.com/111729
Gerjanne te Winkel, Niels van Loon

PORTUGAL

Supreme Court

07/07/2022, Case 2/19.3YQSTR-G.L1.S1, e-Competitions Bulletin, Art. N° 116310
www.concurrences.com/116310
Miguel Miranda, Efigénia Marabuto Tavares

08/03/2022, Case 6/19.6YQSTR-C.L1.S1, e-Competitions Bulletin, Art. N° 116306
www.concurrences.com/116306
Miguel Miranda, Efigénia Marabuto Tavares

16/02/2016, Case 135/12.7TCFUN.L1.S1 AA and BB vs CC, e-Competitions Bulletin, Art. N° 111717
www.concurrences.com/111717
Eduardo Maia Cadete

20/06/2013, Case 178/07.2TVPRT.P1.S1 AUTO-AA vs SC COMÉRCIO and SC-INDÚSTRIAS, e-Competitions Bulletin, Art. N° 111718
www.concurrences.com/111718
Eduardo Maia Cadete, Miguel Mota Delgado, Morais Leitão Advogados

2010, Case 3130/08, A. vs B, judgment publicly available in physical format at Portuguese Colectânea de Jurisprudência, n.º 227, Tomo III/2010, e-Competitions Bulletin, Art. N° 111720
www.concurrences.com/111720
Eduardo Maia Cadete, Miguel Mota Delgado, Morais Leitão Advogados

Court of Appeal

22/03/2023, Case 18/21.0YQSTR.L1, e-Competitions Bulletin, Art. N° 116323
www.concurrences.com/116323
Miguel Miranda, Efigénia Marabuto Tavares

13/07/2022, Case 6/21.6YQSTR.L1-PICRS, e-Competitions Bulletin, Art. N° 116311
www.concurrences.com/116311
Miguel Miranda, Efigénia Marabuto Tavares

04/10/2011, Case 107/2001.L1-7, e-Competitions Bulletin, Art. N° 111719
www.concurrences.com/111719
Eduardo Maia Cadete, Miguel Mota Delgado, Morais Leitão Advogados

Competition Court

10/03/2023, Case 54/19.6YQSTR, e-Competitions Bulletin, Art. N° 116321
www.concurrences.com/116321
Miguel Miranda, Efigénia Marabuto Tavares

08/03/2023, Case 6/21.6YQSTR, e-Competitions Bulletin, Art. N° 116319
www.concurrences.com/116319
Miguel Miranda, Efigénia Marabuto Tavares

30/11/2022, Case 12/19.0YQSTR, e-Competitions Bulletin, Art. N° 116317
www.concurrences.com/116317
Miguel Miranda, Efigénia Marabuto Tavares

06/11/2022, Case 71/19.6YQSTR, e-Competitions Bulletin, Art. N° 116312
www.concurrences.com/116312
Miguel Miranda, Efigénia Marabuto Tavares

Court of First Instance

22/11/2016, Case 1774/11.9TVLSB, e-Competitions Bulletin, Art. N° 111722
www.concurrences.com/111722
Gonçalo Machado Borges

Cogeco Communications Inc v. Sport TV Portugal, case pending.
Daniela Cardoso

SPAIN

Supreme Court

07/11/2023, Case 651/2013, e-Competitions Bulletin, Art. N° 111675
www.concurrences.com/111675
Juan Pablo Correa Delcasso, Laura Pérez Poza and Paula Belén Pérez Chávez

04/09/2023, Case 528/2013, e-Competitions Bulletin, Art. N° 111678
www.concurrences.com/111678
Jesús Almoguera, Juan Pablo Correa Delcasso, Laura Pérez Poza

14/06/2023, Case 949/2023, e-Competitions Bulletin, Art. N° 116233
www.concurrences.com/116233
Belén Irissarry, Fernando Giménez-Alvear and Laura García-Valdecasas

14/06/2023, Case 5855/2020, e-Competitions Bulletin, Art. N° 116273
www.concurrences.com/116273
Rais Amils & Ana Parés

14/06/2023, Case 5408/2020, e-Competitions Bulletin, Art. N° 116273
www.concurrences.com/116273
Rais Amils & Ana Parés

12/06/2023, Case 6019/2020, e-Competitions Bulletin, Art. N° 116254
www.concurrences.com/116254
Rais Amils & Ana Parés

12/06/2023, Case 586/2020, e-Competitions Bulletin, Art. N° 116253
www.concurrences.com/116253
Rais Amils & Ana Parés

07/10/2022, Case 45/2021, e-Competitions Bulletin, Art. N° 116201
www.concurrences.com/116201
Rais Amils & Ana Parés

08/03/2022, Case 4079/2018, e-Competitions Bulletin, Art. N° 116208
www.concurrences.com/116208
Rais Amils & Ana Parés

26/02/2019, Order, Case 262/2018, e-Competitions Bulletin, Art. N° 111694
www.concurrences.com/111694
Rais Amils, Belén Irissarry, Juan Pablo Correa Delcasso, Laura Pérez Poza

08/06/2012, Case 344/2012, e-Competitions Bulletin, Art. N° 111674
www.concurrences.com/111674
Jesús Almoguera, Juan Pablo Correa Delcasso, Laura Pérez Poza

Courts of Appeal

03/03/2023, Case 104/2023, e-Competitions Bulletin, Art. N° 116230
www.concurrences.com/116230
Belén Irissarry, Fernando Giménez-Alvear and Laura García-Valdecasas

14/02/2023, Case 44/2023, e-Competitions Bulletin, Art. N° 116229
www.concurrences.com/116229
Belén Irissarry, Fernando Giménez-Alvear and Laura García-Valdecasas

10/02/2023, Case 65/2022, e-Competitions Bulletin, Art. N° 116228
www.concurrences.com/116228
Belén Irissarry, Fernando Giménez-Alvear and Laura García-Valdecasas

03/02/2023, Case 99/2003, e-Competitions Bulletin, Art. N° 116226
www.concurrences.com/116226
Belén Irissarry, Fernando Giménez-Alvear and Laura García-Valdecasas

17/01/2023, Case 53/2023, e-Competitions Bulletin, Art. N° 116225
www.concurrences.com/116225
Belén Irissarry, Fernando Giménez-Alvear and Laura García-Valdecasas

23/12/2022, Case 375/2022, e-Competitions Bulletin, Art. N° 116224
www.concurrences.com/116224
Belén Irissarry, Fernando Giménez-Alvear and Laura García-Valdecasas

16/12/2022, Case 736/2022, e-Competitions Bulletin, Art. N° 116223
www.concurrences.com/116223
Belén Irissarry, Fernando Giménez-Alvear and Laura García-Valdecasas

02/12/2022, Case 1417/2022, e-Competitions Bulletin, Art. N° 116217
www.concurrences.com/116217
Belén Irissarry, Fernando Giménez-Alvear and Laura García-Valdecasas

11/11/2022, Case 745/2022, e-Competitions Bulletin, Art. N° 116205
www.concurrences.com/116205
Belén Irissarry, Fernando Giménez-Alvear and Laura García-Valdecasas

04/11/2022, Case 1596/2022, e-Competitions Bulletin, Art. N° 116199
www.concurrences.com/116199
Belén Irissarry, Fernando Giménez-Alvear and Laura García-Valdecasas

06/10/2022, Case 1791/2021, e-Competitions Bulletin, Art. N° 116200
www.concurrences.com/116200
Rais Amils & Ana Parés

19/09/2022, Case 84/2020, e-Competitions Bulletin, Art. N° 116198
www.concurrences.com/116198
Rais Amils & Ana Parés

07/09/2022, Case 986/2021, e-Competitions Bulletin, Art. N° 116195
www.concurrences.com/116195
Rais Amils & Ana Parés

18/07/2022, Case 1762/2021, e-Competitions Bulletin, Art. N° 116202
www.concurrences.com/116202
Rais Amils & Ana Parés

27/06/2022, Case 109/2021, e-Competitions Bulletin, Art. N° 116219
www.concurrences.com/116219
Rais Amils & Ana Parés

13/06/2022, Case 1785/2021, e-Competitions Bulletin, Art. N° 116218
www.concurrences.com/116218
Rais Amils & Ana Parés

19/05/2022, Case 292/2021, e-Competitions Bulletin, Art. N° 116213
www.concurrences.com/116213
Rais Amils & Ana Parés

16/03/2022, Case 735/2021, e-Competitions Bulletin, Art. N° 116209
www.concurrences.com/116209
Rais Amils & Ana Parés

15/02/2022, Case 1405/2021, e-Competitions Bulletin, Art. N° 116206
www.concurrences.com/116206
Rais Amils & Ana Parés

07/02/2022, Case 2112/2021, e-Competitions Bulletin, Art. N° 116204
www.concurrences.com/116204
Rais Amils & Ana Parés

31/01/2022, Case 43/2021, e-Competitions Bulletin, Art. N° 116203
www.concurrences.com/116203
Rais Amils & Ana Parés

10/12/2021, Case 736/2019, e-Competitions Bulletin, Art. N° 116337
www.concurrences.com/116337
Rais Amils & Ana Parés

19/11/2021, Case 180/2020, e-Competitions Bulletin, Art. N° 116335
www.concurrences.com/116335
Rais Amils & Ana Parés

01/07/2021, Case 693/2021, e-Competitions Bulletin, Art. N° 116333
www.concurrences.com/116333
Rais Amils & Ana Parés

26/02/2021, Case 2882/2019, e-Competitions Bulletin, Art. N° 116354
www.concurrences.com/116354
Rais Amils & Ana Parés

16/12/2019, Case 1126/2019, e-Competitions Bulletin, Art. N° 111712
www.concurrences.com/111712
Juan Pablo Correa Delcasso, Laura Pérez Poza and Paula Belén Pérez Chávez

16/12/2019, Case 1071/2019, e-Competitions Bulletin, Art. N° 116367
www.concurrences.com/116367
Juan Pablo Correa Delcasso, Laura Pérez Poza and Paula Belén Pérez Chávez

05/12/2019, Case 1169/2019, e-Competitions Bulletin, Art. N° 111709
www.concurrences.com/111709
Jesús Almoguera, Juan Pablo Correa Delcasso, Laura Pérez Poza

24/10/2019, Case 775/2019, e-Competitions Bulletin, Art. N° 111708
www.concurrences.com/111708
Jesús Almoguera, Juan Pablo Correa Delcasso, Laura Pérez Poza, Rais Amils

20/06/2019, Case 180/2019, e-Competitions Bulletin, Art. N° 111699
www.concurrences.com/111699
Rais Amils, Belén Irissarry, Juan Pablo Correa Delcasso, Laura Pérez Poza

03/07/2017, Case 475/2015, e-Competitions Bulletin, Art. N° 111677
www.concurrences.com/111677
Rais Amils, Belén Irissarry, Juan Pablo Correa Delcasso, Laura Pérez Poza

Commercial Courts

02/06/2023, Case 307/2023, e-Competitions Bulletin, Art. N° 116196
www.concurrences.com/116196
Juan Pablo Correa Delcasso, Laura Pérez Poza and Paula Belén Pérez Chávez

01/12/2022, Case 583/2022, e-Competitions Bulletin, Art. N° 116210
www.concurrences.com/116210
Belén Irissarry, Fernando Giménez-Alvear and Laura García-Valdecasas

21/10/2022, Case 148/2022, e-Competitions Bulletin, Art. N° 116212
www.concurrences.com/116212
Rais Amils & Ana Parés

07/09/2022, Case 135/2022, e-Competitions Bulletin, Art. N° 116339
www.concurrences.com/116339
Rais Amils & Ana Parés

08/06/2022, Case 221/2022, e-Competitions Bulletin, Art. N° 116216
www.concurrences.com/116216
Rais Amils & Ana Parés

03/06/2022, Case 969/2021, e-Competitions Bulletin, Art. N° 116214
www.concurrences.com/116214
Rais Amils & Ana Parés

22/03/2022, Case 2250/2019, e-Competitions Bulletin, Art. N° 116211
www.concurrences.com/116211
Rais Amils & Ana Parés

17/02/2022, Case 1639/2022 and 1764/2022, e-Competitions Bulletin, Art. N° 116207
www.concurrences.com/116207
Rais Amils & Ana Parés

30/06/2021, Case 1722/2015, e-Competitions Bulletin, Art. N° 116330
www.concurrences.com/116330
Rais Amils & Ana Parés

18/05/2021, Case 588/2018, e-Competitions Bulletin, Art. N° 116326
www.concurrences.com/116326
Rais Amils & Ana Parés

15/03/2020, Case 52/2019, e-Competitions Bulletin, Art. N° 111696
www.concurrences.com/111696
Jesús Almoguera, Rais Amils, Juan Pablo Correa Delcasso, Laura Pérez Poza

03/03/2020, Case 127/2019, e-Competitions Bulletin, Art. N° 111716
www.concurrences.com/111716
Jesús Almoguera, Juan Pablo Correa Delcasso, Laura Pérez Poza

30/12/2019, Case 317/2019, e-Competitions Bulletin, Art. N° 111714
www.concurrences.com/111714
Jesús Almoguera, Juan Pablo Correa Delcasso, Laura Pérez Poza

02/10/2019, Case 211/2019, e-Competitions Bulletin, Art. N° 111707
www.concurrences.com/111707
Jesús Almoguera, Juan Pablo Correa Delcasso, Laura Pérez Poza, Rais Amils

12/09/2019, Case 501/2018, e-Competitions Bulletin, Art. N° 111705
www.concurrences.com/111705
Rais Amils, Belén Irissarry, Juan Pablo Correa Delcasso, Laura Pérez Poza

27/09/2019, Case 1/2018, e-Competitions Bulletin, Art. N° 111706
www.concurrences.com/111706
Jesús Almoguera, Juan Pablo Correa Delcasso, Laura Pérez Poza

10/09/2019, Case 118/2019, e-Competitions Bulletin, Art. N° 111704
www.concurrences.com/111704
Jesús Almoguera, Juan Pablo Correa Delcasso, Laura Pérez Poza, Rais Amils

30/08/2019, Case 151/2019, e-Competitions Bulletin, Art. N° 111703
www.concurrences.com/111703
Jesús Almoguera, Juan Pablo Correa Delcasso, Laura Pérez Poza, Rais Amils

26/07/2019, Case 117/2019, e-Competitions Bulletin, Art. N° 111702
www.concurrences.com/111702
Jesús Almoguera, Juan Pablo Correa Delcasso, Laura Pérez Poza

03/07/2019, Case 584/2018, e-Competitions Bulletin, Art. N° 116241
www.concurrences.com/116241
Jesús Almoguera, Juan Pablo Correa Delcasso, Laura Pérez Poza

02/07/2019, Case 265/2019, e-Competitions Bulletin, Art. N° 111700
www.concurrences.com/111700
Jesús Almoguera, Juan Pablo Correa Delcasso, Laura Pérez Poza

14/06/2019, Case 338/2019, e-Competitions Bulletin, Art. N° 111698
www.concurrences.com/111698
Jesús Almoguera, Juan Pablo Correa Delcasso, Laura Pérez Poza

07/05/2019, Case 338/2018, e-Competitions Bulletin, Art. N° 111679
www.concurrences.com/111679
Jesús Almoguera

13/03/2019, Case 309/2018, e-Competitions Bulletin, Art. N° 111695 www.concurrences.com/111695
Jesús Almoguera, Juan Pablo Correa Delcasso, Laura Pérez Poza

20/02/2019, Case 287/2018, e-Competitions Bulletin, Art. N° 111693 www.concurrences.com/111693
Juan Pablo Correa Delcasso, Laura Pérez Poza and Paula Belén Pérez Chávez, Jesús Almoguera

23/01/2019, Case 899/2017, e-Competitions Bulletin, Art. N° 111692 www.concurrences.com/111692
Rais Amils, Belén Irissarry, Juan Pablo Correa Delcasso, Laura Pérez Poza

13/12/2018, Case 198/2018, e-Competitions Bulletin, Art. N° 111690 www.concurrences.com/111690
Jesús Almoguera, Juan Pablo Correa Delcasso, Laura Pérez Poza

07/12/2018, Case 644/2017, e-Competitions Bulletin, Art. N° 111689 www.concurrences.com/111689
Jesús Almoguera, Juan Pablo Correa Delcasso, Laura Pérez Poza

27/09/2018, Case 274/2018, e-Competitions Bulletin, Art. N° 111688 www.concurrences.com/111688
Juan Pablo Correa Delcasso, Laura Pérez Poza and Paula Belén Pérez Chávez

10/09/2018, Case 320/15, e-Competitions Bulletin, Art. N° 111687 www.concurrences.com/111687
Rais Amils, Belén Irissarry, Juan Pablo Correa Delcasso, Laura Pérez Poza

05/09/2018, Case 32/15, e-Competitions Bulletin, Art. N° 111686 www.concurrences.com/111686
Rais Amils, Belén Irissarry, Juan Pablo Correa Delcasso, Laura Pérez Poza

05/09/2018, Case 31/15, e-Competitions Bulletin, Art. N° 111685 www.concurrences.com/111685
Rais Amils, Belén Irissarry, Juan Pablo Correa Delcasso, Laura Pérez Poza

08/06/2018, Case 189/2015, e-Competitions Bulletin, Art. N° 111683 www.concurrences.com/111683
Rais Amils, Belén Irissarry, Juan Pablo Correa Delcasso, Laura Pérez Poza

06/06/2018, Case 30/2015, e-Competitions Bulletin, Art. N° 111684 www.concurrences.com/111684
Juan Pablo Correa Delcasso, Laura Pérez Poza and Paula Belén Pérez Chávez, Rais Amils, Belén Irissarry, Jesús Almoguera

06/06/2018, Case 15/1, e-Competitions Bulletin, Art. N° 111680 www.concurrences.com/111680
Rais Amils, Belén Irissarry, Juan Pablo Correa Delcasso, Laura Pérez Poza

07/05/2018, Case 241/2015, e-Competitions Bulletin, Art. N° 111679 www.concurrences.com/111679
Juan Pablo Correa Delcasso, Laura Pérez Poza and Paula Belén Pérez Chávez

Court of First Instance

06/02/2020, Case 342/2019, e-Competitions Bulletin, Art. N° 111715 www.concurrences.com/111715
Jesús Almoguera, Juan Pablo Correa Delcasso, Laura Pérez Poza

SWEDEN

Court of Appeal

21/12/2017, Tele2 v Telia (T 5365-16), e-Competitions Bulletin, Art. N° 111671
www.concurrences.com/111671
Claes Langenius, Sofia Falkne

29/06/2017, Yarps v Telia (T 2673-16), e-Competitions Bulletin, Art. N° 111672
www.concurrences.com/111672
Claes Langenius, Sofia Falkner

19/01/2011, Europe Investor Direct et. al. v Euroclear Sweden (T 10012-08), e-Competitions Bulletin, Art. N° 111673
www.concurrences.com/111673
Claes Langenius, Sofia Falkner

TURKEY

Regional Court of Appeals

22/03/2019, 2015/1008 E., 2017/1325 K. – (Based on the infringement decision of the Turkish Competition Board numbered 8 March 2013 and numbered 13-13/198-100), e-Competitions Bulletin, Art. N° 111670
www.concurrences.com/111670
Şahin Ardıyok

Commercial Court of First Instance

22/06/2022, Ongoing case (Based on the infringement decision of the Turkish Competition Board dated 6 June 2011 and numbered 11-34/742-230), e-Competitions Bulletin, Art. N° 116257
www.concurrences.com/116257
Şahin Ardıyok

UKRAINE

Supreme Court

16/02/2023, Case No 910/14588/21, e-Competitions Bulletin, Art. N° 116262
www.concurrences.com/116262
Danylo Volkovetskyi

03/10/2022, Case No 910/17197/21, e-Competitions Bulletin, Art. N° 116260
www.concurrences.com/116260
Danylo Volkovetskyi

08/02/2022, Case No 916/3563/20, e-Competitions Bulletin, Art. N° 116269
www.concurrences.com/116269
Danylo Volkovetskyi

03/07/2018, Case No 910/4425/16, e-Competitions Bulletin, Art. N° 111636
www.concurrences.com/111636
Daryna Ushchapivsk

26/04/2018, Case No 927/81/16, e-Competitions Bulletin, Art. N° 111631
www.concurrences.com/111631
Daryna Ushchapivska

Commercial Court of Appeal

11/04/2023, Case No 910/1925/21, e-Competitions Bulletin, Art. N° 116267
www.concurrences.com/116267
Danylo Volkovetskyi

28/03/2023, Case No 910/18575/21, e-Competitions Bulletin, Art. N° 116265
www.concurrences.com/116265
Danylo Volkovetskyi

23/11/2022, Case No 910/17196/21, e-Competitions Bulletin, Art. N° 116261
www.concurrences.com/116261
Danylo Volkovetskyi

16/11/2022, Case No 910/147/22, e-Competitions Bulletin, Art. N° 116259
www.concurrences.com/116259
Danylo Volkovetskyi

09/12/2021, Case No 922/3779/19, e-Competitions Bulletin, Art. N° 116268
www.concurrences.com/116268
Danylo Volkovetskyi

16/04/2019, Case No 910/12634/18, e-Competitions Bulletin, Art. N° 111637
www.concurrences.com/111637
Daryna Ushchapivska

UNITED KINGDOM

Supreme Court

17/06/2020, Sainsbury's Supermarkets Limited v Visa Europe Services LLC and others, Supreme Court judgment, e-Competitions Bulletin, Art. N° 111656
www.concurrences.com/111656
Penny Coombs

31/10/2019, 26 January 2015 – Appeal Judgment, BritNed Development Ltd v ABB AB and ABB Ltd, e-Competitions Bulletin, Art. N° 111652
www.concurrences.com/111652
Penny Coombs

Apple Retail UK Limited and others v Qualcomm UK Limited and Qualcomm Incorporated, Jurisdiction judgments in May and October 2018. Case settled, e-Competitions Bulletin, Art. N° 111644
www.concurrences.com/111644
Penny Coombs

16/02/2018, iiyama and Mouse Computer v Schott AG and others, Issued 19 December 2014 – Court of Appeal judgment, e-Competitions Bulletin, Art. N° 111654
www.concurrences.com/111654
Penny Coombs

12/02/2016, Streetmap.eu Limited v Google Inc, Google Ireland Limited and Google UK Limited, Issued 15 March 2013 – Judgment, e-Competitions Bulletin, Art. N° 111655
www.concurrences.com/111655
Penny Coombs

25/09/2015, Microsoft Mobile OY (Ltd) v Sony Europe Ltd and others, e-Competitions Bulletin, Art. N° 111651
www.concurrences.com/111651
Penny Coombs

05/08/2015, Arcadia Group Brands Ltd and others v Visa Inc and others, e-Competitions Bulletin, Art. N° 111658
www.concurrences.com/111658
Penny Coombs

19/12/2014, Vodafone Group Services Limited v Infineon Technologies AG and others, Issued, e-Competitions Bulletin, Art. N° 111653
www.concurrences.com/111653
Penny Coombs

21/12/2010, Safeway Stores Limited and others v Twigger and others, e-Competitions Bulletin, Art. N° 111667
www.concurrences.com/111667
Penny Coombs

18/11/2010, Emerald Supplies Ltd and others v British Airways Plc, Claim issued 18 September 2008; Strike-out judgment, e-Competitions Bulletin, Art. N° 111664
www.concurrences.com/111664
Penny Coombs

23/07/2010, Cooper Tire & Rubber Company and others v Shell Chemicals UK Limited and others [2009] EWHC 2609 (Comm), Issued 22 February 2008 – Judgment, e-Competitions Bulletin, Art. N° 111666
www.concurrences.com/111666
Penny Coombs

15/10/2008, Devenish Nutrition Ltd and others v Sanofi-Aventis SA (France) and others, Issued 14 May 2008 – Judgment, e-Competitions Bulletin, Art. N° 111665
www.concurrences.com/111665
Penny Coombs

29/09/2008, Karen Murphy v Media Protection Services Ltd, e-Competitions Bulletin, Art. N° 111663
www.concurrences.com/111663
Penny Coombs

02/02/2007, Attheraces Ltd & Anor v The British Horseracing Board Ltd & Anor Rev 2 [2007] EWCA Civ 38, Court of Appeal Judgment, e-Competitions Bulletin, Art. N° 111668
www.concurrences.com/111668
Penny Coombs

19/07/2006, Bernard Crehan v Inntrepreneur Pub Company Limited and Brewman Group Limited ([2006] UKHL 38), House of Lords judgment, e-Competitions Bulletin, Art. N° 111669
www.concurrences.com/111669
Penny Coombs

Unlockd Ltd and Unlockd Media Technology Ltd v Google Ireland Ltd, Google Commerce Ltd and Google LLC, Claim withdrawn, e-Competitions Bulletin, Art. N° 111643
www.concurrences.com/111643
Penny Coombs

Competition Appeal Tribunal

31/03/2023, Mr Phillip Evans [as class representative] v Barclays Bank PLC and others/ Michael O'Higgins FX Class Representative Limited v Barclays Bank PLC and others, Issued (class certification), e-Competitions Bulletin, Art. N° 111638
www.concurrences.com/111638
Penny Coombs

07/02/2023, Royal Mail Group Limited v DAF Trucks Limited and others/BT Group PLC v DAF Trucks Limited and others, e-Competitions Bulletin, Art. N° 116318
www.concurrences.com/116318
Penny Coombs

08/06/2022, Road Haulage Association Limited -v- Man SE and others, Issued (class certification), e-Competitions Bulletin, Art. N° 1116642
www.concurrences.com/111642
Penny Coombs

08/06/2022, UK Trucks Claim Limited v Iveco Magirus AG and Daimler AG, (class certification), e-Competitions Bulletin, Art. N° 111641
www.concurrences.com/111641
Penny Coombs

18/01/2022, Justin Gutmann v First MTR South Western Trains Limited and Another & Justin Gutmann v London & South Eastern Railway Limited, Issued (class certification), e-Competitions Bulletin, Art. N° 111640
www.concurrences.com/111640
Penny Coombs

26/05/2017, Socrates Training Limited v The Law Society of England and Wales, Issued 04 April 2016 – Judgment, e-Competitions Bulletin, Art. N° 111649
www.concurrences.com/111649
Penny Coombs

31/03/2017, Dorothy Gibson -v- Pride Mobility Products Limited, Issued 25/05/2016, CAT judgment issued, e-Competitions Bulletin, Art. N° 111646
www.concurrences.com/111646
Penny Coombs

08/09/2016, Walter Hugh Merricks CBE -v- MasterCard Inc and others, Issued – Supreme Court judgment on preliminary issue awaited, e-Competitions Bulletin, Art. N° 111645
www.concurrences.com/111645
Penny Coombs

27/07/2016, Peugeot Citroen Automobiles UK Ltd and others v Pilkington Group Limited and others (1244/5/7/15), Issued 22 December 2015 – Limitation judgment, e-Competitions Bulletin, Art. N° 111650
www.concurrences.com/111650
Penny Coombs

05/02/2016, Shadhid Latif & Mohammed Abdul Waheed -v- Tesco Stores Limited, Issued – Discontinued, e-Competitions Bulletin, Art. N° 111648
www.concurrences.com/111648
Penny Coombs

28/03/2013, Albion Water v Dwr Cymru, Issued 18 June 2010 – Judgment, e-Competitions Bulletin, Art. N° 111662
www.concurrences.com/111662
Penny Coombs

18/12/2012, Case 1241/5/7/15 (T) Sainsbury's Supermarkets Ltd -v- Mastercard Incorporated (2) Mastercard International Incorporated (3) Mastercard Europe SA, Issued, e-Competitions Bulletin, Art. N° 111657
www.concurrences.com/111657
Penny Coombs

05/07/2012, 2 Travel Group PLC (in liquidation) v Cardiff City Transport Services Limited, Claim issued 14 January 2011 – Judgment, e-Competitions Bulletin, Art. N° 111659
www.concurrences.com/111659
Penny Coombs

Commercial Court (now Competition Appeal Tribunal)

25/02/2020, Granville Technology Group Limited, OT Computers Limited and another v Infineon Technologies AG, Micron Europe Limited (and others), Issued: 18 May 2016, Judgment on part of the claim, e-Competitions Bulletin, Art. N° 111647
www.concurrences.com/111647
Penny Coombs

UNITED STATES OF AMERICA

Supreme Court

25/06/2018, Ohio v. American Express Co., 138 S.Ct. 2274 (2018), e-Competitions Bulletin, Art. N° 111620
www.concurrences.com/111620
Benjamin Holt

14/06/2018, Animal Science Products, Inc. v. Hebei Welcome Pharmaceutical Co. Ltd., 138 S.Ct. 1865 (2018), e-Competitions Bulletin, Art. N° 111629
www.concurrences.com/111629
Benjamin Holt

Courts of Appeal

08/04/2022, Olean Wholesale Grocery Cooperative Inc. v. Bumble Bee Foods, e-Competitions Bulletin, Art. N° 16352
www.concurrences.com/16352
Benjamin Holt

07/03/2022, Indirect Purchaser Plaintiffs v. Samsung Elecs. Co. (In re Dynamic Random Access Memory (DRAM) Indirect Purchaser Antitrust Litigation), e-Competitions Bulletin, Art. N° 116351
www.concurrences.com/116351
Benjamin Holt

22/01/2018, In re Processed Egg Products Antitrust Litigation, 881 F.3d 262 (3d Cir. 2018), e-Competitions Bulletin, Art. N° 111625
www.concurrences.com/111625
Benjamin Holt

02/10/2017, Valspar Corp. v. E.I. Du Pont, 873 F.3d 185 (3d Cir. 2017), e-Competitions Bulletin, Art. N° 111617 www.concurrences.com/111617
Benjamin Holt

12/01/2017, In re Apple iPhone Antitrust Litigation, 846 F.3d 313 (9th Cir. 2017), e-Competitions Bulletin, Art. N° 111622
www.concurrences.com/111622
Benjamin Holt

23/05/2016, Gelboim v. Bank of America Corp., 823 F.3d 759 (2d Cir. 2016), e-Competitions Bulletin, Art. N° 111628
www.concurrences.com/111628
Benjamin Holt

TABLE OF CONTENTS

Biographies III

Foreword V

Acknowledgements VII

Introduction XI

Publisher's Note XIII

Glossary XV

EUROPEAN UNION
François Brunet and Pierre Chellet
1. Jurisdiction 2
1.1 Jurisdiction of the Member State where the defendant is domiciled 3
1.2 Alternative jurisdiction 3
2. Relevant legislation and legal grounds 4
3. What types of anti-competitive conduct are damages actions available for? 5
4. What forms of relief may a private claimant seek? 6
5. Passing-on defence 6
5.1 Passing-on defense 6
5.2 Claims from indirect customers 7
6. Pre-trial discovery and disclosure, treatment of confidential information 8
6.1 Main principles that apply to disclosure of evidence 8
6.2 Specific rules to disclose evidence included in the file of a competition authority 9
7. Limitation periods 10
8. Appeal 11
9. Class actions and collective representation 11
10. Key issues 11
10.1 Probative value of the Commission and NCA decisions 11
10.2 Private enforcement and the corporate veil 12
10.3 Civil liability among cartel members 13
10.4 Who can be a claimant? 14
10.5 Entry into force of the Damages Directive 14

AUSTRIA
Andreas Traugott, Bernt Elsner, Lothar Hofmann, Florian Neumayr, Markus P. Fellner, Christoph Haid, Stefanie Stegbauer, Martin Eckel, David Konrath, Philipp Strasser, Guenter Bauer and Robert Wagner
1. **Jurisdiction** 20
2. **Relevant legislation and legal grounds** 20
3. **What types of anti-competitive conduct are damages actions available for?** 21
4. **What forms of relief may a private claimant seek?** 21
5. **Passing-on defence** 22
6. **Pre-trial discovery and disclosure, treatment of confidential information** ... 23
7. **Limitation periods** 23
8. **Appeal** 24
9. **Class actions and collective representation** 24
10. **Key issues** 25

BELGIUM
Gerrit Oosterhuis, Angela Ortega González and Vincent Mussche
1. **Jurisdiction** 30
2. **Relevant legislation and legal grounds** 30
3. **What types of anti-competitive conduct are damages actions available for?** 32
4. **What forms of relief may a private claimant seek?** 32
5. **Passing-on defence** 34
6. **Pre-trial discovery and disclosure, treatment of confidential information** 34
7. **Limitation Periods** 36
8. **Appeal** 37
9. **Class actions and collective representation** 37

BRAZIL
Joyce Honda, Thales de Melo e Lemos, José Gabriel Assis de Almeida and Mickael Viglino
1. **Jurisdiction** 42
2. **Relevant legislation and legal grounds** 42
3. **What types of anti-competitive conduct are damages actions available for?** 44
4. **What forms of relief may a private claimant seek?** 44
5. **Passing-on defence** 46
6. **Pre-trial discovery and disclosure, treatment of confidential information** 46
7. **Limitation periods** 47
8. **Appeal** 48
9. **Class actions and collective representation** 48
10. **Key issues** 49

CHILE

Benjamin Grebe and Andrea Von Chrismar

1. **Jurisdiction** 54
2. **Relevant legislation and legal grounds** 55
3. **What types of anti-competitive conduct are damages actions available for?** 55
4. **What forms of relief may a private claimant seek?** 56
5. **Standard of proof** 56
6. **Confidentiality, discovery, exhibition, leniency** 56
7. **Limitation periods** 56
8. **Appeal** 57
9. **Class actions and collective representation** 57

FRANCE

Sergio Sorinas and Marie Louvet

1. **Jurisdiction** 62
2. **Relevant legislation and legal grounds** 62
3. **Passing-on defence** 65
4. **Pre-trial discovery and disclosure, treatment of confidential information** 66
5. **Limitation periods** 66
6. **Appeal** 67
7. **Key issues** 68

GERMANY

Christian Ritz and Carolin Marx

1. **Jurisdiction** 74
2. **Relevant Legislation and Legal Grounds** 74
3. **What types of anti-competitive conduct are damages actions available for?** 77
4. **What forms of relief may a private claimant seek?** 78
5. **Passing-on defence** 78
6. **Pre-trial discovery and disclosure, treatment of confidential information** 79
7. **Limitation periods** 80
8. **Appeal** 81
9. **Class actions and collective representation** 81

ITALY

Guido Carducci, Irene de Angelis, Jacques Moscianese, Pietro Merlino and Veronica Pinotti

1. **Jurisdiction** 88
2. **Relevant legislation and legal grounds** 88
3. **What types of anti-competitive conduct are damages actions available for?** 89
4. **What form of relief may claimant seek** 89
5. **Passing-on defence** 90

6. **Pre-trial evidence and disclosure, treatment of confidential information** 90
7. **Limitation period** 91
8. **Appeal** 91
9. **Class actions and collective representation** 91
10. **Key issues** 92

KOREA
Cecil Saehoon Chung, Woo Yul Lee and Tae Yong Kim
1. **Jurisdiction** 98
2. **Relevant legislation and legal grounds** 99
3. **What types of anti-competitive conduct are damages actions available for?** 99
4. **What forms of reliev may a private claimant seek ?** 100
5. **Burden of proof** 100
6. **Pre-trial discovery and disclosure, treatment of confidential information** 101
7. **Limitation periods** 102
8. **Appeal** 102
9. **Class Actions and Collective Representation** 102
10. **Key Issues** 103

MEXICO
Ivan Szymanski Curiel and Fernando Ruiz Alva
1. **Jurisdiction** 106
2. **Relevant legislation and legal grounds** 107
3. **What types of anti-competitive conduct are damages available for?** 107
4. **What forms of relief may a private claimant seek?** 108
5. **Passing-on defence** 108
6. **Pre-trial discovery and disclosure, treatment of confidential information** 109
7. **Limitation periods** 109
8. **Appeal** 109
9. **Class action and collective representation** 110

NETHERLANDS
Gerjanne te Winkel and Niels van Loon
1. **Jurisdiction** 112
2. **Relevant legislation and legal grounds** 113
3. **What types of anti-competitive conducts are damages actions available for?** 113
4. **What forms of relief may a private party seek?** 113
5. **Passing-on defence** 114

6. Pre-trial discovery and disclosure, treatment of confidential information 114
7. Limitation Periods 115
8. Appeal 116
9. Class actions and collective representation 117

POLAND
Marcin Trepka and Elżbieta Buczkowska
1. Jurisdiction 122
2. Relevant legislation and legal grounds 122
3. What types of anti-competitive conduct are damages actions available for? 124
4. What forms of relief may a private claimant seek? 124
5. Passing-on defence 125
6. Pre-trial discovery and disclosure, treatment of confidential information 125
7. Limitation periods 126
8. Appeal 126
9. Class actions and collective representation 126
10. Key issues 127
11. Key cases in antitrust damages actions in Poland 127

PORTUGAL
Eduardo Maia Cadete, Miguel Miranda, Miguel Gorjão-Henriques, Gonçalo Anastácio, Leyre Prieto, Nuno Cruz and Miguel Pena Machete
1. Jurisdiction 132
2. Relevant legislation and legal grounds 132
3. What types of anti-competitive conduct are damages actions available for? 133
4. What forms of relief may a private claimant seek? 133
5. Passing-on defence 134
6. Pre-trial discovery and disclosure, treatment of confidential information 134
7. Limitation periods 135
8. Appeal 136
9. Class actions and collective representation 136
10. Key issue 136

SPAIN
Juan Pablo Correa Delcasso, Laura Pérez, Rais Amils, Ana Parés, Belén Irissarry, Fernando Giménez-Alvear and Laura García-Valdecasas
1. Jurisdiction 140
2. Relevant legislation, legal grounds and burden of proof 140
3. What types of anti-competitive conduct are damages actions available for? 142

4. What forms of relief may a private claimant seek? 142
5. Passing-on defence 143
6. Pre-trial disclosure and treatment of confidential information 144
7. Limitation periods 145
8. Appeal 146
9. Class action and collective representation 146
10. Key issues 147

SWEDEN
Claes Langenius and Sofia Falkner
1. Jurisdiction 158
2. Relevant legislation and legal grounds 158
***3. Rationae temporis* application of the Competition Damages Act**... 159
4. What types of anti-competitive conduct are damages actions available for? 160
5. What forms of relief may a private claimant seek? 160
6. Passing-on defence 160
7. Pre-Trial discovery and Disclosure, treatment of confidential information 160
8. Limitation periods 161
9. Appeal 162
10. Class actions and collective representation 162
11. Key Issues 163

TURKEY
Sahin Ardıyok
1. Jurisdiction 166
2. Relevant legislation and legal grounds 167
3. What types of anti-competitive conduct are damages actions available for? 167
4. What forms of relief may a private claimant seek? 168
5. Passing-on defence 169
6. Pre-trial discovery and disclosure, treatment of confidential information 169
7. Statute of Limitation 170
8. Appeal 170
9. Class actions and collective representation 171
10. Key issues 171
10.1The settlement mechanism 173
10.2The De Minimis principle 173

UKRAINE
Olexander Martinenko and Daryna Ushchapivska
1. Jurisdiction 178
2. Relevant legislation and legal grounds 179

3. What types of anti-competitive conduct are damages actions available for? 179
4. What forms of relief may a private claimant seek? 180
5. Passing-on defence 182
6. Pre-trial discovery and disclosure, treatment of confidential information 182
7. Limitation periods 183
8. Appeal 183
9. Class actions and collective representation 183

UNITED KINGDOM
Andrew Bartlett and Penny Coombs
1. Jurisdiction 188
2. Relevant legislation and legal grounds 188
3. What types of anti-competitive conduct are damages actions available for? 189
4. What forms of relief may a private claimant seek? 190
5. Passing-on defence 190
6. Disclosure 191
7. Limitation periods 191
8. Quantification of damages 192
9. Appeal 193
10. Collective claims (including "class actions") 193
11. Key issues 195

UNITED STATES OF AMERICA
Benjamin Holt
1. Jurisdiction 202
2. Relevant legislation and legal grounds 203
3. What types of anti-competitive conduct are damages actions available for? 203
4. What forms of relief may a private claimant seek? 203
5. Passing-on defence 204
6. Pre-trial discovery and disclosure, treatment of confidential information 204
7. Limitation periods 205
8. Appeal 205
9. Class actions and collective representation 205
10. Key issues 206

Table of Cases XVII

The Institute of Competition Law

The Institute of Competition Law is a publishing company, founded in 2004 by Dr. Nicolas Charbit, based in Paris, London and NewYork. The Institute cultivates scholarship and discussion about antitrust issues though publications and conferences. Each publication and event is supervised by editorial boards and scientific or steering committees to ensure independence, objectivity, and academic rigor. Thanks to this management, the Institute has become one of the few think tanks in Europe to have significant influence on antitrust policies.

Aim

The Institute focuses government, business and academic attention on a broad range of subjects which concern competition laws, regulations and related economics.

Boards

To maintain its unique focus, the Institute relies upon highly distinguished editors, all leading experts in national or international antitrust: Bill Kovacic, Mario Monti, Eleanor Fox, Laurence Idot, Frédéric Jenny, Ioannis Lianos, Richard Whish, etc.

Authors

4,000 authors, from 85 jurisdictions.

Partners

- Universities: University College London, King's College London, Queen Mary University, Paris Sorbonne Panthéon-Assas, etc.
- Law firms: Allen & Overy, Cleary Gottlieb Steen & Hamilton, Baker McKenzie, Hogan Lovells, Jones Day, Norton Rose Fulbright, Skadden Arps, White & Case, etc.

Events

Brussels, Dusseldorf, Hong Kong, London, Milan, New York, Paris, Singapore, Warsaw and Washington DC.

Online version

Concurrences website provides all articles published since its inception.

Publications

The Institute publishes Concurrences Review, a print and online quarterly peer-reviewed journal dedicated to EU and national competitions laws. e-Competitions is a bi-monthly antitrust news bulletin covering 85 countries. The e-Competitions database contains over 25,000 case summaries from 4,000 authors.

Concurrences
Competition Laws Review

Concurrences Review

Concurrences is a print and online quarterly peer reviewed journal dedicated to EU and national competitions laws. It has been launched in 2004 as the flagship of the Institute of Competition Law in order to provide a forum for academics, practitioners and enforcers. Concurrences' influence and expertise has garnered contributions or interviews with such figures as Christine Lagarde, Bill Kovacic, Emmanuel Macron, Antonin Scalia and Magrethe Vestager.

Contents

More than 15,000 articles, print and/or online. Quarterly issues provide current coverage with contributions from the EU or national or foreign countries thanks to more than 2,500 authors in Europe and abroad.

Format

In order to balance academic contributions with opinions or legal practice notes, Concurrences provides its insight and analysis in a number of formats:

- Forewords: Opinions by leading academics or enforcers
- Interviews: Interviews of antitrust experts
- On-Topics: 4 to 6 short papers on hot issues
- Law & Economics: Short papers written by economists for a legal audience
- Articles: Long academic papers
- Case Summaries: Case commentary on EU and French case law
- Legal Practice: Short papers for in-house counsels
- International: Medium size papers on international policies
- Books Review: Summaries of recent antitrust books
- Articles Review: Summaries of leading articles published in 45 antitrust journals

Boards

The Scientific Committee is headed by Laurence Idot, Professor at Panthéon Assas University. The International Committee is headed by Frederic Jenny, OECD Competition Comitteee Chairman. Boards members include Douglas Ginsburg, Benoît Cœuré, Howard Shelanski, Richard Whish, Wouter Wils, Joshua Wright, etc.

Online version

Concurrences website provides all articles published since its inception, in addition to selected articles published online only in the electronic supplement.

Write for Concurrences

Concurrences welcome spontaneous contributions. Except in rare circumstances, the journal accepts only unpublished articles, whatever the form and nature of the contribution. The Editorial Board checks the form of the proposals, and then submits these to the Scientific Committee. Selection of the papers is conditional to a peer review by at least two members of the Committee. Within a month, the Committee assesses whether the draft article can be published and notifies the author.

www.ingramcontent.com/pod-product-compliance
Ingram Content Group UK Ltd.
Pitfield, Milton Keynes, MK11 3LW, UK
UKHW020216290926
15470UKWH00001B/220

9 781954 750524